# GOVERNING IN THE SHADOWS

# / AFRICAN
# / ARGUMENTS

African Arguments is a series of short books about contemporary Africa and the critical issues and debates surrounding the continent. The books are scholarly and engaged, substantive and topical. They focus on questions of justice, rights and citizenship; politics, protests and revolutions; the environment, land, oil and other resources; health and disease; economy: growth, aid, taxation, debt and capital flight; and both Africa's international relations and country case studies.

*Managing Editor*, Stephanie Kitchen

*Series editors*

Adam Branch
Alex de Waal
Alcinda Honwana
Ebenezer Obadare
Carlos Oya
Nicholas Westcott

PAULA CRISTINA ROQUE

# Governing in the Shadows

*Angola's Securitised State*

HURST & COMPANY, LONDON

**IAI**    International African Institute

Published in collaboration with the International African Institute.
First published in the United Kingdom in 2021 by
C. Hurst & Co. (Publishers) Ltd.,
83 Torbay Road, London, NW6 7DT
Copyright © Paula Cristina Roque, 2021
All rights reserved.

A Cataloguing-in-Publication data record for this book
is available from the British Library.

ISBN: 9781787385740

This book is printed using paper from registered sustainable
and managed sources.

www.hurstpublishers.com

Printed and bound in Great Britain by Bell and Bain Ltd, Glasgow

# CONTENTS

*Acknowledgements*     vii
*List of Acronyms*     ix
*Map of Angola*     xii

Introduction     1

1. The Component Parts     23
2. A Strategy of Securitised Hegemony: Outmanoeuvring
      the Enemy     49
3. The Shadow Government: Guarding the Guardians     87
4. The Angolan Armed Forces: A Strained National Pillar     129
5. Changing the Guard: João Lourenço's Presidency     169
6. The Time of Monsters: Angola's Response to Covid-19     203

Conclusion     217

*Notes*     235
*Bibliography*     263
*Index*     271

# ACKNOWLEDGEMENTS

This book feels like the closing of a life chapter. It is the product of a fascinating journey through Angolan politics over the course of 18 years. It began as many unpublished papers and reports, with interviews gathered from hundreds of different sources from 2002 to 2020. It was mainly written during the pregnancy of my son Balthazar and through the Covid-19 pandemic. While the world was changing, I spent hours sitting at my desk, attempting to do justice to an important topic while struggling to home-school, do domestic chores and unsuccessfully brush off the sense of prolonged doom with a moment in history that betrayed its transformative impact. My family and friends kept me going. My husband André, my equal partner and best friend, was unwavering in his support and love. He sets a very high bar for what a husband and father should be. Our children, Santiago, Balthazar and Sophia, were extraordinary in their understanding and affection. I also couldn't have done it without Mamosito Agnes Molapo, my children's second mother, or Alice Durão. I am eternally grateful to all of them.

Angola was always special to me. I grew up exposed to its politics, its wars, its destruction and the beauty of its people and land. Songs of liberation and hope marked my youth, their poetry and lyricism incomparable even amongst African musical genius. Generals and military officers, intelligence operatives, diplomats and activists were permanent features of my childhood. Books on war, African politics, international relations and development lined the walls of our homes. Visits with my mother to military and war museums were always amusing, especially around the sections with tanks and armoured

# ACKNOWLEDGEMENTS

vehicles. My mother, Fátima Moura Roque, spent her entire life working, fighting and hoping for a better Angola. She, like many others, lost so much. She will always remain one of Angola's most respected and brilliant economists.

I am indebted to Paul-Simon Handy, Richard Cornwell, Henri Boshoff, Piers Pigou, Sean Cleary, Justin Pearce and many others who challenged me in my analysis of Angola. Rafael Marques de Morais, my brother and dear friend, your kindness, wisdom and support made all the difference. I will never forget when we first met in 1998 after you spoke at the Portuguese Parliament. Your eloquence and courage are unprecedented, and for them, you have been jailed, intimidated, surveilled and tried.

I cannot name the great majority of those who helped me with the most difficult parts of my research. You know who you are. Military and intelligence officers went to great lengths to explain the system's inner workings to me in fair and balanced ways. Your patriotism and love of country were apparent at every juncture. You kept me safe on numerous occasions and taught me so much. I cannot express enough how grateful I am to all of you. One day, when there is democracy and freedom in Angola, I hope you will write your memoirs and your experiences of war and peace.

Thank you to Rafael and Paulo Faria for reviewing the manuscript. My admiration for your knowledge and work is great. Stephanie Kitchen, my editor, thank you for your support, understanding and extreme patience over numerous delays.

It has been a true privilege to learn and write about Angola all these years. In the process, I have met unique individuals whose integrity and strength are limitless. Angola has also caused me much heartache and an experience with PTSD, but I would do it all over again.

This book is dedicated to my children.

# LIST OF ACRONYMS

| | |
|---|---|
| CASA-CE | Convergência Ampla de Salvação de Angola— Coligação Eleitoral (The Broad Convergence for the Salvation of Angola Electoral Coalition) |
| CEMG | Chefe do Estado Maior General (Chief of General Staff) |
| CNE | Comissão Nacional Eleitoral (National Electoral Commission) |
| DDR | Disarmament, Demobilisation and Reintegration |
| DISA | Direcção de Informação e Segurança de Estado (Directorate of Information and Security of Angola) |
| DPCS | Destacamento de Protecção da Casa de Segurança (Reconstruction Protection Unit) |
| FAA | Forças Armadas Angolanas (Angolan Armed Forces) |
| FALA | Forças Armadas de Libertação de Angola (UNITA's Armed Forces for the Liberation of Angola) |
| FAN | Força Aérea Nacional de Angola (National Air Force of Angola) |
| FAPLA | Forças Armadas Populares de Libertação de Angola (MPLA's People's Armed Forces of Liberation of Angola) |

# LIST OF ACRONYMS

| | |
|---|---|
| FLEC | Frente para a Libertação do Enclave de Cabinda (Front for the Liberation of the Enclave of Cabinda) |
| FNLA | Frente Nacional de Libertação de Angola (National Front for the Liberation of Angola) |
| GURN | Government of Unity and National Reconciliation |
| IDP | internally displaced person |
| IMF | International Monetary Fund |
| MINSE | Ministério de Segurança de Estado (Ministry of State Security) |
| MONUA | United Nations Observer Mission in Angola |
| MPLA | Movimento Popular de Libertação de Angola (The People's Movement for the Liberation of Angola) |
| MSF | *Médecins Sans Frontières* (Doctors Without Borders) |
| ODC | Organização de Defesa Civil (Civil Defence Organisation) |
| PIR | Polícia de Intervenção Rápida (Rapid Response Police) |
| PRS | Partido de Renovação Social (Social Renewal Party) |
| SCP | Security Cabinet of the Presidency |
| SIE | Serviço de Inteligência Externa (External Intelligence Service) |
| SINFO | the predecessor to SINSE |
| SINSE | Serviço de Inteligência e Segurança de Estado (Internal State Security and Intelligence) |
| SISM | Servico de Inteligência e Segurança Militar (Military Intelligence Service) |
| SWF | Sovereign Wealth Fund |
| UGP | Unidade da Guarda Presidencial (Presidential Guard Unit) |
| UNAVEM I, II and III | United Nations Angola Verification Missions |
| UNITA | União Nacional para a Independência Total de Angola (The National Union for the Total Independence of Angola) |

## LIST OF ACRONYMS

| | |
|---|---|
| USP | Unidade de Segurança Presidencial (Presidential Security Unit) |
| WFP | World Food Programme |

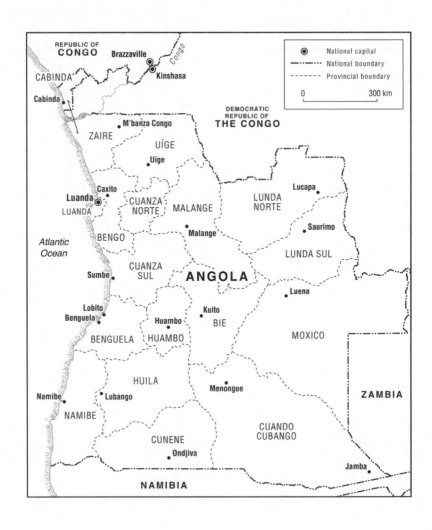

# INTRODUCTION

"There are two types of poison that we use—the herbal kind that is not easily detected and won't show up in blood tests, and the chemical kind that is much more dangerous for the body and will cause irreversible damage. If they targeted you it was because they need you to leave Angola. It was a warning, but it was not meant to seriously hurt you".[1] Returning from a trip to the province of Cabinda in November 2015, where a low-level insurgency contradicted the government's denial of any form of instability in Angola, I was, apparently, poisoned. In the oil-rich enclave, I had met with civil society activists, priests, political supporters of the different factions of the Cabindan Liberation Front (FLEC) insurgency and dissenters on the security services watch list. Every meeting and meal was in either personal homes and offices, or restaurants that had buffets (so the food wasn't poisoned) with cutlery and glasses already on the table (so nothing could be brought in from the kitchen laced with something). It was unclear how it happened exactly, but I had ingested something in Luanda that made me viciously ill for months. Purging that poison took weeks and no number of saline drips helped clear it out. At first, that I had been poisoned didn't seem possible and I dismissed it as having been a very bad form of food poisoning, but a meeting with a sergeant from Military Intelligence introduced the possibility that I had been targeted by the secret services. I was lucky, he suggested, to only have experienced the herbal kind of poison.

This was not the first time I was "warned" to change course. In 2008, following a report on the elections in which I denounced elec-

1

toral fraud, I was harassed with over 50 phone calls from a woman who indirectly threatened my family. This, a top-level official of the South African government confirmed, was the modus operandi of the Angolans and their Soviet/Cuban-inspired tactics. I filed a complaint with the police in Pretoria, the first step before diplomatic intervention. The calls even continued while I was at the station. The police officer spoke to my tormentor, luckily becoming increasingly convinced that I wasn't just a paranoid researcher. I was an obvious target because I was talking to the international press about electoral misconduct and this caught the attention of the external intelligence services operating in South Africa. I was also a target because my mother had been a high-ranking member of the opposition, although she had retired from politics in 1998. We were both in Luanda before the first post-war polls and had been invited to attend the ruling party's closing rally. In line with the overt manipulation of the process and the pattern of showcasing members of the opposition that had defected to their ranks, we were placed on the presidential podium. Once I realised that the invitation was a political trap I walked off the podium, minutes after President José Eduardo dos Santos had taken his place. I realised then that the sophistication and fragilities of the strategies keeping the President in power were a very dangerous combination. The sophistication of political manoeuvrings was matched by the fragilities of upholding perceptions and illusions. Weeks later, the harassment from the intelligence services, coincidentally, stopped immediately when a call was made to the Angolan Presidency.

The second time I was exposed to the far-reaching network of the intelligence services, which had exponentially grown into a political police force, was in 2012, during a trip to the defeated rebels' emblematic wartime capital of Jamba as part of my DPhil research on insurgent state-building. I caught the attention of the intelligence services because I was travelling in a military vehicle and with military personnel. My trip was authorised by the Armed Forces and I was accompanied by officers of the special forces. My research into the rebels' parallel state was a cause for concern to the services because it was historically sensitive. History continued to be dangerous, unpredictable, and interventionist. Nothing happened to me but those who had helped me within the military had to answer more questions than usual. Again, I was told by a senior army general, the Presidency was informed.

# INTRODUCTION

These three instances highlighted the extensive net of the intelligence services monitoring harmless movements and utterances that in no way threatened national security. They did, however, coincide with distinct shifts in the Presidency's heightened perception of danger and insecurity. The 2008 elections, the country's first post-war polls, were key to consolidating power and changing the constitution. They could not be threatened by claims of irregularities. In 2012 the government was in a state of overreactive caution due to the previous year's protests, inspired by the Arab Spring, that had led to a strategy of infiltrating the population and widening surveillance across society. In 2015 the government was starting to feel the impact of the economic crisis that abruptly ended its oil boom years and exposed it to the political costs of poverty. In the worst-case scenario in which all three of these episodes were targeted actions, confirming suspicions (although there was never any hard evidence), the reach and mandate of the security agencies in Angola was intrusive, incestuous and excessive. In the best-case scenario of these being mere coincidences and not instances of encounters with clandestine services, it revealed the reputation and perception of overzealous and nasty Soviet-like agencies among the people who had helped me do my research in Angola over the years. The Russian proverb "fear has big eyes" encapsulated this well, meaning that those who were afraid of something would overestimate its danger or tended to see the danger everywhere. It was equally applied to the President and his elites as it was to the population. This sparked my interest in how the state was supported by mobilising danger and fear but was upheld by astute politicians and elites who were themselves torn between serving the President, their party, and their own interests. Mediating all these conflicting loyalties was a vast operation of security and political control.

Angola was born from war, its state and power edified by war, its history and purpose informed by the political visions moulded by war and survival. These attributes found expression in the governing mindset of the ruling elite, in the long-term strategy of political survival, and the parallel illusionary dynamics of development and democratisation on the one side and securitisation and hegemonic dominance on the other. Within these dynamics were strategies of control and consent by the ruling party. It was about the control of events that could lead to military defeat, unravelling political dissent, social upheaval, or an electoral victory of the opposition. But it was also about consent and surrender. Consent and complicity of elites, the military apparatchiks and the ruling nomenclature that allowed the Presidency to govern over the state as long as they benefited economically and retained the control of Angola's identity. The population was not afforded a choice or their consent required. After decades of war and a political existence of zero-sum strategising, the President and his closest cohorts only really understood their ability to govern as an "us or them" approach. The "them" would mostly be defined by the opposition but also became defined by the general population that the elites chose not to govern. The majority of Angolans governed themselves in the informality of the parallel economy, with communities helping each other and retaining conflicting perspectives of the nation they were born into. Securitising governance was for the ruling elites a safe strategy to contain dissent, subvert demands for better governance, and sabotage any capacity for popular organisation and mobilisation.

Securitisation became the mechanism used defensively and offensively to protect the ruling elites from any forces threatening to undo their hegemony. It referred to a process whereby all spaces of public and private life, institutional and informal, regulated and seemingly uncontrollable organisations were intruded upon by the actions, utterances and policies of a state afraid of change and impotence. The political order it built was intended to defend the interests of the Presidency and ruling elites, relentlessly tackling and undermining perceived subversive and reformist actions by those who contradicted the policies and identity of the post-war state. Securitisation was not predicated on efficiency but utility and complementarity with other political strategies such as neo-patrimonialism and massification of political structures. It wasn't the leading post-war strategy on nation-building but happened to become the default state-building process.

This is an old fight. The search for security had been the ultimate war cry for political actors and communities in search of survival. During the years of conflict, 1975–2002, this struggle was framed by the warring parties as competing versions of Angolan identity, as "a clash of two states and two societies".[2] The battle was for the soul of the country and what it meant to be Angolan. When the ruling

# INTRODUCTION

Movimento Popular de Libertação de Angola (MPLA) and the insurgency União Nacional para a Independência Total de Angola (UNITA) committed to peace in 2002, the country was severely weakened, stratified and politically divided. In the last 18 years of peace this struggle has moved into the shadows of daily life through the insidious encroachment of a securitised existence. For the President and the ruling MPLA that won the war this reflected their need for regime survival and untouchability. For the civilian population it meant a need for socio-economic stability, justice and participation. In their simultaneously and at times mutually exclusive pursuits of security, each group defined the hostile forces threatening their identity, lives and livelihoods. The securitisation of politics, the economy and society had become the strongest regulating force between the state and its population.

This book provides an alternative explanation of Angola's post war state and nation-building exercise. Existing perspectives of Angola's post-conflict transformation have focused on economic success and elite enrichment as avenues for political control leaving out a key element: the role, ethos and projection of the security apparatus in upholding the Presidency and sustaining a system of governance. It explains how power works in Angola, not by dislodging the predominance of patrimonial or neo-patrimonial theories, but by addressing an area that not only complements these existing strategies but is foundational in their capacity to function. Securitisation became the practices, representations, institutional forms, imaginings and utterances that supported all other governing strategies. In this way securitisation was not a competing strategy to patrimonialism or neo-patrimonialism but rather a fundamental part of it. Without the shadows of power and the securitisation architecture that gave it strength the patrimonial system of the 1980s would not have succeeded in Angola. The administrative and military structures that made up this patrimonial system, beholden to the President, were directed and operational through the prism of securitisation. The shadow government became the all-powerful entity that allowed power and control to be manoeuvred from the sidelines of the formal government, privately appropriating economic advantages and managing politics and government through its defensive oligarchic structures. The neo-patrimonial system that developed thereafter in the

1990s, carefully crafted a façade of public norms while creating a system to undermine the functioning of government and the institutional-bureaucratic structures of the state. The different forces that operated under the securitised system allowed the shadow government to extend its reach into different geographical and social peripheries and communities in more effective ways than any other strategy.

The works of Tony Hodges (2004) and Ricardo Soares de Oliveira (2015) established the crucial meta-narratives of wartime and peacetime state-building exercises, respectively, implemented by the MPLA with a focus on the political and economic strategies of regime survival and the entangled interdependent relations of the party, the elites, the military, and their interests in natural resources. Both scholars analysed the concurrent trajectories, by design and by accident, of the personalisation of power, the hegemonic drive of the MPLA and the elites' stranglehold on the economy, describing a country deep in the entrails of cronyism and mismanagement. The brilliance of their contributions in explaining the configuration of power, however, only briefly addressed the important role of the security apparatus. The way Angola's peacetime authoritarian character was described by these and other authors (e.g. Péclard 2008) never fully tied the infrastructure of the security apparatus to the overarching political strategy of the Presidency. This book attempts to provide nuance and information on this empirical silence. It will, like other books on Angola, unavoidably be accused of omissions and misinterpretations given that it is presenting a new narrative. This is not to say that Angola should be read uniquely through a security lens. That would paint a distorted picture of a highly complex country where everything is transactional yet simultaneously rooted in historical divisions and opposing political projects. This book will show that securitisation occurred in tandem with other strategies, where presidential and MPLA objectives of extending control to every domain of social life, while closely guarding economic opportunities and clientelist as well as patronage relations, were possible because of the control extended to them through securitisation. In all its complexity, the pillars for sustaining power in Angola were a contradictory combination of neo-patrimonialism, corruption and securitisation.

A full portrayal of Angola's history and its political and socio-economic system has yet to emerge given the complexities of doing research, navigating partisan narratives, and understanding the nuances of where historical and present-day truth lies. It may be an impossible task to complete. This book aims to build on the courageous and ground-breaking work of Christine Messiant, Tony Hodges, David Birmingham, Ricardo Soares de Oliveira, Justin Pearce, Jon Schubert, Inge Brinkman, Claudia Gastrow, Marissa Moorman, Didier Péclard, Patrick Chabal and Nuno Vidal to name but a few who have provided important perspectives over the years. Several Angolan voices—Rafael Marques, Paulo Faria, Antonio Tomás, Fernando Pacheco, Nelson Pestana, Domingos da Cruz and others—have emerged to complement, contradict and provide nuance on how outsider scholars have viewed Angola. Their analysis has been incredibly important building on their day-to-day experience of political emersion and intrigue, exposing the social realities of the cities and rural areas, navigating complex governance issues with clarity and the insights of those exposed to the contradictions and astuteness of the presidential order and the party-state system. This book does not attempt to rebuke any of the work conducted by these scholars but rather provides a new narrative about Angola that in many ways complements these very diverse and valuable academic voices.

Angola's rise from war, destruction and fragility was visible, exceptional and admired by its African peers and international partners. The ruling elite's capacity to rebuild the country, accelerate economic growth and implement a vision, whilst exclusionary and elitist, towards the future (Soares de Oliveira 2013; Chabal and Vidal 2008) provided an important but incomplete explanation. The political system, depicted as an illiberal state (Soares de Oliveira 2011), a state experiencing authoritarian reconvergence (Péclard 2008), or engaging in competitive authoritarianism (Schubert 2013), was built on the strength of the Presidency and the vast array of security forces. In whichever form this authoritarianism was analysed, it was built with democratic procedures and adopting a mantle of republicanism (Zakaria 1997) while largely excluding the public from national politics. The Presidency's capacity to stabilise political relations through patrimonial, kleptocratic and nepotistic arrangements fuelled corruption, but built a system of adequate loyalty. Elections brought about legitimacy while they destroyed the opposition and silenced their political programmes and values. Society was engineered to accept the fate of MPLA corporatism and assimilation, which hierarchised citizenship and deepened inequality, marginalisation and neutered pluralism. All these processes were neither new nor a phenomenon of post-war Angola. Their origins were historically built during decades of war.

The foundations for all these achievements and strategies were the army, the Presidential Guard, loyal securocrats, intelligence services, political militias, and a militarised police force. Behind the Presidency and the MPLA was a large securitised machinery that provided the institutional, psychological and functional backbone of political control and centralised power. This book will analyse each of these elements of the security apparatus highlighting an area that has seldom received any analytical treatment in Angola's peacetime literature. It will argue that Angola reinvented its path towards peace and development through the shadowing of power in parallel institutions upheld by intrusive and far-reaching security agencies and policies. The post-war political order centralised power in the Presidency and shielded it from extraneous forces (the ruling elites, the opposition and the people). Governing in the shadows was not the aim but the form achieved to centralise power and create systems to manage multiple threats. The intelligence apparatus played a crucial role in controlling the different component parts of the system. The system was fed by revenues from extractive industries and reconstruction funds. It was legitimised through elections and the veneer of democracy. It was shielded from criticism by the complicity of Western countries, and Russia and China, in their beneficial engagements of doing business with the elites, in arms, oil, diamonds, banking, and construction.

Decades of wartime governance had transitioned power away from the state and party into the Presidency that retained arbitrary control over all important portfolios of the economy, society and the political order. With the advent of peace, the strategy became clearer, albeit more discreet in its extension but more important in its efficiency. Peace had to be protected at all costs. Angola's securitised state was perfected in the post-war decade. To protect the state from the citizenry and legal accountability, the Presidency needed arbitrary power operating in the shadows of the rule of law. The Casa de Segurança, the Presidential Security Cabinet (SCP), was one of two vast structures of the Presidency, the other being the Casa Civil (Civil Cabinet), which became the most powerful organs of the state. Together they centralised control of the state, shadowing the government, supervising the work of cabinet, parliament, and the judiciary, monitoring political developments, and advising on the economy and foreign relations. They duplicated many of the formal government's functions and controlled all these areas with the support of key generals and technocrats in a vertical reporting system. These securocrats were given unprecedented power to influence government policy, subverting the powers and mandates of state organs, and entrenching their ability to reprioritise issues for the President.

Angola's shadow government (Roque 2011) operated autonomously and was accountable only to the Presidency. It emerged "from war, from fear of revolution and change, from the economic instability of capitalism. … It (became) the actualising mechanism for ruling elites to implement their imperial schemes and misplaced ideals" (Raskin 1976: 189). The three main intelligence services—external, domestic, and military intelligence—and the Presidential Guard in particular played a defining role in assuring the rule of Angolan President dos Santos. They were put to the service of the MPLA and against the opposition, the military, civil society and political dissenters. Like the police, they became increasingly violent and used as a force to maintain political, not public, order. This shadow government also built in parallel defence mechanisms to avert any move from the armed forces to interfere in politics and contain any potential social unrest. Senior military and political apparatchiks were tied into a system that distributed benefits and privileges, creating complicity in defending the system. The Presidential Guard developed into the best trained, armed and resourced entity of the security apparatus. The socialisation of danger and the bureaucratisation of threats led to the subordination of the nation, society and the state to the overriding importance of security. Securitisation provided the form, ethos and structures for the President's "politics of protection" (Huysmans et al. 2006). Securitisation achieved its ultimate goal of protecting the President and the post-war order but entrenched inequality, poverty, fear and impunity.

## Theorising Angola's Securitisation

In this book, securitisation refers to an architecture of power and strategy to ensure the survival and longevity of a political project. It is an inherently political process aimed at creating a web of centralised control of information, people, and politics in support of a hegemonic leader and his elite towards their survival and benefit, using a combination of multiple security forces and intelligence services, surveillance, paranoia, pre-emptive or reactive violence and an overarching sense of ubiquity. This type of securitisation usually follows complementary strategies of patronage and clientelism, the instrumentalisation of democratic procedure and in many cases strategic partnerships with international donors and financial allies. For the Angolan government, this strategy arose because few others had the capacity to ensure such a rapid degree of order and relatively benevolent control. This form of securitisation went beyond the building of illiberal states and their political economy of authoritarianism as defined by Jones, Soares de Oliveira and Verhoeven (2013). A securitised state viewed threats to the regime and the political survival of the elites as a threat to national security. National security objectives were prioritised with the rise in importance, funding and size of military and security sectors aimed at defending a political project that entailed squashing internal dissent and neutralising any actions or perceived threats that were contrary to its interests. For the securitised state the mere questioning of historical identity and official narratives, or popular protests, were existential threats to the state not just the regime, creating a symbiosis of incestuous survival or demise. It was a monolithic entity, born out of war and unable to transition effectively into peacetime politics by the very divisive outcomes of peace and victor's justice. Securitisation directly tied that fate of the state and society to the survival of the regime, as a necessary condition to avoid chaos, the unravelling of decades of unaddressed fault lines and systemic pathologies.

Securitisation as a concept has however generated competing interpretations, making it an imprecise categorisation influenced by the subjective nature of 'security'. As an intersubjective concept it had no specific objective meaning but was "what people ma(d)e of it" (Williams 2007). Securitisation theory greatly expanded upon the actors who securitised, the threats defined, the referent object for whom there was a threat, why and under which conditions security was evoked. Insecurity, threats and vulnerabilities were socially constructed, rather than objective conditions (Buzan et al. 1998: 50–51). Breaking away from the traditional threats to state security, the Copenhagen school took the concept from purely military and political sectors into broader areas outside of traditional security studies. Securitisation could therefore occur in the non-security areas of the economy, society, and the environment, mobilising other problems such as poverty, unemployment and immigration. Invoking 'security' was first a speech act, whereby the utterance of the word would move state-representatives in particular directions (Waever 1995: 55). In this way security became part of a transitory process that involved the passing of one social order to another. Everyday politics shifted to the realm of emergency (Holbraad and Axel Pedersen 2012: 2). When issues were defined as matters of security they became an existential issue in need of a political response and the adoption of extraordinary measures. The act of securitising involved several components: the actor that defined the issue, the threat identified as existential, the object in need of protection, the audience that accepted the issue as a security threat, and the strategy of extraordinary means enacted to respond to the threat. The enactment of emergency measures also occurred in the absence of public debate (Williams 2003). One serious limitation of this theory is that it did not adequately explore the reasons why actors chose to securitise issues (McDonald 2008) even if an issue portrayed as a security threat was highly subjective. The choice to securitise was always political and embedded in specific social, political and historical contexts that helped determine why some issues were deemed as necessary for securitisation while others remained unthreatening.

Initially, the theory was applied to the political contexts of Western states. In questioning 'democratic bias', several scholars expanded the securitisation process to totalitarian or non-democratic contexts where it became almost impossible to identify the shift from 'normal' to 'special' politics (Vuori 2008: 69). In China, much like Angola, securitisation is used to reproduce and protect the political order, and for controlling society. It is upheld by a symbiotic party-state dynamic, with a defined ideology sustained by strong propaganda mechanisms. The illocutionary act of making pronouncements about security and national threats are only one aspect of how securitisation occurs. Unlike China however, securitisation in Angola was not webbed into the nationalistic mindset or projected as a form of order to protect "the revolution" or even as a stability mechanism to keep citizens engaged (Vuori 2008). The nationalistic mindset was abandoned in peacetime and forms of social cohesion that could rally behind a political project were linked by patronage and economic survival imperatives rather than conviction or political identity. In this way, Angola's form of securitisation differs. It is in this case a modality and pathology of governance rather than a stabilising and unifying factor. Securitisation was the type of politics enacted and the form of power defined by the Presidency that placed the act of governing above the reach of and disconnected from citizens. In this way the President and his shadow institutions acted with a degree of autonomy over his subjects, as if "belonging to separate ontological realms (where) the people themselves and the political structures and the social process to which their lives (we)re subject exist(ed) in relative autonomy from each other" (Holbraad and Axel Pedersen 2012: 6). It altered the relationship between the government and the governed. Governing became more an act of guarding the elites and the Presidency from the people.

The Angolan case brings together several elements of the existing literature on securitisation but it also highlights the different features of a securitised state. As a process, it continued to rest on three pillars: agents, discourses and acts. The agents were the actors pushing the security agenda—in this case the wide universe of the Presidency and the SCP in particular that managed the military, the police, the parallel presidential army, and the intelligence services. The actors were also the audience and the silenced subjects (Gaudino 2020) that were fed the existential threats discourse or became the threats themselves. The discourses were influenced by the historical context and the political identity of the actors, while the acts themselves translated the need for security into policies, institutions, practices and utterances. The process of securitisation in Angola was simultaneously a speech act, a political strategy, an infrastructure, and a post-conflict state-building effort. The Presidency and the elites securitised to survive, to deter behaviour and future acts, for control (Vuori 2008; 2011) and for cohesion. In Angola, security was evoked at every juncture, a call rallying collective purpose, as a reminder of political control, a badge of honour, and as a deterrence to disruptions. Expressions of political protest and peaceful contestation became framed as national security threats, risking the hard-won stability of peace. Consistently, the MPLA and the Presidency placed themselves as guarantors and guardians of peace. Their removal would result in the risk of civil war restarting. The evoking of two massacres—1977 and 1992—during these times were explicit threats to society.

The survival of the state was the goal in most securitisation processes where the urgency of an issue was an existential threat to the state. However, in Angola securitisation was aimed at the survival of shadow power and the political project of the elite. The state was a hollowed-out shell, useful but weak in its capacity to implement the same political control and level of power of the Presidency. It lacked sufficient human capital, management systems and administrative infrastructure and was unable to deliver services to its citizens. It did however extend control to the party, lower-level officials and business elites to extract value and power. Interlinking the parallel shadow structures, arguably more efficient and better resourced, with the state created an illusion of minimal functionality. Because of this shortcoming, Angola's securitised state became preoccupied "with the management of the marginalised and socially excluded" (Hallsworth and Lea 2011) so that social fragmentation could not undo the concentration of power. The state acted like an agency for social control "which supervis(ed) whole populations whose collective status justifie(d) their banishment" (De Giorgi 2006: 85).[3] Growing inequality, entrenched political prejudices, and polarised class structures were managed by the securitised state by coercing and surveilling the most disenfranchised populations.

Securitisation also referred to the infrastructure built to support the form of governing. Either as national security states, illiberal states functioning with Soviet-era intelligence units, or militarised governing elites operating within broad coalitions and democratic procedure, the infrastructure of securitisation varies widely. In the national security state, power permanently shifts towards security and intelligence bureaucracies, giving rise to an emergent autocracy in the guise of a democratic state (Glennon 2015). The structures upholding this system include a network of managers and enforcers in the intelligence, military and law enforcement bureaucracies who become "responsible for protecting the nation and who (come) to operate largely immune from constitutional constraints" (Glennon 2015). These managers have all the incentives of keeping politics operating at a level of emergency, not wanting to fully identify or eliminate threats. The threats the SCP and the intelligence chiefs "uncovered" were to a large degree fabricated to retain their power and standing with the President. The three examples of national security threats, described in Chapter 3, point to the overreactions and the disproportionate response of the security forces in neutralising what were instances of protests and organisational life outside of the MPLA-mandated structures.

Despite this, Angola did not fully share the traits of a national security state. Angola did not place the military as the highest organ of power. In fact the military was politically weakened by the Presidency as a way to ensure that no military leader would challenge dos Santos. Angola did not fully rally the church to mobilise resources for the state, rather financial resources were captured by a small elite controlling natural resources, rents and opportunities. Whichever social resources were mobilised, this was done more effectively by the traditional authorities, the local cells of the ruling party and the intelligence services. What Angola did share with the national security state was that 1) it maintained the appearance of democracy but viewed democratic procedure with contempt; 2) its security sector wielded considerable economic and political power; 3) it became obsessed with enemies (although it doesn't come across as institutionalised paranoia) and that these enemies were ruthless; and 4) it restricted public debate through secrecy and intimidation (Nelson-Pellmeyer 1992).

Several conditions have allowed the securitised state to emerge in Angola. They are predicated on historical experience, war, inequality, resources, distorted patriotism and the paternalism of a political elite. None of these combined would have naturally led to a securitised state. This was a choice, based on the distinct interpretation of threats and how power became structured overtime. Firstly, a long, divisive and brutal war militarised politics and instituted a survivalist mentality of governance that was never shed in peacetime. This conditioned politics. It had allowed for the rise of a generation of securocrats that were instrumental in helping the ruling party win the war while undermining it by transferring power to the Presidency. The structures of war—logistics, intelligence, command, training, arms, and mission—were adapted to guard the nation from itself.

Secondly, social and ethnic stratification, built over almost a century with colonial, liberation, and post-independence politics, created deep antagonisms aligned with privilege that needed protecting on one side, and marginalisation that needed reinforcing on the other. This conditioned identities and their place in the pyramid of power. This marginalisation was however graded and hierarchised between those that were politically aligned and those that were potential dissenters and needed containment. The way these divisions became embedded into the political and economic system meant that for some to succeed others had to fail, which created deep-seated fears within the ruling nomenclature.

Thirdly, wealth from the extractive industries meant the government could govern without negotiating with its citizens. Oil rents countered the need for aid conditioned on reform or economic policies that included citizens. Rather revenue and capital accrued by the ruling elites through their dominance of the oil industry, the diamond sector, the use of sovereign guarantees for loans, and the wide array of global business partners, provided an incentive to securitise. Sustainable development, underpinned by economic distribution and greater equity across society, threatened elite interests. This required effective mechanisms to contain such a threat. Extractive wealth also allowed the Presidency to build a vast empire of security around himself, his elites, and the mechanisms of power heavily tilting the national budget towards defence spending. Few forces existed that could inject accountability and distributive participation into the system. This conditioned citizenship even further. It also conditioned development and inclusion. Oligarchs positioned their efforts into instituting a feudal-like system distorting social relations and economic imperatives and embedding patronage. Lastly, the nature of the MPLA's sense of historical purpose and righteousness equated the nation to the party. This was informed by a deep-seated conviction that it was the only political force capable of taking Angola into the future by building a new social and political order. This conditioned the prospects for democracy. It disqualified all other actors and potential for political pluralism, muting alternative visions and undercutting competing values and needs. This also meant that political alternance would be construed as fatal.

The securitised state that ensued had several key traits. Its main feature was a strong Presidency that centralised power and patronage and designed, coordinated and fuelled the system. It served very narrow interests. It was supported by an amassed albeit weakened ruling party that webbed control through local structures, linking political support to access and services, and was key in broadening the control of the Presidency. The interests of both were upheld by a shadow government and a parallel "bureaucracy that administered things without concern for ends or assumptions" (Raskin 1976: 189). National rhetoric and ruling party messaging ensured that the country understood that peace and stability were assured under its guidance and survival. Steps to mobilise against it were positioned as a threat to stability and peace. Widespread infiltration, co-optation and surveillance of social and organisational life allowed the government to control reform and the pace of change and maintain a balance of power that favoured it. A complex security system that webbed control, counter-control, intelligence, counterintelligence, shadow powers and parallel institutions in a way to 'guard the guardians' ensured regime survival and maintained a state of readiness for war. It protected against social uprisings, a palace putsch, military coup, and democratic devolution. Combined, all these features brought about a new kind of securitised politics upheld by a vast infrastructure that privileged the identity, vision and exclusive political order of the MPLA. Over a million Angolans were linked in one way or another to this security universe, through active participation, in retirement, in reserve, or in clandestine form.

Securitisation had several effects. It resulted in society's belief that the system was built to undermine it and that it was incapable of treating citizens fairly. It was a system rigged against the population by treating them as subjects. The more elites benefited from the system, the greater the distance with the population, building on perceptions of greater threat. The availability of natural resources, neopatrimonialism connecting elites, and the power of the security apparatus together delinked political power from the masses. As a result, the MPLA was unaccountable to the vast majority, even if it demanded absolute loyalty. This de-linkage was further aggravated by the inability of the MPLA to provide services to the people, a situation that began at independence and remained the underlying characteristic of the government for 40 years. It also resulted in the state failing to do its duties and administer the country. Decades of undermining moves in parliament, the judiciary and the cabinet entrenched dysfunction that was routinely tapered over by the availability of money to create the illusion of government action. This dysfunction was a side-effect and not so much a stated strategy, although it served well the need to dissipate the power of competing institutions. Infrastructure projects, development programmes, or surgical distributive actions were used to show the government was operating for the people even if these barely made a dent against poverty and unemployment.

Angola wasn't exceptional in its choice of securitisation as a gover nance strategy. In Africa several ruling parties and their presidents opted to use the same tools of empowering securocrats, extending surveillance, containing dissent through infiltration and fear, and allowing military and security elites to economically benefit. Rwanda, Ethiopia, Eritrea, Uganda, South Sudan and Chad, which "were governed by military personnel and relied on the use of force to maintain order and legitimacy" (Fisher and Anderson 2015: 136), also adopted differing levels of securitisation. The authoritarian states they built were interventionist and controlling, managing a captured economy and surveilled society, as an attempt to establish durable political orders. Rwanda, Uganda and Ethiopia in particular used and instrumentalised military assistance from Western donors to ensure regime stability, reconfigure power and build militarised states. Under the guise of humanitarianism this "securitisation" (Duffield 2001) took the form of defence transformation initiatives and other security sector reform programmes, peacekeeping operations or direct military assistance. These countries in turn used the process of securitised aid to enhance the capacity and effectiveness of their authoritarian actions against internal dissent and threats on their borders (Fischer and Anderson 2015). Securitisation in these countries however was more pervasive and certainly more instrumentalised by ruling elites than merely the strategic use of foreign aid for the consolidation of authoritarian rule. It was also aimed at ensuring a narrative and identity (Rwanda), in managing the coexistence of governing partnerships (Ethiopia) and weaponising national security concerns stemming from opposition politics and popular protests (Uganda).

Surveillance strategies have become deeply embedded in the political strategies of survival. Ethiopia's use of abusive surveillance has a long and well-documented history of efforts to monitor critics inside the country and abroad.[4] Just like China and Saudi Arabia, Rwanda also uses social networks and spyware to harass dissidents and extend repression transnationally.[5] The rendition of Paul Rusesabagina from Dubai in August 2020 became the most recent example of Kigali extending its control of people, ideas and perceived threats to national security beyond its borders.[6] The use of coercive networks of embassies and expat organisations to intimidate people also spread to countries like South Sudan where intelligence services began kidnapping its citizens from neighbouring countries.[7] South Sudan's National Security Service's (NISS) threat of surveillance has terrorised journalists, opposition members and activists, sowing a web of generalised fear even when their interception and spying capabilities were not particularly sophisticated. NISS penetrated the daily life of its citizens and transformed how society interacted.[8]

Elsewhere on the continent securitisation processes occurred as part of the political landscape of competing political elites from within the ruling parties, as strategies to both contain divergence and protect factions. South Africa, which had robust public institutions and an established culture of democracy, has also experienced a rise in the power and influence of securocrats. These officers within the security apparatus were given prominence in the architecture of party and government policy during the presidency of Jacob Zuma (2008–17). Zuma used securocrats to advance his agenda and squash internal dissent, subverting democratic processes by using the armed might of the state to force through a political project (Duncan 2015). The Marikana massacre of 2012, where a group of protesting miners were gunned down by an overmilitarised police response, became the main identifier of this "tectonic shift" that had placed the military, police, and intelligence officers at the service of a small elite against the people (*ibid.*). The insidious use of the intelligence services to counter investigations into corruption, governance malfeasance and any other actions threatening the power of a faction of the ANC was also part of this securitisation. Like Angola, South Africa securitised its response to the Covid-19 pandemic with measures that empowered the military and employed war-like rhetoric against an existential threat. In Zimbabwe a similar trend emerged. Security agencies became deeply involved in the succession battle within the ruling ZANU-PF party with military intelligence and the civilian-led central intelligence organisation each supporting a different faction (Tendi 2016). Mandaza (2016) has described Zimbabwe as a "securocrat state" where the military-security apparatus was the dominant force in the structuring of power. In this perspective President Robert Mugabe, much like dos Santos, centred executive power in the Presidency, used the security agencies in order to execute different political programmes and kept securocrats individually beholden to him by personally facilitating the participation of the chiefs of the military, police and intelligence in the extractive industries.[9] Like the MPLA, ZANU-PF attempted to engulf society through the use of local administrators, traditional leaders and the military-security complex (*ibid.*).

*Structure of the Book*

The following chapters briefly cover the strategies of the MPLA and the Presidency in securitising power over a period of 30 years. The chapters do not follow a chronological order but provide a narrative rooted in historical explanation. This book cannot claim to represent a holistic and complete picture of the security apparatus in all its complexity. Rather it aims to begin a conversation about the role played by the security apparatus in deconstructing the nation and state in postwar Angola. Given the inherent difficulties of researching a system built on secrecy, intimidation, and the management of violence, information was gathered through interviews, research papers and media reports. Information on the country remains tightly controlled by the government. Fear and paranoia were particularly evident with informants who provided insights into the different areas of the security apparatus. It would take over ten years, and demonstrative commitment to their anonymity for them to discuss sensitive information.

Based on research conducted since 2002 with over 300 interviews in Luanda and six other provinces (Huila, Huambo, Bie, Moxico, Cabinda and Kuando Kubango) these first-hand insights provide a glimpse into the role of the security apparatus in Angola's peacetime politics. Because "securitisation occurs in a field of struggles" (Balzcq 2011: 15) where subjective understandings, interpretations and perspectives dispute different perceived and imagined realities, securitisation as it occurred in Angola had many versions and experiences. Interviews were conducted with former UNITA and MPLA commanders, with active and retired army generals, with ex-combatants that experienced the three sets of demobilisation, with officers within the Presidency and military intelligence, and with influential MPLA officials. All information from interviews conveys the knowledge, subjectivity and experience of each interviewee. Their names are kept anonymous to protect them and their families.

Chapter 1: The Component Parts introduces the component parts of Angola's political and social system. It provides a short and brief history of the ruling party and the Presidency in order to contextualise the usurpation of power described in the following chapters. The opposition and organised civil society are also introduced as elements that competed with, collaborated with or were deeply conditioned by the securitised system and the political and economic strategies of hegemonic control. This chapter provides the necessary background to the political components that upheld the many strategies of post-war governance in Angola and were built on an array of security interventions and forces.

Chapter 2: A Strategy of Securitised Hegemony contextualises the emergence of the President's securitised policy. It begins with the breakdown of the 1992 peace process and the securitised strategies that undermined efforts for political resolution on both sides of the conflict. The chapter provides the background to the last decade of war and the shifting priorities of elite survival that informed the post-war rebuilding strategy. It briefly describes the steps taken by the Presidency to ensure an outright military victory over UNITA. This chapter explains Angola's post-conflict stabilisation strategy, bringing to the fore the many contradictions that began to take root. The 'Angola rising' perspective was crafted on the ambitions of a self-defined exceptionalist stance of modernity, development, and untouchability. The country transitioned from armed conflict to armed peace.

Chapter 3: The Shadow Government details the shadow government and the edifice of power that was built to ensure the MPLA's longevity but more importantly the survival of the presidential circle. It explains the structures upholding the securitised and shadow state, dominated by the Casa de Segurança (Security Cabinet of the Presidency, SCP). It briefly describes the central structures and the multiple portfolios it managed which allowed it, via a vertical reporting system, to command the security apparatus and key areas of the cabinet. This chapter explores the contours of the SCP and the parallel army that sustained it. It analyses the role played by the three intelligence services that took on a broader surveillance role, spying on the elites and opposition and infiltrating society. I use the example of three cases—the book club "coup", the Kalupeteka religious sect massacre and the assassinations of activists Cassule and Kamulingue—to highlight the dysfunctions, overactions and violent underpinnings of the system.

Chapter 4: The Angolan Armed Forces traces the trajectory of the Angolan Armed Forces (FAA) as a founding pillar of the state, albeit a weakened one, in the post-war years. For decades the army was a vital conduit between the people and the government. As the only remaining institution of the peace process that retained former UNITA officers in leading positions and was racially and ethnically diverse, the FAA would experience several pathologies in peacetime. It would begin a re-edification process aimed at modernising and transforming the military while remaining a large and inactive army, with a depleted air force and a residual navy. With equipment in disrepair and corruption running deep inside the command structures, the FAA was impacted by the Presidency's manipulation, subverting professionalism, effectiveness, and morale. The chapter briefly discusses the FAA's foreign deployments in Africa, and ends by analysing its domestic role in two of the most marginalised and underdeveloped areas: the oil-rich enclave of Cabinda and diamond-rich Lunda-Norte and Lunda-Sul provinces.

Chapter 5: Changing the Guard analyses the 2017 presidential transition and the end of the dos Santos era. The new President, João Lourenço, became Angola's first head of state with a military background. Weeks into his Presidency, Lourenço reshuffled the leadership of the different branches of the security apparatus and slowly began dismantling the dos Santos family's grip on the economy. He rapidly understood that saving the image of the party and the economy had to become his first priorities if he was to survive a crippling recession and deep popular disillusion. He began a targeted corruption drive purging the ruling party and recovering assets to inject into the failing economy but replicated many of the same dynamics of his predecessor. In order to protect himself and his reform agenda the new President fell back on the securitisation strategy. Lourenço took the reins to reform but failed to understand that the securitisation policy had become the cornerstone of the country's inequality, citizen disenfranchisement, and governance failings.

Chapter 6: The Time of Monsters is dedicated to Angola's response to the Covid-19 pandemic. When, in 2020, coronavirus struck, the country was ill-prepared and unable to implement the measures needed to save lives and livelihoods. The fragilities created by dos Santos began unravelling as the twin shocks of the oil crisis and the pandemic plunged Angolans into greater poverty and despair. Signs of social rupture and an increase in protests suggested that change could come from the demands of the street, not the tempered reforms of the palace. Lourenço's governing mistakes were also a sign of his unwillingness to desecuritise. The concluding chapter looks at the broader issue of securitisation and its legacies. The country is facing a difficult crossroads. Policies enacted could either lead it down a path of entrenched securitisation and militarisation or to a process of desecuritisation and democratic emancipation. Either way, politics as usual will have to end.

# 1

# THE COMPONENT PARTS

This book is not about the MPLA, nor is it focused on President José Eduardo dos Santos. It is about a system of governance that included members of the MPLA and was built by President dos Santos but operated with many other intervenient forces. A complex group of political, security, commercial and financial agents helped the Presidency ensure dominance over the state, society, the economy and elite interests. Together they formed Angola's edifice of power. The Presidency stood at the pyramid's apex, providing strategy and everyday direction while generously distributing state loot. However, the Presidency was tied to the political structures of the ruling party, unable to override the MPLA entirely. The MPLA provided the political and legal front for the Presidency to control the state and society, building on local party cells to engulf non-partisan spaces. While this book focuses on the security apparatus as the conduit between all other underlying elements of the system, a brief introduction of the MPLA, the Presidency, the opposition and civil society provides some context with which to measure the impact of securitisation on the direction that Angola took in two decades of peace. While the MPLA, politico-party elites, the middle class, urban and rural populations, and organised civil society are presented in this section separately, they interacted, fused and at times collaborated for diverse reasons in a way that exemplifies the complexity of Angolan social, security and political relations. This chapter contextualises the political and social forces that collaborated with, contested and empowered the security apparatus. Chapters 3 and 4 describe the diverse intelligence and security units that upheld the securitised system at length.

## The MPLA

The MPLA was once considered one of Africa's most progressive parties, inspiring a generation of activists and intellectuals across the continent, but it ultimately became synonymous with corruption, marginalisation and an emasculated political hegemony. For decades it operated as if "Angola belonged to it", partly because of its visceral belief that it was the only legitimate and capable political force to govern the country (Vines et al. 2005). It insisted on its "exclusive ownership of Angolan nationhood ... (which viewed) any opposition as tantamount to treason" (Pearce 2016). Its electoral slogan of "O MPLA é o Povo e o Povo é o MPLA" (The MPLA is the people and the people are the MPLA) epitomised this national imperialism. From independence in 1975, the MPLA operated the state not as a separate entity but as part of its centralised structures. The party-state of the 1980s–1990s would slowly be overtaken by the force with which the presidential-state controlled and directed the war and, later, peace.

Upon its inception, the MPLA was a party led by intellectuals and mestiço (mixed-race) Luso-Angolans, with a predominantly urban and Mbundu-based constituency. The predominance of a creole aristocracy created a complex relationship with rural populations and pointed to the inherent contradictions of having a set of privileged colonial descendants launching a rebellion against the Portuguese and attempting to build a party of the people. For decades its political opponents would enhance these contradictions and present the MPLA as a narrow and exclusionary party unable to understand those it was meant to represent. While the MPLA was a political project, it was also an identity project based on the cultural ethos of a Mbundu/Creole constituency bent on advancing multiracial and multinational nationalism and articulating visions of cosmopolitanism (Moorman 2008). To be effective, the MPLA attempted to "appropriate categories of consciousness", like the idea of Angolanidade (Angolanness) so that it could "replace the nation itself" (Tomás 2012: 238–331). Its version of Angolanness was urban, modern, developmental, Westernised and hybrid, taking its identity beyond its founding ethnic-regional-linguistic character (Vidal 2019). The *Grande Familia do MPLA* (MPLA's Great Family) was a strategy to co-opt other political forces into its ranks, uniting different political families, regions and intellectual strands aligned with (or at least not repelled by) its vision for Angola. It became a united political community with strategic objectives, motivated to impose its vision of the world while dominating state structures (Paredes 2010).

The institutional and behavioural DNA of the MPLA was marked by centralised control. The establishment of "a monolithic political system" (Hodges 2004) began post-independence during one-party rule with the centralising role of the Marxist party. Angola's first President Agostinho Neto proclaimed on Independence Day that the party's organs would take precedence over the organs of the state. Under Neto, any dissidence and differing viewpoints capable of threatening party cohesion and centralised control were either suppressed or co-opted. Historically the MPLA was plagued by divisions and elite contestation. From 1962 to 1977, the movement would experience various political crises, including Viriato da Cruz's dissidence in 1963–4 (Bittencourt 2011) and the Eastern Revolt of Daniel Chipenda in 1969–1974 (Mabeko-Tali 2001) around racial and ethnic contentions. These disintegrative tendencies, made more prominent by the Active Revolt in 1974, were only halted by the massive purge of 27 May 1977.

Divergence within the nucleus of the MPLA's leadership would persist in the 1980s in particular among the pragmatic-nationalist faction (of dos Santos) and the progressive-socialist faction (of Lucio Lara, Iko Carreira and others) (Vidal 2016) aligned with regional (Luanda-Catete vs Malange) and racial (Luso-descendants and black leaders) cleavages. However, none of these classic threats grew to destabilise the President's power and political dominance, partly because of the massive purge of 1977 that eliminated leaders and forcefully ensured loyalty.

The need to install order and 'rectify' dissident political views within the MPLA had its roots in immediate post-independence politics. On 27 May 1977, two members of the central committee, Alves

Bernardo Baptista "Nito Alves" and José Vieira Dias Van Dunem, were accused of launching a coup against Neto. The two men led a reformist faction. They accused the ruling elite of prioritising personal wealth and power over the wellbeing of the people and the country. Tensions within the MPLA had been mounting for several months. Nito rallied great support in Luanda, having organised the party committees known as *poder popular* (popular power) during the 1975 transition, which later fought during the civil war.[1] Versions of events contrast greatly. Some sources claim a coup was the faction's desired outcome (Wolfers and Bergerol 1983; Pawson 2007), while survivors and MPLA dissidents claim that the two men seized the radio station to call for mass demonstrations in order to pressurise Neto to clean up his government. Under the command of Rafael Moracén, who operated within the Presidential Guard, Cuban forces were vital in repelling the alleged coup and began a sweep of supporters. Defence Minister Henrique Teles "Iko" Carreira played a crucial role in the extra-judicial trials and execution of Nito Alves in the army barracks of Grafanil.[2] The state's Directorate of Information and Security (Direcção de Informação e Segurança de Angola, DISA) subsequently proceeded with house-to-house searches looking for the Nitistas. Thousands were arrested, tortured, and killed. Persecutions continued for two more years as traitors were presented on television before being executed. Over 15,000 people were exhibited and killed in this way (Mateus and Mateus 2007). Although authorities never released an official number, between 30,000 and 90,000 MPLA supporters and leaders could have been killed.[3] The massacre became memorialised by the party as a necessary response to an imminent threat. Families of the disappeared and survivors claim that allegations of a coup were used to neutralise a powerful faction within the MPLA.[4]

The 27 May purge would set the preventive tone for future protests in Angola, with fear permeating any idea of taking to the streets in Luanda. "If they did this to their own comrades, imagine what they would do to others".[5] This episode also signalled an irreversible shift by the Presidency to weaken and contain the MPLA through security operations and control. It signalled the utility of having a strong and autonomous Presidential Guard whose mission was first and foremost about keeping the President in power. The clampdown that followed broke the collective leadership structures of the party, depleted its ranks, and severely scarred the intellectual and popular elites. Following the purge, the MPLA signed a 20-year Friendship and Cooperation treaty with the Soviet Union. In December 1977 it fully committed itself to Marxism-Leninism, becoming the MPLA-Partido do Trabalho (Labour Party). This brought about an era of centralised control and a hard-line stance whose lasting effects were felt within the MPLA and broader society. With an economy in tatters, a growing insurgency, a collapsed agricultural system, and an inefficient centralised socialist system unable to deliver services, the MPLA fell back on its narrower support base to stabilise its rule. This meant that rural populations and those from the interior were not assigned roles in the post-independence political order: this naturally fed UNITA's reformist agenda.

The political aftershocks of the purge allowed for a peaceful transition of power after Neto's death in September 1979. Cohesion within the ruling party had always been contingent on the President's overriding power, which invariably weakened party elites and upended the distribution of power within the different organisational structures. When dos Santos took the Presidency he inherited a smaller and more contained party. The MPLA's membership had fallen from 60,000 in 1975 to 16,000 in 1979 (Tvedten 1997) but would grow vertiginously to nearly 4 million by the time dos Santos could fully control politics in the post-war years.[6] From 1982 to 1985, dos Santos secured absolute control of the patrimonial apparatus, institutionalised the power of the Presidency and secured emergency powers allowing him to override the government and the party and insulate the petroleum sector (Vidal 2016).

The system of centralising control was also a result of a collapsed bureaucracy and administration. The mass exodus of state officials and public servants in 1975 contributed to a dysfunctional state bureaucracy. Faced with a system that was unable to deliver, power became concentrated in the Presidency and key party elites that micro-managed the everyday business of state affairs and government administration. In 1986 a steep fall in oil prices, corresponding to a loss of $200 million, coupled with corruption, excessive bureaucratisation and incompetence, had virtually led to economic collapse (Gleijeses 2013). The party began questioning the economic model imposed by its founding ideology, leading it away from the most stringent forms of central planning. In 1987 it devised the Saneamento Económico e Financeiro (Economic and Financial Rehabilitation programme) to rehabilitate the economy. It was meant to create a culture of entrepreneurship to foster a national bourgeoisie and the private sector (Tomás 2012). Liberalising the economy was more representative of the utility of the state apparatus towards the private appropriation of capital (and an extension of presidential clientelism) than a full transition towards a market economy (Vidal 2016). With the withdrawal of Cuban troops in 1989 and the end of the Cold War, the already strained system had few options but to transition away from state socialism.

In 1991 the MPLA signed the Bicesse Agreement with UNITA, bringing about far-reaching economic and political reforms. The MPLA recast itself in the run-up to the 1992 elections as the party for peace and reconciliation. It contrasted its image with a far more bellicose and intimidating UNITA whose leader Jonas Malheiro Savimbi's charisma and totalitarian tendencies terrified elites in Luanda who had begun developing their own interests and patronage networks in the wake of the reforms. The threat of a UNITA electoral victory risked undoing their political and economic control. As a result, the second securitised response was enacted to counter another significant existential threat. In October 1992, following tense negotiations to address the electoral impasse, the Halloween massacre (dealt with in Chapter 2) pushed UNITA back into war and permanently reversed any political legitimacy it had in the international community. For the MPLA, the system had opened up too quickly, and reforms had made it vulnerable to multiple threats. Decades of war taught the MPLA not to surrender political space without mechanisms to manage reforms and bypass them when necessary.

In 2002, the MPLA was presented with the opportunity to secure its political sovereignty and shape the country to its vision of development and modernity. It grew exponentially in the post-war years, becoming the only source of services, employment, and patronage. The strategy of placing intelligence operatives in every sector during the previous decades shifted and instead emphasis was placed on strengthening the party. The party's specialist committees would ensure that professionals in all areas were at the service of the MPLA and that MPLA members secured employment. Committees of political action (CAPs), the base structures of the party, were everywhere. The CAPs were meant to unite the MPLA "family", expelling and disciplining rebellious members while repelling any threats to the party (Rodrigues 2010). By 2008 the ruling party had over 35,600 CAPs spread across the country.[7] "To become a director of a school you had to be a member of the MPLA. If you wanted to rise in your career—as an engineer or doctor—you had to belong to a specialist committee".[8] The threat transitioned. In wartime, the state was in danger. In peacetime politics, the threats were to the MPLA.

The MPLA may have witnessed the gradual dissipation of its power by the Presidency but the underlying premise remained that they needed the President to maintain control. Members of the elite would cycle between various roles. Under dos Santos, the MPLA became less instrumental and increasingly surpassed by the power of the Presidency (Vidal 2019). The replacement of old party barons, the rotation of power between party elites that fell in and out of grace with dos Santos, aided this personalisation of power. "There was never stability within the MPLA as a party and dos Santos understood that if people were occupied with their personal interests they'd refrain from factionalising so the possibility of a split was remote until now".[9] For the first time since 1977, members of the MPLA and civil society began witnessing a new era of political reckoning under the Presidency of João Lourenço, who took over in 2017. It injected a sense of persecution, displacing fear from wider society to the elites.

*The Presidency*

Since 1979, the Presidency has become the most powerful institution in Angola. Dos Santos was simultaneously the head of state, the president of the party, the commander-in-chief of the armed forces, arbitrator of the economy and the principal advisor to everyone else involved in running the country (Roque 2011). As President, he would vigorously pursue a war against UNITA. He would steer the MPLA away from a Soviet-style centrally planned economy with the pragmatism that would become characteristic of his shifts to accommodate change and increase his chances of political survival. Following Savimbi's death and the Luena Accord in April 2002, he would be lauded for his magnanimity in accommodating the remaining UNITA military and political leaders in Luanda. For 38 years, he kept the MPLA and the government in check by expanding a highly efficient system of patronage that rewarded a loyal elite of politicians, family members and the military. He also contained their political influence by appointing and transferring powers to his security chiefs and their securitised agendas. Angola's presidential-state was effectively run by two support megastructures, revealing the design and sophistication of dos Santos' strategy to divide, rule, consolidate and securitise.

Trained and schooled in the Soviet Union as an oil engineer, he would serve as the country's first foreign minister, and in late 1978 would become the Minister of Planning. Dos Santos finished what Neto had started in December 1978 by pushing aside the party's old guard and bringing in young technocrats who would rise through the ranks and advise him in the Presidency. He would learn from Neto's rebalancing of ethnic, racial and regional groups and continue to integrate dissident members who had defected. During the war, personal loyalty to the President was the most important criteria for an MPLA member waiting to be appointed to a position of power.

Power would become increasingly concentrated within the Presidency even as it changed in form, name and ideology. The MPLA had not intended for this to happen. In fact, in 1975, the President had a coordinating and supervisory role of the organs of state, retaining few personal powers (Araújo 2017). In the central committee's opinion, the President would not have executive functions. Numerous constitutional reviews (undertaken in 1976–9) gradually began transferring all legislative, executive and provincial commissary powers to the President. Until 1980, Angola had no parliament. Instead the Council of the Revolution (Conselho da Revolução) became the supreme state organ. This council would be superseded by the People's Assembly (Assembleia do Povo), which became the first legislature but had little influence over state matters. These assemblies were primarily organs of the party. Within a few short years, dos Santos would become the head of the army and the president of the people's assembly (Araújo 2017).

In the 1980s, dos Santos was increasingly facing an intransigent and powerful insurgency that denied the MPLA the full benefits of sovereignty. UNITA, having recovered from its near defeat in 1976, was posing a serious military threat. It ran a parallel wartime state with its capital in Jamba, that governed civilians, and began training an army of cadres to serve as civil servants (Roque 2017b). This threat led the MPLA to grant dos Santos special powers in 1982, which allowed him to appoint Regional Military Councils (RMCs), reporting directly to the Presidency. The RMCs were positioned above local, provincial and administrative bodies and military courts were given preponderance over civilian tribunals (Vidal 2008).[10] Military officers became ministers and provincial governors, allowing the armed forces direct public administration involvement (Hodges 2004). Increasingly the centres of power had shifted from the party to the President. At the same time, the military was placed into the party-state structures, with the President mediating the different factions (Messiant 1992).[11]

In 1984, the Defence and Security Council (DSC) became the country's top decision-making body, eclipsing the power of the MPLA's Political Bureau and functioning like an inner cabinet that supervised all the affairs of the state (Hodges 2004: 53). The DSC decisively removed power from the party organs into the security elites loyal to the President. The council was composed of the President, the Ministers of Defence, Interior, State Security, Planning and Provincial Coordination, and the military's Chief of Staff. This would arguably become the first shadow supra-structure commanding control over all aspects of the state's survival. The DSC extended its reach provincially by having the regional military councils report directly to it, becoming a form of martial government with unlimited power across the country, including financial dealings (Vidal 2008: 133). The DSC would be dissolved in 1991 with the Bicesse accord, which propelled the Presidency to further vertically align powers within its structures.

In the 1990s, dos Santos perfected transferring and shadowing powers from the state to the Presidency. He further personalised and centralised control, governing from the presidential compound of Futungo de Belas in the outskirts of Luanda. Futungo was upheld by a coterie of generals and technocrats that together ensured the political longevity of dos Santos, diffused internal MPLA tensions, and governed in the shadows of the formal state institutions. Informal networks of patronage and security webbed together diverse interests and ensured that government business ran first and foremost through the Presidency. In Futungo, the two supra-structures of the Presidency—the Casa Militar and the Casa Civil—provided the infrastructure of counterpower to political and military elites. They became the key strategising fora that would allow dos Santos to survive another decade of war. The Casa Militar was the first format of the SCP. It was preceded by the Secretaria da Defesa (Defence Secretariat) that had General Antonio José Maria as its secretary, one of President dos Santos' most loyal and most aggressive generals. General José Maria would become a key pillar of the securitised strategy after 2002, playing an instrumental role in spying on the MPLA and the army and sowing political intrigue and dysfunction within the security apparatus.

The political transition of the 1990s reintroduced the need to strengthen the MPLA party structures, not as a way of enhancing the President's power base but to engage fully in electoral politics and extend the patronage system. In 1991 the one-party state dissolved, shedding the mantle of Marxism. A new constitution was enacted. The constitutional revision laws of 1991–2 formed a multi-party political system, created political space for the press and civil society, and provided for the decentralisation of power through the establishment of local government. Despite these essential changes, the constitution enshrined the President's powers. It allowed him to nominate and remove his government and ministers, all provincial governors, and several other organs of the state. UNITA had accepted this on the assumption that Savimbi would win the elections and formalise the powers he already retained in his parallel rebel state. The need to build on the structures of the party became imperative ahead of the 1992 elections. As a result, the President began reviving local party structures and multiplying party cells across the country. In 1990 the party had registered 65,000 members and by the end of 1992 had increased its membership by over 540,000 (Vidal 2008: 139). Because the MPLA controlled the legislative and the judiciary, "there was no institutional, political or legal check on a process of predation that favoured the President's networks" (Messiant 2008: 102). Although a Prime Minister theoretically headed the government, there were times during the last ten years of war that this post was either vacant or mostly ineffective. Advisors and unelected officials retained greater power than ministers and members of parliament. The tendencies to shadow would continue and increase with the establishment of the 1997 Government of National Unity (GURN) following the signing of the Lusaka Peace Agreement (explained in the next chapter). With UNITA's entry into the GURN, Angola experienced some semblance of political pluralism. Debates in parliament allowed for important policy directions to be discussed, but the legislature remained ineffective. Just as the 1992 elections had provided international legitimacy, the creation of the GURN and the implementation of the Lusaka Agreement allowed the government to continue consolidating power and resources on the sidelines. UNITA officials in the unity government had no significant power. They were forced to implement MPLA policies: "Behind every UNITA held post in the GURN was a more powerful MPLA official that retained real influence in what that ministry or department was doing".[12] Every politically sensitive competence that came with the different positions attributed to UNITA was transferred to an MPLA member. While UNITA retained the portfolios of Commerce, Mines and Tourism, as per the peace agreement, the respective ministers had only minor influence on the directions their ministries took.

In 1999, dos Santos was given a "blank cheque" by the party and parliament to use any means necessary to win the war (Araújo 2017). This provided dos Santos with the legal shield to remove authority from all other areas of government. The process of presidential securitisation was gaining heft and endurance, but it was in peacetime that it expanded. In peacetime, the 'state of exception' and the special powers he accrued over time to fight UNITA were formalised and regularised as a governing strategy. Dos Santos normalised the 'state of exception' by formalising it in the 2010 Constitution. He also combined features of the former Soviet-inspired Marxist order with parliamentary democracy and market economy (Tomás 2012). In the form of the Presidency, the presence of the state became omnipresent, combating any forces capable of exposing its unlawful practices.

The utility of democratic procedure was never more pronounced than during the first post-war polls of 2008 that dissolved the

33

GURN. The MPLA's overwhelming victory allowed the President to change the constitution in 2010. It concentrated executive powers in the Presidency and replaced provisions for direct presidential polls, instead having the head of the party with the largest number of votes in the legislative become the head of state. The constitution was the work of a commission guided by Carlos Feijó, then the Minister of State for the Civil Cabinet of the Presidency (CCP), who countered accusations that the President was all-powerful by placing one caveat of MPLA control. Unlike the 1992 constitution, the President would no longer be able to dissolve the parliament, which would be directly elected and charged with nominating the President. Ironically, Angola became governed by a presidentialist system in which the population would never elect the President. The new constitution, labelled as "hyper-presidentialist"[13] (Moreira 2010), allowed the President to dismiss or appoint ministers, vice-ministers, judges of the Constitutional, Supreme, Audit and Supreme Military Courts, governors of the Central Bank, and the board of the state-owned oil company Sonangol, and retain legislative powers. He could appoint all security and military chiefs and could at any point declare war or a state of national emergency (Thomashausen 2014). Constitutional experts equated the powers granted to the President as similar to those established under the authoritarian regime of Portugal's right-wing dictator Antonio de Oliveira Salazar in the 1930s (Miranda 2010).

The President became the ultimate arbitrator of state power, coordinating institutional links and the political design of every aspect of governance. With the new constitution, the role of Prime Minister was replaced by a Vice-President, who became an auxiliary organ to the President in his executive function. The government also became an auxiliary organ to the President, who was no longer politically accountable to the national assembly, which lost its powers to criticise the President. In a masterful stroke, the president tightened his stranglehold over politics, the economy and society. The system was beset by conflicting economic needs (of the poor, the elite, foreign investors, and the middle class), political perspectives (within the MPLA, the opposition, and civil society), widespread inequality and unaddressed grievances. It was shored up by the security apparatus. The frailty of the post-war order had to be corrected and strengthened through the only institution that was hierarchically conditioned to abide by presidential command and respected enough to control other competing MPLA interests. Securitisation of the state and the nation was in full operation after 2010.

## The Others

On the margins of this mammoth institution that had become the Presidency were the opposition parties, the population, civil society, the media, the youth, the churches and traditional authorities. As alternative forms of political pluralism, they were threats to the Presidency. This category of the others does not take away their fundamental importance, nor is it meant to amalgamate distinct forces and groups. It doesn't reduce their complexity or the fact that the others are the vast majority in Angola. They are depicted as the mass numbers of politicians, intellectuals, activists, professionals, rural and urban populations that existed and operated outside the Presidency. They were of little importance to the ruling party, the President and the state, except when they were useful or decided to mobilise and demand reform. Yet these groups—party-political elites, the middle class and the general population—were widely different and heterogeneous in their composition, support for the ruling party, and collaboration with and against the system. They are referred to here as "others", following a popular expression that "there is an Angola for some and an Angola for others"—a way of expressing the murky, contradictory and complex binaries of Angola. Some of these forces stood directly at odds with the ruling party and the Presidency, while others silently opposed dos Santos but surrendered to the inevitability of the MPLA governing Angola for many more decades. Many supported the ruling party through conviction or estrangement with other opposition parties but they also fell outside the MPLA's circle of patrons, and were, therefore, in the broader category of powerless and expendable others. Because the MPLA presented itself "as the legitimate heir of resistance", it colonised and imprisoned the public and non-political spaces (Faria 2013) as well as shadowed them by creating opposition parties, media outlets and NGOs. This was historically underpinned by the sectarian and monolithic character of the

MPLA's socialist state in the 1970s and 1980s (Pacheco 2009) that attempted to control all independent social forces.

The securitisation of society was not a coherent presidential strategy. While Angola was certainly a militarised society due to the war and the army of civilians, securitisation occurred because of infiltration and how economic, legal, familial, social, organisational problems were handled by the state (Schuilenburg 2011). While society fell away from its role as a counterpower to the system, organised civil society began emerging as a hub for alternative thought, questioning the elites and securitised governing strategies. The MPLA and the Presidency sought to create alliances across the different segments of civil society, reflecting "a desire to control the uncertainty of the future" (Crawford 2003: 490).[14] Actions to socially engineer a modern society that had left behind the importance of sub-national and complementary identities led society into retreat. This was not a signal of defeat but a recognition of the superior power of the security forces and those commanding them. It was a strategy to carve out peaceful normality as a negation of the political contestation that fed the war. With society's retreat came more enhanced forms of structured domination, fuelled by the fear that whatever threat existed was not easily seen. For many years, securitisation and the parallelisation of social forces took the power out of citizen participation, cultural and social self-expression, and economic development.

In wartime, as much as in peacetime, the population tactically withdrew from demanding a political voice, avoiding the attention of security agents and police, with self-censorship and political apathy. Their experience of war had removed any interest in protest. Still, dissatisfaction and resentment ran deep in the slums of Luanda, in the millions of unemployed youth, and in the rural communities that were unable to drag themselves out of poverty. The population governed themselves, fighting for daily subsistence and receiving inadequate and scarce services. Housing, healthcare, clean potable water, electricity, education, employment, and public sanitation systems were either insufficient, in disrepair, or completely lacking in many areas of the country. This forced the population to structure their lives on the margins of the state and the formal economy. Nothing about Angolan society was simplistic, even if it was depicted as marginalised and excluded populations. Ordinary Angolans had different strategies to regain agency, in the way they negotiated with and at times reproduced the system (Schubert 2018). Outside partisan political spaces, civilians came up with solutions to their problems. They showed themselves to be resilient, creative and pragmatic.

The informal economy provided income for millions, with over 70% of the population dependent on the sector, but it also reflected the state's maladjustment to the collective interests of society.[15] The economic model and post-war development priorities were ill-adapted to the socio-economic reality of the vast majority. The formal economy could not generate sufficient employment as diversification failed, with numerous barriers to small enterprise and with corruption preventing the implementation of development interventions. Of the $225 million generated monthly from the economy in the capital, 50% was generated by goods and services in the informal economy.[16] This created unique spaces and logistics chains with *quitandeiras* (suppliers), *zungueiras* (market sellers), *kupatata* (transporting merchandise), *kinguilas* and *doleiros* (forex dollar dealers), and *candongueiros* (taxi drivers) feeding a counter-system. In Luanda, Africa's largest outdoor market, Roque Santeiro, became a symbol of this informal economy. A sprawling enterprise, it fed Luanda's parallel economy, allowing millions to survive during years of war and economic hardship. Its market stalls stretched over 3 kilometres, selling everything from household goods and food, to weapons, assassinations and other services. It represented the informal economy but also showed the resilience of the Angolan people and their alternative forms of resistance.

For 40 years (during the anti-colonial struggle 1961–75 and the civil war 1975–2002), opposition in Angola was an armed and violent affair. The war for independence saw three movements build distinct nationalist ideologies, each principally representative of an ethnic group, a social class and a region of the country. They fought each other with the same intensity as they fought the colonial power, Portugal. These movements shared the objective of a free and independent Angola but diverged in their strategy, support base and ideology. UNITA waged war against the MPLA for three decades. Founded in 1966 and led by Jonas Malheiro Savimbi (until 2002), the movement believed that the exclusionary, narrow and elitist stance of the ruling party, upheld by foreign support, would perpetuate inequality and deny the majority of Angolans a place in society. UNITA fought the Marxist outlook of the MPLA, its alliance with the Cubans and Soviets, and the discrimination against rural and African populations. Its main support base was the Ovimbundu (the largest ethnic group of the central high plateau) and other southern and eastern people. For over a decade (1979–91), UNITA ran a parallel state, headquartered in its rear base in Jamba, governing millions of Angolans with effective but repressive structures. Its totalitarian state nevertheless provided healthcare, mandatory education, and skills training for its troops and cadres, developed food security and ran diverse manufacturing plants while creating a parallel society (Roque 2017b). For millions of Angolans, UNITA's defeat in 2002 rendered them "nationless" despite the movement's conduct and political mistakes.

From 2003, Isaias Samakuva directed the difficult task of shedding UNITA's belligerent image and rebuilding a severely damaged support base. UNITA was crushed at the 2008 polls, reducing its presence in parliament from 70 to 16 seats, but would build its vote share in all subsequent elections. This was evidence of growing support which increased its membership to over 2 million supporters. In 2019 Adalberto da Costa Junior was elected President of UNITA.[17] The government tried vigorously to interfere with the process, fearing that his election would bring new impetus to the party. He combined eloquence, youthfulness, and urban sophistication, all of which the MPLA had tried to deny as traits of UNITA's leadership.

The National Front for the Liberation of Angola (FNLA), founded in 1956 as the União dos Povos Angolanos (UPA), was composed mainly of the Bakongo (the third largest ethnic group) and was led by Holden Roberto. Its initial military strength and political astuteness positioned it as the strongest liberation movement before independence. Its 1976 military defeat at Quifangondo by MPLA forces led the FNLA to retreat into Zaire. It would only return to the political scene after the 1991 Bicesse agreement. As an opposition party, it would remain weak and ineffective, divided by internal factionalism exacerbated by the death of its founder in 2007. After Roberto's death, Ngola Kabango assumed leadership of the party, splitting the Bakongo support between the FNLA and the Democratic Party for Progress—

Angolan National Alliance (PDP-ANA). The PDP-ANA was founded in 1991 by M'fulumpinga N'landu Victor, a charismatic and outspoken university professor who had belonged to the FNLA. M'fulumpinga's leadership and strong Bakongo support made the party a threat to the MPLA. In July 2004, he was assassinated, which destroyed the party. Having lost its capacity to mobilise the masses, it joined the coalition group CASA-CE in 2012.

In March 2012, a coalition of smaller parties[18] converged under Abel Epalanga Chivukuvuku, a leading UNITA politician who defected from the party. The Convergence for National Salvation—Electoral Coalition (CASA-CE), a broad coalition proposing a third way for Angola, grew to become the second largest opposition party. Created a mere six months before the second post-war elections, it managed to secure 6% of the vote in 2012 and in 2017 increased its vote to 9.4%, doubling its representatives. It rapidly positioned itself as a bridging organisation between MPLA and UNITA constituencies, given the composition of its leaders, and as a home for different political affiliations. Several leaders from civil society, UNITA and the MPLA joined it. Admiral André Mendes de Carvalho "Miau", who was the deputy defence minister and from a family of strong nationalist and MPLA stalwarts, became a prominent MPLA defector. He was made CASA-CE's vice-president. CASA-CE's political ascendance would be halted by internal divisions, in particular ahead of the 2017 polls. In 2019 Chivukuvuku would be deposed as leader of CASA-CE and replaced by his deputy "Miau". He would move to establish his own party, Partido do Renascimento Angolano—Juntos por Angola (PRA-JA), but faced legal hurdles and politically motivated blockages at the constitutional court.[19]

Like the FNLA, the Party for Social Renewal (PRS) had strong ethnolinguistic representation. It also suffered from internal divisions. Formed in 1990, it participated in the 1992 elections in support of the MPLA's presidential bid. Led by Eduardo Kuangana, its key constituency was the Chokwe population in the rich Luanda diamond region. Although the party presented a proposal for a federalist constitution in 1998, it gained national appeal and secured eight seats in the 2008 elections. It lost credibility by voting with the MPLA on the electoral package in 2011. The PRS, like the FNLA and several other parties, could not withstand the MPLA's political attrition. Smaller opposition parties were unable to survive unscathed the 1992 and 2008 polls, and few reached the 2012 elections. After the MPLA consolidated its supremacy in 2008, it would interfere and nullify any attempts at political pluralism and multiparty debate.

Politically, Angolans remained deeply divided despite years of peaceful coexistence. Identities were built and altered during the war, entrenching further sentiments of political ostracisation and ethnic, racial and class divisions. Angolans didn't unite behind a foundational moment like achieving independence, with nationalist fervour, nor did they unite at the end of the war, when all were desperate for peace. Common to these two moments were the denialism of identity and historical justice on all sides. In many ways, both UNITA and the MPLA continued to embody the identities they built during the war. The MPLA depicted itself as representative of the nation, showcasing its military heroism. UNITA built its image on the nationalism of the excluded and the suffering. Neither of these images were real or helpful for Angolans. The narratives and images used to justify these divisions blocked key moments for political and national dialogue. Securitising peace only made this more pronounced. The threat of UNITA kept otherwise fractured MPLA elites united, too afraid of unpredictable reforms and unable to fathom an existence with a "rural, backward and ethnicised party" leading Angola into the future. The population, poor and lacking serious political representation, would also become a psychological threat to the MPLA and the Presidency.

Outside the ugly business of electoral politics, the opposition's growing strength revealed complex dynamics that characterised the country's social fabric. While the war masked some of the underlying social prejudices instrumentalised by the parties, peacetime politics brought these to the fore. For many in the opposition, no member of the Ovimbundu, Bakongo, Chokwe or other ethnic group would ever be able to hold powerful positions in government or the MPLA, outside of token nominations. Class distinctions that were formulated during the colonial period and sustained during the war continued to influence political positions and perceptions of party enmity. The MPLA would continue to be perceived as representing the petit bourgeoisie of the acculturated and "civilized" black Angolans deriving from the educated strata of society in Luanda (Cleary 2001). UNITA and the opposition more broadly were perceived by the MPLA as representing the residual peasantry of "native" Africans who lacked the vision, know-how, and national representation required to govern the country. Around these formulations were class, ethnic, racial and regional prejudices that permeated across generations. The choice was between urban modernity or an ethnic hinterland, both of which failed to represent all Angolans. However, one levelling dynamic emerged. Informers, soldiers, police and intelligence agents could be mobilised and recruited from all areas to create the massively inflated structures of the security apparatus. In the service of securitisation, all were provided with a role, irrespective of the perceived, existential or actual divisions and historical cleavages.

In the post-war era, Angola continued to claim one of Africa's largest armies. It also had a massive structure of competing and parallel forces that, including ex-combatants and intelligence officers, easily exceeded a million individuals (in a population of 31.8 million) formally linked to the security apparatus. This included the Angolan Armed Forces (FAA) with 120,000 active personnel, over 150,000 police,[20] as many as 100,000 intelligence operatives posted across the 18 provinces,[21] 10,000 from the Presidential Guard units, over 290,000 ex-combatants from the different DDR processes, 50,000 private security guards, and an unknown number of reserve units in the national guard, civil defence, and political militias. Had the government chosen another governing strategy, outside of securitised options, a heavily militarised and armed population would remain a defining legacy of the war and the parties that fought it. The military unofficially estimated that every household in Angola could own a firearm. Civilian disarmament campaigns from 2005 to 2007 resulted in the destruction of over 372 metric tons of weapons and 281 metric tons of explosive devices.[22] Yet Angola remained awash with small arms. In February 2003, the police established that a third of Angolans were still armed, pointing to a figure of over 4 million weapons (Weigert 2011: 170). By 2017 that number had decreased to 2.98 million privately owned firearms,[23] although estimates from military intelligence privately placed that number at 5 million.[24]

Civil society became the counterpower to the agents of securitisation, albeit small and weak, seeking participation in questions of politics and the economy denied to them. Four decades of war crushed any possibility for organised civil society to emerge outside the parties' parameters. In government and UNITA areas, youths were made to sing party slogans and political anthems to build a collective identity. In schools, in the army, at rallies, they were part and parcel of the political ideals of the warring factions. In this way, women, youths and sectorial professionals were socialised into the different political orders they advocated for. It was only in the 1990s that civil society began to develop in strength autonomously.

Efforts to strengthen civil society in the 1990s opened new opportunities for the church, private media, human rights organisations, NGOs and community groups to create a multi-party culture. In 2001 over 95 international NGOs and 365 national NGOs were registered (Vines et al. 2005). However, when groups became too powerful or inconvenient, they were either infiltrated or legally disbanded. In the post-war era, the government introduced new controls to regulate NGOs, the press and access to information, alongside the creation of MPLA-friendly civil society organisations.[25] Some organisations, however, survived these efforts to control and suppress their operations. These included Mãos Livres (Free Hands), Mosaiko, ADRA and AJPD, and faith-based organisations like Caritas.[26]

The President would begin an incursion into civil society and traditional institutions that would help him control the image of the MPLA and retain influence over how these social forces operated. Extending clientelist networks and patronage outside of the political and military elites allowed the President to begin influencing society in more benevolent ways. Two initiatives were emblematic of this approach. The first was the creation of the NGO O Nosso Soba (Our Soba) and the Associação Angolana de Autoridades Tradicionais (AATA) which allowed the MPLA to extend its patronage to the traditional authorities (Sobas) in the provinces. The MPLA's attention towards the Sobas was a strategy to inculcate the party in the rural areas and guarantee its hegemony in the periphery. Because of the chaos that ensued after the war and the mass displacement of people across the country, traditional authorities were the only recognised form of leadership in rural areas. The MPLA would harness this as a conduit for popular organisation and influence in the post-war era. This strategy was particularly effective during the 2008 elections, where Sobas were seen on television receiving bicycles, computers, money and other benefits. They were found with ballot boxes and ballots in their homes during the 2008 and 2017 elections.[27] As a result, the Sobas were no longer perceived as objective intermediaries but disseminators of the MPLA political message. State media would report on the MPLA's efforts to work with the "philanthropic" organisations O Nosso Soba and Causa Solidaria in post-war reconstruction efforts.[28] These organisations "operated within the MPLA's cabinet for citizenship and civil society" (Faria 2013: 170). By 2012, over 41,500 traditional authorities, out of 50,000, were on the government's payroll, costing the state an estimated 8 billion kwanza (equivalent to $13 million) a month (Soares de Oliveira 2013).[29]

The second strategy to neutralise non-partisan and autonomous spaces in society resulted in the creation of the Fundação Eduardo dos Santos (FESA), which allowed the President to take credit for any social activities in the areas of education, health and other donor-funded interventions (Messiant 2008: 104). FESA was established in 1996 and served to enhance the personal power and prestige of the President and extended his influence over civil society through the funding, creation, and activities of NGOs linked to him. FESA officially focused on cultural, social, and scientific issues to develop the educational sector, stimulate the economy, and assist private and public institutions in providing social services. Unofficially it served to neutralise civil society and co-opt any opposition to Futungo. The creation of pro-government NGOs that functioned as "chains of transmission" for its policies and strategies (Pacheco 2009) undermined genuine efforts towards creating a civil society movement. All those unsympathetic to the MPLA struggled to survive and faced challenges at every level. Other NGOs with connections to the government included the Lwini Social Solidarity Fund (set up by the first lady), and Criança Futuro (under the supervision of an intelligence chief General Miala) among others. These allowed the Presidency to create a politically manipulated and cooperative "civil society" operating within the logic of patrimonialism (Vidal 2008).

Efforts to control and direct the media led the MPLA elites to create their own media outlets. Independent media struggled to survive this strategy, as well as overcome the legal constraints brought against them. Before 1991 there was no private press in Angola. Criminal defamation laws, open censorship and the persecution of journalists restricted freedom of expression and the free press even after the 1991 reforms. Radio Ecclesia, one of the most vocal and independent outlets, was allowed to begin broadcasting in Luanda in 1997, rapidly gaining a reputation for independent and critical reporting. It was created in the 1950s but had been banned in 1978. While it operated in the capital, it had been barred from broadcasting throughout the country until 2018. It had been forbidden from using relay stations to broadcast in the provinces, one of many legal hurdles placed by the government to shut down an independent political and social voice. State media, particularly the *Jornal de Angola* newspaper, the Televisão Public de Angola (TPA) and the Radio Nacional de Angola, became mouthpieces for the MPLA. Their directors and journalists were elected onto the party's central committee, directing propaganda and political misinformation across the country.[30] Numerous "independent" television stations and newspapers were directly linked to the MPLA. The Media Novo group, belonging to three of dos Santos' closest advisors, Generals "Dino" and "Kopelipa" and former vice-president Manuel Vicente, owned several of the private press outlets including the channel TV Zimbo, the newspaper *O Pais*, and Radio Mais. Another group, Interactive Empreendimentos Multimedia, which owned TV Palanca and Radio Global, was owned by Manuel Rabelais, the former head of Communications of the Presidency.

Several newspapers survived years of infiltration, economic strangulation and legal barrages against them. *Folha 8, Angolense, A Capital and Agora* were some of the only ones that were both critical and, at times, antagonistic towards the MPLA. In the immediate post-war years, these papers began reporting on elite corruption and the fortunes of MPLA politicians, which resulted in direct threats by security services against their journalists, cases of defamation meant to bankrupt them, and lengthy interrogations by the police.[31] Curbing press freedom was not always benevolent. The Cabindan-born journalist Ricardo De Melo, director of Imparcial Fax, was killed in January 1995, allegedly for exposing corruption. No one was ever charged with his murder. From 1999, journalist Rafael Marques de Morais would also become a leading enemy of the state. His exposés on corruption and human rights abuses over the years would frequently land him in jail and in court. William Tonet, editor of *Folha 8* and later a founding member of the opposition party CASA-CE, would also suffer relentless intimidation. Many others would lead the charge against misinformation and repression at great risk to their lives and livelihoods.

While the control of chiefs, the media and NGOs aimed to defang forms of protest and bring social forces under the control of the MPLA, a more intrusive strategy accompanied it. This included building a system of human surveillance. Intelligence operatives pretended to be journalists, members of the opposition, activists, and bureaucrats in public institutions, banks, and private sectors. They were placed strategically in key areas of the capital and countryside. "In 2011, the government began a systematic process of infiltrating society with security and intelligence agents because of their fear of the Arab Spring".[32] People believed that the presence of these agents extended into the intimacy of their homes. "The security forces were everywhere and infiltrated families. Within their own homes, people didn't know who the informer that the services had recruited was".[33]

The church did not escape the divisions of society and the political groups. The Church's influence on the political consciousness of the anti-colonial leaders spanned across the liberation movements (Messiant 2000; 2008) and had a long and important history in Angola. The Catholic Church, representing over 14 million followers in Angola, was the most powerful, with 18 dioceses, three archdioceses in Luanda, Lubango and Huambo, and over 3,000 priests at its service (Jensen and Pestana 2010). In September 2019, the President signed a framework agreement with the Holy See, long requested by the Catholic Church, formalising its position of privilege as the government's main religious interlocutor.[34] This ratified a relationship that had over the years led to several priests openly supporting the MPLA. It was also an attempt to counter the expansion of new evangelical churches outside the control of the government and in areas where the state had a weak presence. Less than a year later, Luanda ordered the closure of one of Brazil's largest evangelical churches—the Universal Church of the Kingdom of God—accusing it of fraud and other fiscal crimes. The move signalled a continued effort to bring parishes and churches across the country under the MPLA's control. The government created a coalition of 1,200 "illegal churches" that were instructed to vote for the MPLA in the 2012 polls. Known as the Christian Coalition of Angola, this was led by an alleged regime-affiliated pastor Antunes Huambo.[35] The authorities subsequently persecuted those refusing to join the coalition.

One case in particular revealed the MPLA's efforts to homogenise all sectors under their influence. In December 2014, Rome was voting to elect the next archbishop of Angola. The Catholic Church in Angola was deeply divided on whom to support. On one side was Filomeno de Nascimento Vieira Dias (from an MPLA family), and on the other was Dom Gabriel Mbilingue (associated with UNITA), who had many votes within the Vatican. Dom Mbiligue was the president of the influential CEAST, the Catholic Bishops Conference of Angola and São Tomé. Both dos Santos and the Cardinal of Luanda, Dom Alexandre do Nascimento, a revered figure among the MPLA's political elites, lobbied for the election of Vieira Dias, who won the vote. Just as the Archbishop was selected from the MPLA's ethnic constituency, "The Cardinal of Luanda (would) always be a Kimbundu when, in fact, there were more Ovimbundu bishops".[36]

All these dynamics served to contain areas for independent expression and protest. However, a small group of youth activists managed to shake the Presidency single-handedly, becoming the voices of defiance for their generation. Their bold and brave actions cost them their health, their lives and their sanity. In the wake of the Arab Spring protests that inspired youths around the world to rise against authoritarian and entrenched regimes, a small group of activists took the forefront of their generation's fight against dos Santos. Created on 7 March 2011, the group's membership would remain small and leaderless but effective in mobilising public opinion and rattling the security apparatus. As this group of "revolutionary" youth grew, who became known as the "Revus", so did coordinated aggressions of the state security apparatus with mass arrests, beatings, torture and kidnappings. These demonstrations were also an indication of the changing social fabric in Angola. After 2002, music increasingly became a form of protest in the urban areas, eloquently accusing the political establishment and exposing their failures. Rappers like MCK, Kid MC, Ikonoklasta and many others gave voice to the contradictions in Angola, narrating the difficulties faced by the population. Born out of the suburbs of Luanda, different styles like *kizomba* and *kuduro* had counter-hegemonic tones, "de-centering the asphalt in favour of the *musseques* (the slums)" (Tomás 2012: 316). Unlike the revolutionary songs of the past, these became songs of anger and disappointment, of a country betrayed by its leadership.

2

# A STRATEGY OF SECURITISED HEGEMONY

## OUTMANOEUVRING THE ENEMY

Angola's securitised state has long antecedents. Its edifice of power was shaped by decades of conflict, incomplete transitions, and the political mutations of a system that was consistently underpinned by combative and survivalist imperatives. Having fought for nearly six decades to attain or retain power, the MPLA would continuously find ways to shield itself from any threats. While the way it governed in the preceding decades informed how the party and Presidency would continue to organise power around the security apparatus, the nature of the current strategy began in the 1991–2 transition. The need to control the pace of change and reform led the President and his governing elites to devise strategies to undercut political transformation, popular accountability, and international scrutiny. The transition to multi-party politics pushed the mechanisms of control and power into the shadows.

With each stage of war, the Angolan state morphed further into a securitised entity, driven by policies of regime survival, detached from its responsibilities to its citizens, and with a concentration of power in the Presidency. The first, 16-year, war (1975–91) was a conflict of ideologies and competing visions for the nation fed by Cold War proxy dynamics. When this post-independence war ended, there was military parity in terms of strength and capacity between the two sides. The second war (1992–4) was a vengeful war of political betrayal and disillusion. The high levels of destruction and militarisation were unprecedented. This war had no ideological underpinning and was driven by mutual fear and the unmeasured ambition for power on both sides. Both the MPLA and UNITA restructured their militaries, armed and funded through access to natural resources. The national security threat of an enraged and wounded UNITA was justification enough for a policy of securitisation. Despite that, securitisation occurred because of political threats, not just military ones. In some respects, the President and MPLA chose securitisation to replace the vast security apparatus of the Cubans and Soviets, tying the need to internally securitise to changing internal political dynamics (the externally imposed reform process) but also a changing international environment. In other respects, securitisation was a mere continuation of a policy that already existed. The presence of UNITA politicians, international mediators and diplomats in Luanda in the 1990s created the need to shadow institutions so that a veneer of reform could operate in tandem with the centralisation of power in the Presidency. The third war of 1998–2002 became the war to end all wars. With policies of scorched earth and the indiscriminate targeting of civilians, it plunged the country into new depths of despair and suffering. UNITA had been reduced to a guerrilla army, no longer retaining the capacity to engage in conventional warfare. When peace was declared in 2002, Angola was destroyed on many fronts. There was a mass underreported humanitarian crisis of 5 million in need of emergency aid; infrastructure and cities had been decimated; the countryside was mined and fallow with few communities left that weren't uprooted by the conflict. At war's end, securitisation intensified as a form of extended administration of people, fear, forced reconciliation and reconstruction. It allowed the ruling party to ensure stability with an armed peace rather than a political vision that could unify a broken nation.

This chapter traces the key moments that led to the current state of securitisation and how each phase contributed to the hegemonic control of the MPLA. It explores the events that led to the resumption of war following the 1992 elections. It describes the conduct of the war on both sides and the events that led to UNITA's defeat in 2002. The humanitarian crisis that ensued in peacetime and the government's response provides insight into the disconnect between the state and society, characteristic of the existing dynamic of inequality, marginalisation and a divided society. It describes how reforms in Angola were more a reflection of the need to adapt to change to maintain control of the state—and to control the rate at which any change occurred—than a genuine opening of the political space (Roque 2011). The chapter ends with an overview of the key decisions made by the Presidency towards reconstruction and the emergence of the Angola rising spectacle.

## Unravelling of the Bicesse Agreement

Every country has defining moments that lead them down unexpected paths. The unravelling of the 1991–2 peace process was one such moment. Events during the 1992 transition could have taken many different forms resulting in distinct paths for the country. Yet the outcome that prevailed was one laced with political distortions and incomplete transitions. An economic and political reform process brought about a system of multi-party politics yet centralisation never stopped. The Presidency became the most powerful institution even if dos Santos was never officially elected, having deflected the second run-off polls in the country's first elections in 1992, thereby taking control of the country by underhanded means. The army was formed using troops from both sides, with the intention of unifying forces and building trust, but it was heavily dominated by the MPLA's military ethos and was sent to war immediately after edification. The international community, aiming to play a constructive role, would increasingly find itself unable to change the course of politics. Events in 1992 prepared the ground for another decade of war, despite intermittent years of tense peace.

The leadership and supporters of both sides temporarily overcame high levels of distrust, resentment and estrangement after the signing of the 1991 Bicesse Accord. UNITA returned to Luanda for the first time since 1975. There was renewed hope for peace. The agreement formalised a ceasefire and outlined the steps for national reconciliation during a transitional phase that would culminate in multi-party elections and a unified national army. There was a genuine belief that the

51

political process would provide the space for both UNITA and the MPLA to alter the terms of their engagement. Both parties, however, failed to demobilise and continued to operate with a zero-sum mentality. The failure of the peace process poisoned subsequent attempts at a negotiated solution. With each failed attempt, the brutality of the war increased while decreasing any political efforts to justify their need to continue fighting.

The peace process was never expected to be easy. Both UNITA and the MPLA had entrenched their mutual animosity for over two decades through highly divisive propaganda strategies, social mobilisation for war, and the belief that only eliminating the enemy would allow the country to continue its righteous path to development and nation-building. Power-sharing would never have been an easy and acceptable outcome for either dos Santos or Savimbi. Access to resources for the government (oil) and UNITA (diamonds) meant that both continued to have the capacity to wage war and procure arms. Politicians on both sides acknowledge that there should have been more time for the demobilisation process and that elections should have never occurred while both parties were still armed. Several external factors also explain why the process collapsed. The United Nations' mission in Angola was criticised for having an inadequate mandate, mission size and commitment. The international community lost leverage on both sides and was overcome by the events on the ground. The UN's selective application of sanctions also had a negative impact on prospects for peace. UNITA was repeatedly condemned in UN Security Council (UNSC) resolutions for persistent violations of the accords, and punished with sanctions.[1] UNSC Resolution 864 (September 1993) applied Chapter VII for the first time in UN history to a non-state entity as UNITA's fight was defined as a threat to international peace and security. The more isolated UNITA became, the more brutal the war, with the government feeling empowered by international recognition. For its part, UNITA continued fighting for a degree of credibility it would never regain while the war raged.

The UN Angola Verification Mission II (UNAVEM II) was tasked with overseeing the Bicesse peace process. The existing UNAVEM I[2] mission that had monitored the withdrawal of Cuban and South African troops from Angola was transformed into UNAVEM II in 1991, following UNSC Resolution 696. Russia, the United States and Portugal (the Troika) acted as guarantors who could use their influence to assist implementation. The mandate was weak from the onset, given that it was merely a monitoring mission rather than an implementation one. The 17-month operation involved 350 military observers, 126 police and 200 support staff and cost $132 million (Weigert 2011: 106). The mission that would replace it in 1995, UNAVEM III, would, in comparison, have a budget of $23 million per month (Maier 1997). The UN tried to do peacekeeping on the cheap during the most sensitive moment of the post-independence political transition. This minimalist presence on the ground was clearly a contributing factor in the failure to keep both parties engaged. However, the blame for Bicesse's failure lay mainly with both UNITA and the MPLA. Actions taken in the aftermath of the elections revealed the MPLA's intention was never to give up power.

Implementation of the agreement fell to the parties. Several joint commissions were created, with the Political and Military Joint Commission (CCPM), the Joint Commission for the Formation of the Armed Forces (CCFA) and the Joint Ceasefire Verification Monitoring Commission (CCVCF) taking the lead. The CCPM was, in its majority, composed of military leaders, each delegation with six generals, and three Troika observers. The Troika, however, was not empowered to overrule UNITA or government members. The new national army, the Angolan Armed Forces (FAA) would be created with troop parity between UNITA's Forças Armadas de Libertação de Angola (FALA) and the MPLA's Forças Armadas Populares de Libertação de Angola (FAPLA), a total of 50,000 men. The FAA would have 40,000 troops, 4,000 officers, 6,000 sergeants and 30,000 support staff for operations and administration. The government was expected to demobilise 114,000 troops and UNITA was placed to demobilise 37,000 soldiers. Because UNITA had neither a navy nor an airforce to integrate into the FAA, its soldiers would be incorporated into other units. The cantonment, disarmament and demobilisation of troops were slated to occur before the electoral process but encountered numerous delays and obstacles. Both parties deflated their troop number, adding to the suspicion that they were holding armed units outside of the integration and demobilisation process. A year earlier, in October 1991,

UNAVEM II reported that 20% of the government's troops were unaccounted for, representing a force of 30,000 men.[3]

With elections rapidly approaching in September 1992, the government had disbanded less than 20% of its forces while UNITA had demobilised only 4%, even though it had 80% of its troops in cantonment areas (Weigert 2011: 107). The slow rate of demilitarisation was due to the lack of confidence between the two parties and the reluctance to hand over weapons. On 27 September, days before the polls, the FAA was symbolically inaugurated. The new national army was composed of a mere 8,000 men. The party that won the polls would then nominate the Chief of Staff of the FAA. Leading the entire process were UNITA's General Abilio Kamalata Numa and the MPLA's General João de Matos, who were both nominated to the top command of the armed forces. Years later, generals from both sides would state that the military had found the tools, willingness, and channels to work together and it was political interference that led to the resumption of war. When the war restarted, the FAA had 32,000 men, of whom only 7,000 were from the former FALA (4,000 of them later defected back to UNITA).[4]

The agreement also foresaw the integration of UNITA members into the national police force, although the government rejected UNITA's demand to contribute 6,000 to the joint force. In March 1992, the government transferred 1,000 of its elite troops into the newly created Rapid Reaction Intervention Police (PIR), later known as the "Ninjas". The Ninjas became one of the most highly trained paramilitary units of the security apparatus, used to clamp down on dissent at all levels. Trained by Spain's Rural Anti-terrorist Group of the Guardia Civil, the force grew from 4,000 to 20,000 in just a few years.[5] Spain also provided the PIR with weapons worth $26 million in 1992. The creation of the PIR was a key mechanism for the securitisation of the state through games of fear and overt violence. As a militarised police force initially better trained and armed than the FAA, the PIR would become a symbol of the calculations that outmanoeuvred UNITA.

In the run-up to the polls, tensions were high. UNITA's behaviour and discourse had been aggressive. Its bodyguards, given police status under the Bicesse accords, often behaved in a threatening manner, using excessive force against perceived threats, including journalists.

The lack of an independent media fed the existing fear of UNITA in the capital. Two decades of exposure to propaganda and indoctrination had left civilians on both sides fearing the future governance of either party. During the elections, many used the expression "the MPLA steals, but UNITA kills", reflecting the impressions of both parties in Luanda. While UNITA's electoral campaign focused on Savimbi, who often campaigned in fatigues and used bellicose rhetoric that alienated many voters, the MPLA's campaign portrayed dos Santos as a leader that could take Angola into the modern world (Maier 1997). Despite this, many within the MPLA and Western capitals believed UNITA would win the elections given the disenchantment felt with MPLA's one-party rule. UNITA certainly expected to win at the polls. Western diplomats recognise that in 1992 it was Savimbi who lost the elections and not the MPLA that won them.[6]

On 29 and 30 September 1992, Angolans voted for the first time to elect their parliament and President. Voter turnout was above 90%, with 4.4 million casting their vote. The historic elections were "at once peaceful and violent, free and threatened, successful and irrelevant" (Meldrum 1992). As soon as voting began, mutual accusations of irregularities and intimidation occurred. On the night of 30 September, just after voting ended, a massive blackout in Luanda shut down the electoral commission's computers. Although power cuts were common in Luanda, UNITA would later claim that the electoral commission's software was purposefully manipulated to alter results. Legislative results gave the MPLA 54% of the vote, equivalent to 125 seats in parliament, with UNITA trailing behind with 34% of the vote, equivalent to 70 seats. The presidential race was much closer, with dos Santos receiving 49.6% of the vote while Savimbi received 40%, requiring a second round of voting within 30 days. The fact that the MPLA gained a larger share of the vote than the President would haunt dos Santos for the remainder of his tenure. Dos Santos would, in this way, never be directly elected by popular vote, rather being nominated by the party in 2012 as the head of state as per the 2010 constitution.

On 2 October, six opposition parties, including UNITA, FNLA and PDP-ANA,[7] held a joint press conference denouncing the electoral process and outlining all the irregularities that pointed to widespread fraud. UNITA sent several letters to the National Electoral Commission

(CNE), UNAVEM II, the CCPM and the Troika, accompanied by reports and evidence of irregularities and violations of the electoral law. In one of these letters, dated 14 October, UNITA claimed that in seven of the 18 provinces, there were irregularities corresponding to 30% of the results. The opposition demanded that the results be revised, and demanded to know the real number of electoral ID cards distributed, and what happened to the extra ballot papers (7 million ballots were printed, but only 4.3 million were used). They also demanded investigations into the disappearance of ballot boxes and the creation of ghost polling stations. Officially, there were 5,579 polling stations, yet the results issued by CNE computers revealed an additional 408 "supplementary and non-identified" polling stations that corresponded to 489,600 votes.[8] These strategies became the MPLA's cheat book for future polls, replicating similar voter disenfranchisement and result tampering in 2008, 2012 and 2017. In protest, UNITA withdrew 11 of its generals from the FAA on 5 October.

Two weeks later, the opposition issued a declaration calling for a new process aimed at national unity and finding a peaceful resolution to the impasse. On 17 October, the UN Special Envoy for Angola, Margaret Anstee, ratified the electoral results declaring them "generally free and fair", foreclosing any possibility for the opposition to find political redress. While Anstee recognised that there had been irregularities, she asserted that they did not significantly affect the overall results. However, former US Assistant Secretary of State Chester Crocker claimed that observers had no way to evaluate the elections (Simpkins 1996). The UN had 400 election observers for 6,000 polling stations. Two days earlier, Savimbi had formally accepted the results at a press conference in Huambo. This was later reported in the state's newspaper, *Jornal de Angola*, on 17 October.[9] The UN Security Council Resolution 793 (1992) also referred to UNITA's acceptance of the electoral results. The post-electoral crisis that unfolded was not a result of UNITA rejecting the results, as is widely argued across Angola's wartime and peacetime literature, but because of the way the MPLA undercut negotiations and bypassed a second round of presidential polls by unleashing a strategy of violence. Actions by the MPLA pushed UNITA back into war as a way of avoiding democratic political reversal. Between 22 and 31 October, the CCPM met several times to negotiate a solution to the electoral impasse and prepare a second round of presidential polls. UNITA was concerned that the practices that had led to electoral fraud remained unaddressed ahead of the second round. Delegates of the CCPM were aware of the importance of finding a consensus to avoid a return to war. The parties agreed to recommit to the ceasefire and halt all offensive operations staged on both sides; they discussed the holding of the second round of presidential elections; they recommitted to the DDR process and the creation of the FAA.

Tensions were high as sporadic fighting had occurred throughout the previous weeks. However, bipartisan discussions within the CCPM made some headway, with agreement on several issues, except the formation of a transitional government. On 31 October, CCPM negotiators planned to reconvene to approve a document outlining measures to resolve the electoral crises, in the presence of the Troika observers, the UN Special Envoy, UNAVEM II representatives and several regional ambassadors. The Halloween Massacre began before the meeting could take place. Like the 1977 purge before it, this massacre was implanted in the collective consciousness of future dissenters and protesters and set the tone for the subsequent securitisation of elections in Angola. Future polls in peacetime (2008, 2012 and 2017) became sites for contestation and insecurity, perceived as necessary exercises but simultaneously placed as potential threats. Securitisation discourses became a subsequent strategy for electoral manipulation.

The killings began at 2 pm. Claiming that it was responding to a coup attempt by UNITA, the government staged a major clampdown on the leadership of UNITA and its supporters. The first attack occurred against the Turismo hotel. It was followed by the bombardment of UNITA's provincial party offices at 2:20 pm, the Motel at 2:40 pm, the barracks Comandante Economia at 3 pm, and the party's General Secretariat at 3:20 pm, and from 4 pm onwards it became a generalised attack on UNITA supporters (Moura Roque 1994: 146). Foreign journalists present in Luanda during the massacres question the integrity of the government claims that UNITA was staging a coup: "How is it that the only offices, residences and hotels to be destroyed belonged to UNITA?" (Maier 2007: 100). The Halloween massacre aimed to decapitate UNITA's leadership, showing the international community the rebuttal of electoral results and UNITA's need to continue fighting.[10] It was also meant to avoid a second round of elections. Several elements point to a well-orchestrated and premeditated massacre of UNITA supporters, including others who were killed just for being from the south. The arming of civilians, the coordinated action of the police and the PIR, the reactivation of civil militias, and the intense propaganda aimed at creating fear of UNITA created a powder keg. No one knows who masterminded this strategy but the coordination of such forces implied an intervention by the presidential securocrats. Journalists on the governments' side were even preemptively told to take shelter before the massacre began. "At 11:00 am we were told to leave our offices and go home as there was going to be trouble. The killings began that day and spread rapidly. In my neighbourhood the initial killings were done by the population—neighbours attacking people from the south—but after that it was the police that took over".[11]

Weeks earlier, the government had distributed weapons to civilians, demobilised soldiers, party activists and unemployed youths—a fact that the international community was well aware of.[12] The MPLA would unleash a similar strategy on the eve of independence when it armed supporters in the *musseques* (slums), later referred to as *poder popular* (people's power) (Maier 2007: 95). In 1992, the government used popular militias, known as the people's vigilante brigades (BPV) and the youth Jovem Justiceiros to launch a campaign of ethnic cleansing against the Ovimbundu population (Maier 1997). "The attack consisted of heterogeneous forces which included the PIR, demobilised combatants and the population. ... The intention was to annihilate in accordance with the Marxist thinking that where there is antagonistic contradiction there is a need to exclude".[13] The three main arteries to exit the capital (Viana, Cacuaco and Samba) were closed off with roadblocks on the morning of 31 October to stop any movement in and out of the city. UNITA had planned to stage a mass protest that day, an event it had been planning for two weeks, but cancelled the rally because of the road closures and the government's unwillingness to allow the gathering. Many supporters were wearing UNITA t-shirts because of the planned march, which made them easily identifiable targets.

Several of UNITA's top leadership were killed, including Vice-President Jeremias Kalandula Chitunda; the head of UNITA's Delegation to the CCPM, Elias Salupeto Pena; the party's Secretary-General, Adolosi Mango Paulo Alicerses; and Brigadier Eliseu Sapitango Chimbili. Thousands of UNITA supporters were allegedly burnt alive in containers or shot on the streets.[14] Over 430 of UNITA's leadership and senior cadres would be held prisoner in the Turismo, Tropico, Presidente and Costa do Sol hotels as well as different military locations. Savimbi's house in Miramar would be completely destroyed by helicopters, tanks, the PIR and armed popular militias. In total, over 2,000 cadres and supporters were detained including women and children. Many news agencies recorded images of the massacres. Several bishops and politicians made appeals in interviews published by Portuguese newspapers to stop the killings. Horrifying survivor testimonies tell stories of unprecedented levels of personalised cruelty. Throughout Luanda, people "armed with kitchen knives, pistols, clubs, machetes, went from door to door massacring anyone they suspected of belonging to UNITA" (Heywood 2011: 322). Attackers selected victims for merely being from the south of the country and of the Ovimbundu ethnic group.[15] Bodies lay on the streets in Luanda, family members too afraid to collect their dead relatives for fear of being shot by snipers stationed on the rooftops of buildings.[16] The government used UNITA's threatening behaviour in the capital in the preceding months to create the impression that the killings resulted from a popular uprising. The killings had not been spontaneous, as later claimed by the MPLA, but were orchestrated anger, armed by the government and supported by the security apparatus. A church report claims that over 20,000 were massacred in Luanda over three days.[17]

According to UNITA, the killings stopped when General Abilio Kamalata Numa reached the outskirts of the capital in Caxito with his troops, ready to take Luanda. The threat of UNITA's troops on the capital's doorstep, when FAPLA's forces were in disarray and Cuban soldiers weren't present to defend the palace, halted the massacre. Many UNITA leaders were saved and incarcerated by their MPLA counterparts while many others would be killed. The stories of mercy and savagery were many. Mop-up operations across several provinces against the Ovimbundu and the Bakongo would continue for several months, including in the cities of Benguela, Malangue, Lobito and Lubango. The Bloody Friday massacre of Bakongo on 22 January 1993 would become the second most visible episode of ethnic cleansing in the immediate aftermath of the elections. An estimated 3,000 members of the Bakongo were killed in Luanda's open-air markets by armed civilians after the government claimed that Zairean mercenaries had assisted UNITA in capturing the oil town of Soyo in the north.[18] People were identified by their accents, clothing and haircuts. Extrajudicial executions also occurred on a lesser scale in towns across the country.

As a strategy, the Halloween Massacre was, despite its cruelty and criminality, effective and revealed a government intent on never relinquishing power to the opposition, either on military or political terms. Elections became tools for international legitimacy and power grabs. They provided the façade of constitutionality that allowed the government to undercut the transformative elements of the peace process. The alignment of international and MPLA interests would shut out any real opportunity for political accommodation, democratic devolution, and national unity. With the transition to multi-party democracy and the return of the opposition to Luanda, the government made some important changes that set the tone for the securitisation of politics. Before 1991, Luanda was defended by the FAPLA and a brigade-size Presidential Guard. After the war restarted in 1992, the Presidential Guard grew exponentially. Several units were armed, trained and given greater fighting capacity because of the creation of a joint national army. The Presidency had to ensure its ability to retain control of the forces, which led it to strengthen its pocket of shadow power in Futungo de Belas.

The deployment of the PIR, their first operation in civilian areas, was a simulation of how effective they would become in clamping down on any perceived subversive activity. The distribution of small arms to civilians led to the expansion of government militias and their political utility. Formally known as the BPV, with over 600,000 members in the 1970s and personnel stationed in every village, these groups later became the Organisation for Civil Defence (ODC).[19] Society had been militarised during the 1970s and 1980s due to the war of ideologies, propaganda, and visions. But it became far more so after 1992 due to the mass inclusion of civilians in operations as part of paramilitary groups, and forced conscription on both sides.

After the Luanda massacre, UNITA started capturing many areas in the north and the east. By November, it controlled 57 of Angola's 164 municipalities and half of its landmass, including the diamond-producing areas (Maier 2007: 115). In January 1993, the rebels launched a nationwide offensive with fighting spreading to 15 of the 18 provinces. UNITA would subsequently conquer 80% of the territory in a matter of months. Collective punishment and atrocities against those perceived to be government supporters ensued, even in areas UNITA considered their heartland. By November 1994, UNITA had lost several strategic urban strongholds, including Huambo, Soyo, Uige and Mabanza-Congo, with the government managing to reduce UNITA's territorial control to 40% of the country.

## Second War 1992–4

The level of brutality and efficiency of the destruction in the 1992–4 war was unprecedented. In only two years, the conflict claimed over 400,000 lives, numbers equal to the war of 1975–91. The UN estimated that 1,000 people were dying every day,[20] with as many as 3.7 million in need of life-saving aid. The country's infant mortality rate was the highest in the world in 1993, with 300 per 1,000 perishing due to starvation, war and injuries.[21] While the UN struggled to fund its $226 million appeal (by January 1994 it had only received $60 million), the government's callousness in responding to the humanitarian crisis was becoming increasingly visible, with spending on health reaching a mere 0.3% of its budget.[22] Two battles became symbolic of the viciousness of this period: the UNITA siege of government-held Huambo that lasted 55 days and the battle for Kuito that lasted 21 months. UNITA's bid to take both provincial capitals from the government in its ethnic stronghold and symbolic support base severely damaged its image within these communities.

The FAA would take the lead in fighting UNITA but because of the initial level of disorganisation with troops cantoned in different areas, units dismantled, and command and control structures in disarray, the government resorted to, among other measures, seeking the help of Executive Outcomes (EO). In early 1993, it signed a $140 million contract with the South African private security firm that deployed 400 mercenaries to train thousands of FAA troops and plan operations.[23] Their intervention in Angola became a force multiplier due to their tactical advice, training, combat support and direct involvement in combat. Other private security companies like UK-based Sandline International and US-run Military Professional Resources Incorporated were also used to train government forces.[24] By 1994, the government was still only fighting with 60,000 troops which led it, in April 1994, to decree the conscription of all men born in 1974. In addition, the government would begin mortgaging its future oil revenues to buy weapons. These factors helped the FAA recapture a large portion of territory lost to UNITA and begin turning the tide of the war in their favour in 1994–5.

The Bicesse Agreement had defined a Triple Zero clause that prohibited both parties from acquiring new weapons supplies. In June 1993, the government unilaterally revoked the clause, which catalysed a massive arms race. In 1993–4, the government spent over $3.5 billion on weapons. It purchased a range of weapons from small arms to tanks and aircraft from Portugal, Russia, Brazil, Ukraine, North Korea, and Spain, among others.[25] The MPLA had already accrued a $6 billion debt to Russia for weapons supplied in the 1980s.[26] With the production of 500,000 barrels a day, equivalent to $2.75 billion in 1993, the government was spending over 60% of its budget on weapons. During these years, the government would find sophisticated and intricate deals to bypass international restrictions. One of these deals, known as "Angolagate", related to a $130 million arms deal in 1993 involving key members of the French political establishment and arms dealers Pierre Falcone and Arkady Gaydamak.[27] In September 1993, the UNSC imposed its first set of sanctions on UNITA in the form of an arms embargo. UNITA became very effective at circumventing the blockade by bringing arms in through friendly governments. Zaire was a major logistical hub for UNITA and would serve as a transit area for diamond sales and weapons transfers.

Both parties resorted to the most atrocious violations of humanitarian and war laws in the campaigns and battles that followed. While the previous conflict was fought in the countryside and focused on the rural areas, this new war took the fighting to the urban centres, placing populations that had not been exposed to the 16-year war at the heart of military campaigns. Front lines were drawn across city blocks while the surrounding countryside was sown with landmines. Heavily armed troops fought in close quarters across buildings and along streets of residential areas. The siege warfare around Huambo and Kuito destroyed these urban centres and introduced a new era of cruelty towards civilians. The 55-day war for Huambo would kill 15,000 people, while the 21-month siege of Kuito killed as many as 30,000.

The sieges of Huambo and Kuito would mark a generation forever. Capturing these two towns was strategic for UNITA as launch areas for attacks in the country's centre. They were also symbolic of UNITA's Ovimbundu support base, which meant it would seek to overwhelm government forces at any cost. The battles became indicative of UNITA's mindset of permanent threats and betrayal. By encircling these two towns, UNITA cut off any communications and the reinforcement of supplies and materials, intending to get the government to surrender. They also starved civilians living in the towns. The 55-day Huambo war (January–March 1993) was merciless. UNITA forces shelled the city daily with long-range artillery. Civilians attempted to build rudimentary bunkers to shelter themselves from government MiG bombardments and UNITA mortars. Combat occurred in the streets between UNITA and the PIR as well as the amassed armies of both sides. Both parties stopped any humanitarian interventions from reaching the populations. UNITA, in particular, was reported to have shot at several World Food Programme (WFP) flights and attacked relief convoys. In the later stages of the battle, a UNITA human wave attack meant that densely concentrated infantry formations, intent on overrunning enemy lines, swept through the city, showing the lengths they would go to in order to declare victory. Huambo would fall to UNITA on 9 March. The town of 400,000 people, the second largest in the country, known for its beautiful colonial buildings and wide avenues, suffered widespread damage. Columns of thousands of civilians trailed behind government forces along the 400-kilometre retreat to Benguela. UNITA would only occupy Huambo for 18 months.

The siege of Kuito was even more bloody. It became known as Angola's Stalingrad (James 2004). While the most destructive part of the siege lasted nine months, the city would continue to be divided between UNITA and government forces for many more months. From a prolonged military blockade to hand-to-hand combat, the battle involved police, military and armed civilians. UNITA used up to 1,000 shells a day, attempting to seize as many blocks as possible in the city. For months (June–October 1993), the local population, trapped between the two armies, survived off grass, leaves and toasted maize. Civilians resorted to digging tunnels across neighbouring walls of buildings to shield themselves from sniper fire while moving through the city. Because the cemetery was in the part of the city controlled by UNITA, people buried the thousands of dead in the government-controlled area in gardens, rooftops, sidewalks and front yards. Six months into the siege with UNITA fighting building to building, over 40,000 civilians, soldiers and militias had become trapped in an area of just ten blocks.[28] Groups of civilians would organise themselves into *batidas* (expeditions) to venture outside the city to get food. As time passed, the *batidas* had as many as 500 men and women desperate to get any sustenance, with losses as high as a third of the group. When the ceasefire was declared in September only 18 yards separated the two armies. Not a single house or building was unscathed.

In October 1993, UNITA publicly recommitted to the Bicesse accords. The UNSC had threatened sanctions and an oil embargo against both parties unless they reaffirmed their commitment to talks. Negotiations began in Lusaka that same month, chaired by UN representative Alioun Blondin Beye. Throughout the 1990s, the government pursued a two-faced strategy, attempting to diplomatically and politically isolate UNITA on the one hand and to achieve reconciliation on the other, to encourage UNITA to lay down arms. The pragmatism and realism displayed by the President allowed Futungo to centralise power further, even as it swayed through moments of political compromise. More importantly, the MPLA shifted international perceptions and controlled the narrative of the war. UNITA became defined as an intransigent rebel group fighting against a legitimate government.

The cruelty and destruction of the decade that followed informed the political engagement of populations on both sides and determined the parameters of accountability. Neither side was fully held accountable for the atrocities committed. This last decade of war also informed the MPLA of its capacity to shield itself within the confines of sovereignty using the overriding economic imperatives of international partners to proceed unbounded in its quest for security. The political groundwork of mobilising the population with a 'hearts and minds' strategy was unnecessary from the government's perspective given UNITA's conduct and the superiority of its military apparatus. The people of Angola would remain casualties of war in every sense.

## The Breakdown of the 1994 Peace Process

The Lusaka Protocol was signed in November 1994. It provided for, among other things, the reestablishment of the 1991 ceasefire, the DDR of all UNITA forces, the integration of UNITA generals into the FAA, the repatriation of foreign mercenaries, and the disarmament of the civilian population and the "Ninjas" PIR police force. The protocol was implemented in the midst of fighting, under threat of war and numerous ultimatums by the international community. This time the UN was assigned a participatory role. The new mission, UNAVEM III, authorised a military contingent of 7,000 personnel with 350 military and 260 police observers. A second round of DDR was meant to reintegrate the UNITA combatants that had left the FAA in 1992 and integrate an additional 5,000 UNITA troops (4,920 to the army, 70 to the airforce and ten to the navy). Both parties continuously missed deadlines and violated the terms of the agreement. By 1995 the mission had recorded nearly 15,000 ceasefire violations. The government would only begin the repatriation of mercenaries in January 1996, although Luanda may have retained their services by proxy with private security firms Alpha 5, Branch Energy and Saracen International employing Executive Outcomes personnel to assist in securing oil facilities.[29]

In April 1997, the Government of Unity and National Reconciliation (GURN) was inaugurated, but the country remained physically and psychologically divided. UNITA was given four out of 28 ministerial posts (Commerce, Geology and Mines, Tourism and Health), and seven of the 55 vice-ministerial posts (Defence, Finance, Social Reintegration, Information, Agriculture, Home Affairs and Public Works). UNITA was also given six ambassadorships, three provincial governorships (Kuando Kubango, Uige and Lunda-Sul) and seven deputy governorships and over a hundred local level administrators of municipalities and communes. The GURN lasted for 11 years until the first post-war elections of 2008. UNITA's participation in the unity government and the relocation of key leaders to Luanda created a situation of unique contradictions. While the Luanda-based UNITA represented the political engagement of the movement and the GURN, the Huambo-based UNITA represented the belligerent and harder faction that continued fighting until 2002. The formation of the GURN effectively shifted real political power away from the government and MPLA to the Presidency. The strategy of shadowing institutions and creating a veneer of operations would be replicated at all levels. Executive power and decision-making on all matters concerning the day-to-day running of the country and the economy were effectively administered from the Presidency in Futungo, in particular after UNITA joined the government, parliament and local level administrations. The existence of the unity government consolidated the existing strategy of neutering any state organ that could operate outside the control of the Presidency.

In December 1996, over 70,000 UNITA troops were in cantonment. By January the following year, 5,500 had been integrated into the FAA, with an additional 14,000 also expected to join the ranks of the national army.[30] Of those that joined, nine were generals, eight colonels, ten lieutenant colonels and 19 majors. In June 1997, the UNSC voted to replace UNAVEM III with a smaller observation mission (MONUA) that was meant to oversee the remaining disarmament of UNITA troops and the extension of government control into UNITA areas. As negotiations continued to fail, MONUA found it increasingly difficult to justify its existence. Even as war loomed in early 1998, the UN mission shrank from 7,000 to 1,000.

Events within the region contributed to the unravelling of the agreement. Angola seized the opportunity to intervene in the Democratic Republic of Congo (then Zaire) against Mobutu Sese Seko in what became one of the most strategic decisions of the government in decapitating UNITA's logistical capacity. UNITA had used Zaire as a key logistics channel, arms depot, rear base and diamond trade hub. Altering the political design of the region would significantly isolate the rebels. To this effect, Luanda began installing friendly regimes in both

Kinshasa and Brazzaville, extending its securitisation across borders and ensuring that the presidents they helped would retain power. In January 1997, Angola deployed its 24th regiment to eastern Zaire to support Laurent Kabila's Alliance of Democratic Forces for the Liberation of Congo-Zaire (ADFL). UNITA also deployed forces to the aid of Mobutu. Kabila would capture Kinshasa in May 1997.

In September 1997, Luanda intervened in the Republic of Congo in support of Denis Sassou-Nguesso with 5,000 troops (Weigert 2011). Sassou-Nguesso took power from Pascal Lissouba in October. I will expand the FAA's interventions in these conflicts in Chapter 4. These regional interventions and other military operations by the FAA effectively signalled to UNITA that they were losing the diplomatic battle. Luanda was never sanctioned for having helped topple a democratically elected government in Congo or intervening in Zaire. UNITA, on the other hand, was again sanctioned for failing to meet MONUA deadlines. In August 1997, the UN Security Council, under Resolution 1127, decided to ban UNITA officials from international travel, close all UNITA's offices in foreign countries, and ban all aircraft from flying into or out of UNITA-controlled areas (Hodges 2004).

The insurgency would continue to lose territory and control of several diamond areas. By early 1998, its territorial presence was reduced to a number of towns, with Andulo, Bailundo, Nharea and Mungo being the most strategically important ones. The UN accused both parties of taking actions that would lead to war.[31] The continuous non-compliance of the insurgency led the UN to vote on another set of sanctions in June 1998, banning the purchase of Angolan diamonds that were not accompanied by a government certificate of origin and freezing UNITA accounts. In early September 1998, UNITA's secretary-general Manuvakola issued a proclamation suspending Savimbi as the head of the movement and calling for a new party congress. With little support from the base of the movement, from the military wing and even moderate politicians in Luanda, this proclamation nevertheless resulted in the creation of UNITA-Renovada (Renovated-UNITA). The government used this situation to determine that Savimbi was a war criminal and that it would only deal with the new UNITA. In July 1998, João Lourenço, then head of the MPLA parliamentary caucus, steered through a resolution in the national assembly allowing the government to restart the war. Months earlier dos Santos had been diplomatically aligning support from the region and key allies Portugal, France, Russia and Brazil. His trip to Moscow secured six MiG-29 fighter jets, 12 Mi-35 attack helicopters, six Antonov planes, and four Ilyushin-76 cargo planes.[32] A new military strategy was devised by dos Santos, with his Chief of Staff, General Matos; national security advisor General Manuel Hélder Vieira Dias "Kopelipa" (later placed as the head of the Security Cabinet of the Presidency); and MPLA Secretary-General Lopo do Nascimento. It focused on four theatres of operation. The first aimed to retake UNITA's last remaining strongholds of the central highlands with airstrikes from Catumbela base. The second involved a ground offensive in Moxico along the Zambian border. The third was a strategy to contain UNITA in Luanda with a state of emergency. The final strategy aimed at removing UNITA forces from the diamond areas of the Lundas provinces.[33]

## The 1999–2002 War and the Armed Peace

The Lusaka Accord was formally broken in December 1998 when President dos Santos stated, at the Fourth MPLA Congress, that war had to be waged in order for peace to be achieved (Hodges 2004). The option for negotiation was indefinitely postponed. Dos Santos sought to remove Savimbi from the political scene, destroy UNITA militarily, and deal with a more manageable and more compliant opposition (the Luanda-based party Renovated-UNITA). Dos Santos also ended MONUA's mandate and requested the UN to withdraw. The war that ravaged the country from 1999 until 2002 was fought with sustained brutality and graphic violence. The warring factions deliberately perpetrated acts of extreme violence against civilians (including forced displacements, rape, conscription, and summary executions) and deprived them of food and basic resources.[34] The rural areas were the most affected, especially with the laying of 9 million anti-personnel mines near water sources or around farmland, aimed at maiming but not killing. Luanda, Huambo, Uíge and Kuito became packed with those displaced by war, overwhelming any response to contain the humanitarian disaster.

In September 1999, the FAA would launch Operação Restauro (Operation Restoration) to retake UNITA areas of Bailundo and

Andulo. Under extreme pressure from military offensives, Savimbi began purging commanders and cadres that he believed had failed to follow orders or were ready to betray the movement. Key defections from FALA generals in 1998–9 gave the government a huge advantage. Many of these generals were placed within key positions in the FAA. In late December 1999, the FAA began to overtake the satellite bases surrounding UNITA's "capital" Jamba and, on 31 December, took the rear base. Operação Restauro succeeded in bringing down one of the war's biggest and most powerful symbols of resistance and is a constant reminder that the sovereignty of Luanda had been contested for almost two decades in portions of the country.

The fighting in 1998–9 was still organised around frontlines so populations could organise their lives away from combat areas. However, from 2000, government forces moved into areas that had never experienced fighting in an attempt to corral the insurgency. This hardened the warring factions' attitudes towards civilians and exposed them to extreme cruelty.[35] FAA Operations Hexagono and Triangulo in mid-2000 aimed to push Savimbi into a smaller area of the country and destroy UNITA's defensive capabilities (Weigert 2011). UNITA was, however, still capable of staging operations in 15 of the country's 18 provinces. In January 2001, dos Santos replaced General Matos with General Armando da Cruz Neto as the FAA Chief of Staff, who reorganised the army's senior command. Neto was thought to have been the strategist behind the scorched-earth tactics used to hunt down Savimbi (Pearce 2005: 72).

By late 1999, the government's strategy to secure sufficient funds for war had exposed it to accusations of corruption and economic mismanagement. The Global Witness report "A Crude Awakening" led the charge on exposing the government's diversion of oil revenues to support the aspirations of the elites and the business interests of key generals and arms dealers. The organisation referred to the Presidency, the national oil company Sonangol and the national bank as the "Bermuda Triangle", where money disappeared through the dealings of an untouchable oligarchy. The Bermuda Triangle was thought to have comprised 100 of the leading MPLA families (James 2004). International oil companies were accused of hypocrisy and complicity. The report astutely identified several key generals inside the Presidency and the security apparatus as the untouchables. These included Generals Kopelipa, José Maria, and Fernando Miala, the President, his unofficial business manager Elision Figueredo, Vice-Minister for Petroleum Desiderio Costa, and arms runner Pierre Falcone (who was involved in the Angolagate scandal) and his partner Antonio "Mosquito" Mbkassi.[36] The entourage of the shadow government and the generals that would later take the lead in sharpening the focus, infrastructure and efficiency of the securitisation strategy were already coming together.

Despite attempts to revive the peace process in mid-2001, the government continued to pursue the military option with counterinsurgency sweeps in the provinces of Kuando Kubango, Moxico, Uige and Bie. In October, the FAA launched Operation Quissonde (Brave Ant) in the province of Moxico, which, together with Israel's assistance in locating Savimbi's whereabouts through the detection of his personal telephone calls, allowed the FAA to close in on the group's top leadership (Weigert 2011). UNITA's leadership had dispersed into smaller groups, with most of their families placed across the border in Zambia. Savimbi was aware that he was going to die in Angola, having turned down the offer of exile from the South Africans.[37] UNITA's commanders, cadres and top leaders had spent many months in the bush evading the FAA. The majority were malnourished and sick.

Jonas Savimbi was ambushed and killed on 22 February 2002. His body, riddled with bullets, was paraded and humiliated on national television. In light of this significant victory, the government began to observe a unilateral ceasefire that culminated in a formal agreement in April. The Luena Memorandum of Understanding established that an amnesty law for all crimes committed during the conflict be passed and that 5,000 UNITA soldiers be integrated into the FAA, and provided a timetable for demobilising the remaining UNITA forces. The MoU was signed on behalf of the government by General Geraldo Sachipengo Nunda (a former UNITA commander who defected in 1993) and by General Abreu Muengo Ukwachitembo "Kamorteiro" on behalf of UNITA. The agreement was essentially a military ceasefire that would dictate the terms of the DDR process as an addendum to the existing political structures set up by the Lusaka Protocol of 1994.

Three decades of conflict had seen the deaths of a million Angolans, the displacement of 4.1 million, the fleeing of 450,000 to neighbouring countries, the maiming of 100,000,[38] and the all-encompassing militarisation of society. While the country rejoiced in what appeared to be the lasting prospect of peace, few saw its immediate dividends. Angola was plunged into a severe humanitarian crisis that had international agencies struggling to address the situation's complexity. For almost four years, parts of the country had been completely inaccessible to humanitarian agencies who before 1998 were already caring for vulnerable populations by providing minimum services and aid. High levels of insecurity had led many NGOs to close down operations. The government also actively restricted access to people outside of provincial capitals and in UNITA areas. By late 2000, the government controlled over 90% of the territory and began to talk about normalising the country, echoed by the UN and their agencies, who started planning to reduce their aid span. This was aimed at creating a façade of stability when facts on the ground revealed an abandoned population.[39] When, in 2002, international agencies were finally able to assess the situation, they were horrified by what they witnessed. "The policy during the war was that everything that was outside the government or the MPLA's control was enemy territory. The bush was indiscriminately bombarded for two years and we lived atrocious moments".[40] The worst and most violent counter-offensives by the FAA occurred in 2001, when nothing was spared. Compounding the effects of a systematic scorched earth policy, with civilians dying from violence, hunger and disease, was the complete isolation from any external assistance. When the war ended over 5 million people needed life-saving assistance.

In 2002, NGOs began alerting the world to a man-made famine with mortality rates in remote villages reaching six in every 10,000 daily, six times the emergency threshold. Malnutrition rates were among the highest seen in Africa in over a decade.[41] Over 600,000 people were near death, with "one child dying of hunger every 3 minutes in Angola".[42] Cities were overstretched in their attempts to provide infrastructure and assistance to uprooted populations. Rural areas were far worse, with millions displaced. In the central highlands, particularly the province of Bie, there were only three doctors providing assistance to one million people. The destruction and abandonment of 80% of schools had left 70% of children between the ages of six and

14 functionally illiterate.[43] Landmines littered over 85% of the country, meaning that few areas were ready to allow communities to start subsistence farming. At the end of the war, the UN's renewed mandate was primarily a political, albeit toothless, mission aimed at providing technical advice. Its role was constrained by the narrow limits assigned to it by both UNITA and the government. It took two months of difficult negotiations between the government and the UN to agree on how it would assist in the humanitarian crisis. Above all, the government wanted to control external engagement, even if this meant limiting the span of aid.

*Citizens and Visitors: The Humanitarian Crisis*

The war left indelible scars on Angolan society. The most visible and immediate legacies were the millions without recourse to food, security, shelter, and aid. These masses included demobilised soldiers and their families, internally displaced populations (IDPs), and the refugees that began slowly re-entering the country. Throughout 2002–4, this massive humanitarian crisis remained underreported and underfunded. International agencies scrambled to assist, knowing that they were only allowed to operate if they did not embarrass the government by calling for more aid and exposing the chaos. But their silence resulted in a lack of donor support and vastly circumscribed operations.

The post-war context was, as expected, heavily politicised, which significantly impacted the effective assistance and protection of vulnerable groups. After two years of peace, embarrassing reports of state corruption, and pressure for transparency from aid donors, the government's credibility was exposed as it came under fire for only spending a small portion of its budget on humanitarian assistance. In 2002 it reportedly committed $140 million to relief efforts which corresponded to 4.3% of its oil revenues.[44] Hunger, material instability, and physical insecurity rose without remedy, most notably after the government announced the end of emergency assistance in 2004. The government proceeded to rush through the return and resettlement process in two years so that it could move beyond the stage of emergency aid to development assistance. It began adopting the discourse of development, stating that the country was in a phase of recovery.

This rapid and premature transition, which saw the phasing out of OCHA and several NGOs, left millions in desperate situations and set back many more who had restarted farming but were still dependent on humanitarian assistance. In this way, recovery and development was achieved at the cost of the Angolan people. The assistance packages for rehabilitation and reconstruction were invariably different from emergency packages, and the resources needed for stabilising vulnerable populations were directed elsewhere.

Few places met the five return and resettlement pre-conditions established by law (mine clearance, quantity and quality of land, water, state administration, and access to services). State administration may have existed within the municipalities, but no one had the capacity and authorisation to deliver services. Angolan ministries were unable and unwilling to replace the work of NGOs and the UN agencies. Many IDPs, returnees and ex-combatants began resettling without food security, access to secure land and tenure, household items, agricultural and construction materials and the additional government benefits that could have helped them restart their lives. They were confronted by the confounding absence of infrastructure, basic services and state administration in their areas of origin and lived with the threat of concealed landmines and even greater numbers of unexploded ordnance (UXOs).

Government officials echoed well-rehearsed slogans of reconciliation and a united country, but the reality on the ground was radically different. The authorities largely abandoned those who were perceived to have belonged to UNITA to their fate. Communities rejected each other, with administrators in several provinces actively segregating residential areas by political affiliation. Intimidation was rife and the denial of assistance was widespread. Some of this was justified on the basis that the government lacked the capacity to manage and coordinate such a large operation, with dozens of agencies each mandated to take care of a particular area, but a portion of this behaviour was informed by decades of enmity between people. It was a very difficult journey for Angolans to navigate in the immediate aftermath of peace. Both UNITA and the MPLA had "abandoned" their populations in the last stages of the war by instrumentalising, tormenting or targeting civilians in their quest for survival or victory.

After the war, neither of the parties provided the necessary political leadership to help communities recover their political and social standing. Interviews conducted in displaced camps, quartering areas and refugee reception areas in 2004 revealed how estranged people felt from the government that now ruled them. MPLA supporters and people unsympathetic to UNITA viewed government aid as merely symbolic, with the heavy lifting being implemented by international agencies. To them, hunger during peacetime was unexpected. For the UNITA people, two expressions stood out for their resigned poetry: "We are now just visitors" and "this land no longer belongs to us".[45] They referenced the deep disconnect people felt from the state, and the political dominance of the MPLA. Individuals on the "losing" side were left behind by the rapid political shifts of power. They understood they could not expect to benefit.

People were forced to join the MPLA or face greater hardship. The effort to create order in the immediate aftermath of the war inadvertently classified people either as those who were to receive assistance or those left on the side-lines of protection. The government was responsible for screening the areas where IDPs, demobilised soldiers and their families needed help and for coordinating efforts with the international agencies.

"The Red Cross and WFP assisted the groups identified by the government and no one else. These lists classified people."[46] In Huambo, a province that was one of the most affected by the war and had a large concentration of ex-combatants and IDPs, the MPLA flag was flown on the building of the World Food Programme (WFP).[47] This very political gesture, in Ovimbundu heartland, was a clear message that to benefit people had to succumb to the MPLA. Flying the party flag in villages also meant that people were identified as worthy of assistance. "The MPLA flag in the village meant that the population belongs to the government—and that when the elections come we will be given ID cards so that we can vote. It is only in the village that this will happen—not in the bush. Here there are no UNITA people, only local people."[48] This segregation of people exposed them to differences in assistance, in protection and in representation. The explicit distinction and marginalisation of groups on the basis of their political affiliation put their economic and social survival at risk.

In the space of four years (2002–6), over 400,000 refugees and 4 million IDPs (30% of the population) would relocate and settle in new areas. Only 1.5 million were registered as IDPs by humanitarian organisations, and only 123,000 refugees were officially repatriated by the UNHCR or IOM, with the remainder returning spontaneously.[49] The hardship faced by spontaneous returnees worsened once they entered Angola. The authorities barred their access to the transit centres because they were not covered by formal repatriation agreements. Access to the assistance of humanitarian organisations was also equally restricted. These layers of vulnerability increased with the number of political and institutional hurdles. When donors and international agencies were allowed to intervene, the government happily transferred its responsibility for the welfare of the people to them. When agencies left or did not renew funding for programmes due to concerns over corruption, the government would abandon people until they needed to be mobilised for elections.

Unlike the previous peace agreements, the Luena Accords made no provision for international monitoring of the demobilisation process by the UN and the Troika. The Joint Commission in the Peace Process, composed of UNITA, government and Troika state members, mainly dealt with political issues. This meant that the government managed the entire DDR process. Overseeing the DDR process was the Joint Military Commission (JMC) and a Technical Group (TG). The Ministry for Assistance and Social Reintegration (MINARS), together with the FAA and the Institute for Social and Professional Reintegration of Ex-soldiers (IRSEM), were charged with monitoring the demobilisation process, providing transportation after the closure of the camps, registering individuals for assistance, and ensuring that resettlement areas were inhabitable. However, the FAA was primarily responsible for the quartering, registration and screening of combatants, issuing military ID cards, and distributing the benefits of demobilisation. These benefits were meant to include ID cards, five months' salary, an additional US$100 for travel expenses, resettlement kits with non-food items (NFI), food aid, WFP cards and access to vocational training. The government committed $157 million to the two-year process, with donors providing an additional $89 million. The FAA were also responsible for assisting the camps and securing provisions for approximately 425,000 ex-combatants and their families for a period of 18 months.[50] Increasingly the management of the process caused disagreements with the FAA. A military observer noted that "The FAA wanted to get this right and complain(ed) about the central government not giving the resources to make it work".[51] The process was rushed. In 2002 it only took 90 days to set up quartering areas to accommodate almost half a million people, compared to the process under the UN in 1994 that took over eight months to establish the first camp for 8,000 soldiers.

UNITA combatants and their families were assembled in 35 designated quartering areas. The support required was a huge task given the needs and the numbers involved. The demobilisation process descended into chaos. For the first six months of their existence, beginning in April 2002, no international agency was given access to the camps. The UN was accused of being too slow to react, with OCHA insisting on first securing government permission to enter the camps (Porto and Parsons 2003). UNITA soldiers and their families had already entered the demobilisation process with high levels of malnutrition and disease. The lack of conditions in the camps led to a heavy loss of human lives. "In Sambo camp, thousands of people spent 18 months in very precarious conditions. Our children are buried there today. There were between 12 and 15 deaths a day".[52] A quick assessment of the camps by IOM in late 2002 confirmed that seven children were dying a day in some areas.[53] Despite this, the quartering areas were considered to be priorities for food and assistance above the needs of the IDP camps. A long-time DDR military observer commented at the time that the conditions were the worst he had ever witnessed. "They were unfed, had no water, were sick, and hadn't received anything".[54]

Between March and April 2003, all of the quartering areas were closed by the FAA. Many were abruptly closed under the threat of violence and the use of physical coercion against the demobilised.[55] "People were forcibly evacuated and threatened that if we didn't get out that war would restart. We were threatened again with war. We then moved ... but a legal journey is a journey where we have a choice".[56] The government issued a verbal decree, passed on the national radio and transmitted by local administrators, stating that people were only allowed to resettle in their exact areas of origin and nowhere else. The FAA then destroyed camp infrastructures by burning houses and crops after families evacuated them to prevent resettlement. UNITA modelled the QA with village-like structures, similar to agricultural administrations, which caused confusion between resettlement sites and temporary camps. The dispersion and disbanding of former UNITA soldiers was a security concern for the government and a priority for peace consolidation.

Many families remained behind because they had neither received their ID cards, nor their kits, nor their money. It was clear that when the government declared that the QA were officially closed, the demobilisation process was not over. "Demobilisation was ended through a political decision and not a military decision".[57] In this last round of demobilisation, UNITA would incorporate 5,007 troops into the FAA and 40 men into the police force, including 30 generals, 200 superior officers, and 150 captains. By the end of the process, UNITA had demobilised 74,041 and retired 25,195. By 2005, over 33,000 FAA combatants were expected to be demobilised and awaiting their DDR. The majority of these troops were never formally demobilised and never received their subsidies. The three formal DDR processes (1992, 1994 and 2002) demobilised almost 290,000 combatants, of which, according to MINARS, 164,000 were from UNITA and 124,000 were from the government.[58] The distribution of benefits and retirement packages would become a source of protest during dos Santos' remaining years as President, threatening to create instability in the capital. An FAA general commented that "the demobilisation process should have been done in another way. Angolan society is highly militarised. Every home had one member who belonged to the military. All the children over the age of 13 will have this well established in their memories".[59] He was referring to the lack of dignity and the lack of integration of ex-combatants into society. The government lacked the political will to address this issue but also initially lacked the administrative infrastructure and capacity.

Attempts to extend the presence of the state administration into territory ungoverned by the MPLA during the last few years of war were, at first, done with the security forces. The task was complex given the lack of qualified administrators and the almost abandonment of the rural areas during the war. Nearly 80% of local administrators were concentrated in the provincial capitals, with only 19% stationed in the municipalities. However, the state's institutional absence did not mean there was a vacuum of regulating power. Early post-war administration was a combination of police, the army and civilian militias. The MPLA apparatus came much later and, in many rural areas, became the face of the state (Soares de Oliveira 2013). In interviews, many IDPs, returning refugees and ex-combatants mentioned how security forces gave them guidelines and reminded them who they were now to receive orders from. The show of force allowed the state to establish its presence on the ground, providing deterrence against any form of political or social activity that went against the vision of an MPLA victory. It also allowed the government to convey authority.

While there was peace, violence was a default response in instances of political intolerance. This was made worse by the number of armed groups and weapons in the hands of civilians. Many communities were intimidated by the civilian militia, the Organisation of Civil Defence (ODC). The ODC, an MPLA paramilitary group created to secure cities and towns recaptured from UNITA by government forces, was remobilised at the end of the war. It was legalised in March 2002 and received an increased budget for "mobilisation", despite its members being accused of indiscriminate violence.[60] By 2007 there was an effort to begin demobilising the ODC, though information on this process was scant. Many former ODC members became part of the dormant Protecção Civil (a National Guard of sorts). While precise numbers were unknown, the group could have had around 90,000 members (5,000 per province) and fell under the supervision of General Leal Monteiro "Ngongo".[61]

As a result of the military defeat and the severe blow to the political structures of the party, UNITA was drastically weakened. It was learning how to operate as an unarmed political party that was subject to the administrative rule of its long-time foes. Its leadership was transported to Luanda and accommodated with housing by the President. To his credit, dos Santos could have had many military commanders killed on the battlefield but spared them. Instead, he allowed them to rebuild their lives. However, the perception amongst supporters and ex-combatants about their leaders' luxurious city lives created a divide within UNITA's support base. Its leadership in Luanda was also largely separated from its support base in the Central Highlands, and the party faced internal power struggles between key military and civilian leaders. UNITA and the MPLA held their first post-war party congresses in June and December 2003, respectively. The UNITA congress transferred power from their interim leader, General Paulo Lukamba "Gato", to Isaias Samakuva, a diplomat. With the use of secret ballots, Samakuva won a landslide victory. However, UNITA remained incapable of providing the government with any real opposition, especially when the party was financially dependent on the government, receiving $13 million a year.[62] The MPLA congress reaffirmed President dos Santos' leadership of party structures and was elected in a show of hands without any opposition to the party's Presidency.

*Angola Rising*

As the "architect of peace", dos Santos gradually built Angola to mirror his vision of greatness, independence and untouchability. He did this by rewarding loyalty and managing dissidence and divergence within the party through the extension of patronage and enrichment opportunities. If everyone were invested in maintaining the system, they would not work to bring it down. For those in his army, party and opposition that were not corruptible, he built a wide-reaching structure of surveillance and intelligence to keep them under control and infiltrated and subverted. He created parallel organs of power for his own security forces, fighting capacity and counter-intelligence, built with more resources, training, and strategy. The people were kept in poverty and "influenced" by MPLA party cells, propaganda outlets in the national press, and the presence of spies. In the rural areas, traditional authorities were folded into the system of popular regulation. None of this was done in neat, structured or fully functioning ways but took place within controllable chaos and sporadic dysfunction.

The economy had to become more efficient to feed this system, even if it was highly distorted by extractive growth. Between 2002 and 2008, Angola would experience a mini golden age with the average annual growth rate reaching 14.9%.[63] The vision that prevailed was described as top-down, accelerated economic development with an emphasis on investment, big projects and borrowing to build infrastructure (Vines et al. 2005). The government initiated grandiose projects across Luanda to portray a country rushing into modernity, fuelled by rapid growth and reconstruction. But as expected many of these projects were either badly managed, badly conceived or became instruments for patronage and corruption. One such project was the Kilamba Kiaxe city on Luanda's outskirts, which cost over $3.5 billion. It was touted as the model city for the new Luanda with 80,000 apartments. Still, far from becoming the face of a rising middle class, apartments fell into disrepair and were too expensive for their targeted population. Thousands of kilometres of rebuilt roads fell into disrepair, too, laden with potholes only a few years after reconstruction. Large projects like the Benguela Railway, once a vital trade tool crossing 1340km from the coast to the border with the DRC, brought great promise of economic transformation. But like other mass construction projects, they employed Chinese workers instead of local labourers. In 2012 Angola had an estimated 260,000 Chinese workers.[64] These and other significant public works projects failed to yield lasting benefits to the country's economy. They didn't create jobs or leave behind much-needed skills. Instead, foreign labour took jobs in almost all sectors, from bricklayers to managers. Any social utility was reversed by cost, outsourcing and disrepair, with few sequential and complementary policies that allowed underprivileged communities to work their way out of poverty. Between 2005 and 2009, the government spent $4.3 billion annually on massive infrastructure projects, including rehabilitating roads, railways and ports.[65] By 2017 the country had allegedly spent $120 billion on reconstruction, with portions of those funds pocketed by national and foreign business and political elites.[66]

The system was also upheld through the diversified engagement with foreign powers. The MPLA had learnt to manage different interests strategically. Dos Santos came to understand the value of balancing conflicting and contradictory relations by setting aside ideological alignments for profit, leading Angola to engage with Russia, Israel, the US, Portugal, numerous Arab states, Brazil, China and North Korea, all with differing transactional objectives. Its experience with decades of military involvement and international interests provided Luanda with key directions for its realpolitik approach. The approach was pragmatic, flexible and sophisticated. President dos Santos' most important lesson was that diversified partners, not being subservient to one or beholden to a few aligned interests, would allow him the ability to shape Angola in the way the MPLA wanted. Angola became China's most important trading partner on the continent. It continued to regard Russia as its chief military ally and the US as its most crucial oil partner. It embedded itself in the economies of Portugal and Brazil. It managed to ensure influence within the African Union and regional systems and within the UN system by providing support for the election of Antonio Guterres as Secretary-General. Its interventions in Africa, particularly the political patronage and security it provided for the regimes in the two Congos, were aimed at deepening key alliances and creating sufficient financial and diplomatic buffers to assert its own version of African solutions to African problems.

Engagement with China allowed Luanda to proceed with its development priorities without conditions attached. A donor conference was not forthcoming at the end of the war, which led the President to look east for oil-backed loans to start rebuilding the country. The political implications of Luanda's financial independence meant that international aid and pressures from donors did not affect government policy. In 2004, China's Export-Import Bank (Exim Bank) would provide a $2 billion oil-backed loan, the first of many loans mortgaging the country's oil wealth. Banks granted other loans in 2007 ($2.5 billion) and 2010 ($6 billion) and after that (Power and Alves 2012). With this injection of money, unconstrained by demands for political and economic reform, the President proceeded to structure the state to ensure hegemonic control.

China became the main source of external funding, a key infrastructure development partner and the biggest crude oil customer. In 2006, Angola surpassed Saudi Arabia as China's leading oil supplier. By 2019 Angola was supplying China with 13% of its oil. Oil-backed borrowing allowed the President to determine spending priorities, bypassing the inefficiencies of the traditional financial system and contributing to a widespread system of corruption (Vines et al. 2005). Oil-backed credit lines from divergent sources, like Brazil and Portugal, also provided guarantees for companies investing in Angola and further entrenched the reliance on revenues from the extractive industry.

This relationship secured China's special political consideration. Following the 2004 loan, the government established the Office for

National Reconstruction (Gabinete de Reconstrucção National, GRN), run by the head of the Security Cabinet of the Presidency (SCP). The GRN was created to kick-start large infrastructure projects at the heart of Angola's reconstruction programme. The argument made at the time was that the GRN would facilitate the administration of funds and ensure better execution of the different projects. Critics argued Chinese financing enabled "a string of political measures aimed at perpetuating the power of the President's inner circle, while setting back internal dialogue on national reconstruction" (Marques 2011).[67] All Beijing credit lines were underwritten by oil contracts and other concessions. Over the course of several decades, China would loan Angola almost $50 billion for reconstruction and infrastructure development, including $4.4 billion in return for support for Beijing's expansionist One Belt One Road initiative. The relationship was underpinned by complex private and public interests, offshores, joint ventures and transnational partnerships spanning across different industries. The China Petroleum and Chemical Corporation (Sinopec) secured privileged access to production rights, exploration and refining, and became a key partner for Sonangol. In March 2004, Sonangol (45 per cent) and Sinopec International (55 per cent) announced a joint venture. China Sonangol became the sister company for the China International Fund (CIF) that operated within the universe of companies linked to the controversial Queensway group. Investigations into the Hong Kong-registered syndicate Queensway revealed an opaque structure managing private and public interests, wracked by corruption scandals but key in advancing China's Africa quest (Burgis 2015). This partnership became a key driver of Sonangol's expansion which invested billions in key infrastructure projects.[68]

Between 2003 and 2008, over $20 billion was invested in Angola's oil exploration capacity.[69] In 2008 it produced 1.89 million barrels a day (up from 1 million in 2004), fast approaching Nigeria's output as sub-Saharan Africa's top oil producer. Sonangol became an all-powerful entity that controlled assets and funds whose value far surpassed the budget of most African countries. Within a decade, the Sonangol Group (worth $22.2 billion) became the fundamental economic motor of the country and the patronage system that sustained the Presidency. It ranked as the second-largest African company behind Algeria's

Sonatrach (worth $58.7 billion).[70] It also became the financial arm of the President's foreign policy. As well as employing 10,000 people, the company's investments cemented and guaranteed elite interests, generating rentier and clientelist relations domestically and with target states. It offered the select few opportunities for enrichment in return for loyalty.[71] Over the years, Sonangol diversified into banking, telecommunications, real estate, shipping, air transport, and an array of Liquefied Natural Gas (LNG) related activities; oil recovery and deep drilling, seismic data and other services related to the oil and gas industries. It had clinics and many other services outside of its core business. With over 30 subsidiaries and overseas facilities (including Brazzaville, Hong Kong, Houston, London and Singapore), it had two full-service banks, major telecommunications (MSTelcom) and its own airline, Sonair. One of Sonangol's key investment arms, the African Investment Bank (BAI), operated several subsidiary companies that assisted in developing different services for the oil sector. These included Sonangol Distribuidora dealing with downstream activities, Sonangol Shipping that provided maritime transport, and the AAA insurance company, among others.[72]

Angola's indicators were impressive. Inflation was slashed from 108% in 2002 to 14% in 2010; GDP skyrocketed from $15 billion in 2002 to $128 billion in 2012. The oil boom had earned Angola as much as $600 billion in revenue over the previous decade. Over a period of 15 years, Angolan companies and individuals invested almost $200 billion abroad in listed companies and private estates. Angola became a developing country that provided more Foreign Direct Investment than it received. By 2010, Luanda had invested $2.4 billion in the Lisbon Stock Exchange and owned more than 10% of Portuguese listed companies. By 2015 Angolan investment in Portugal had risen to $15 billion, making it the place of choice for Angolan capital flight, with elites investing in real estate and other assets that anchored their wealth portfolios abroad.[73] Sonangol owned 20% of Portugal's largest private bank, Banco Comercial Português (BCP), making it the largest single shareholder. In 2012, Angola's Banco Internacional de Credito (BIC) purchased the Portuguese bank Banco Português de Negocios (BPN) for €40 million and planned to use a further €760 million to expand the number of branches in Brazil and make other strategic acquisitions.

Portugal would remain Angola's largest trading partner supplying 14.7% of imports, followed by China with 12.6%.[74] Over 9,000 Portuguese companies operated in Angola, employing 150,000 Portuguese nationals and exporting €4.9 billion.[75] Before the 2008 financial crisis, which forced Portugal to seek a €78 billion bailout, its foreign direct investment in Angola peaked at €775 million annually.[76] Relations between Lisbon and Luanda soured in late 2011 over Portuguese criminal investigations into the irregular financial dealings of key generals and the Angolan elite.[77] The Portuguese foreign minister publicly apologised to appease tensions but was criticised for questioning the judiciary.[78] Portugal was also criticised in a June 2013 Organisation for Economic Cooperation and Development (OECD) report for its unwillingness to tackle bribery.[79] Corruption seeped into the corridors of power and business interests in Lisbon. Lisbon, however, remained the place for Angolan elites to secure assets, properties, and bank accounts as future safety nets.

The Angolan economy was heavily controlled by the President and his entourage, who wielded power through personalised clientelist networks. Informal power networks subverted formal state institutions (Vine et al. 2005). Accountability, transparency, and efforts to achieve macroeconomic stability geared towards long-term sustainability did not factor into the strategies of the Presidency. Instead, short-term gains merged into a system of elite accumulation. The regulation of foreign investment in the country meant that little was done to create the backbone of development. Rent-seeking and corruption continued to hijack the country's ability to build a stable socio-economic foundation for growth. Sustained levels of widespread poverty negated the idea of a country in the throes of development and growth. Poverty grew despite the oil boom years. A popular expression summed up this predicament: "Oil growth led us towards greater poverty".[80] The poor were not essential contributors or the primary focus of development; instead, they were excluded from the promises of reconstruction (Gastrow 2016). The essential aspects of reconstruction that would directly benefit the population, such as providing drinkable water, low-cost housing, electrification, agricultural infrastructure, schools and working hospitals, received little attention and led to the most damaging legacy of the dos Santos government: inequality.

The disparity caused by the 'resource curse' was defined by the extremes of a small elite of multi-millionaires and the impoverished population. Over 6 million lived on less than two dollars a day, with 20% of the wealthiest receiving 59% of the income and the poorest receiving only 3%. In 2008, half of the population remained under the poverty line, a number that would grow exponentially in the next four years. By 2012, Luanda was considered the world's most expensive city,[81] due to the oil economy, the presence of expats, and the deep disparity between the spending of the elites and the parallel economy of the poor. In 2018, despite the crippling effects of the 2014 oil crisis, it remained the world's sixth most expensive city, with expats paying as much as £3,647 monthly in rent for a flat and £7,866 for a house.[82] Life in Luanda and the rest of Angola revealed two very different countries and social realities. Efforts to modernise the capital collided with the poor living in the *musseques* (slums). Urban development forcibly evicted populations that, in most cases, were never resettled. Multiple mass demolitions, affecting hundreds of thousands, have been conducted since 2002, aimed at clearing away areas for exclusionary modernity. Some of these demolition campaigns resembled military operations with helicopters and hundreds of FAA, police and other security agents.[83]

As Angola celebrated the 40th anniversary of its independence on 11 November 2015, the country was appreciably moving in the direction of decline. The 2014 oil crisis had severely impacted the availability of oil revenues to feed the patrimonial system and uphold the presidential apparatus. Dos Santos' administration would find itself challenged, even if mostly symbolically, by the exposure of its corrupt practices, the unravelling of its distorted economic development plan, a bolder and more robust opposition, and a generation of youths demanding reform. In 2016 dos Santos began expanding the economic reach of his family, a mistake that would come to cost him dearly. He had appointed his son, José Filomeno dos Santos, as the chairman of the Sovereign Wealth Fund in June 2013, but the appointment of his daughter, Isabel dos Santos, as chairwoman of Sonangol in June 2016 would spark huge controversy. This emerging kleptocracy deepened animosity across all levels of society, delegitimised the ruling party and exposed the elites to several anti-corruption drives. Attempts to protect elite and party interests sustained the need for securitisation. Despite the progressive and modernist ambitions, at its core, the ruling party remained deeply conditioned by the legacy of its Marxist and state-socialist underpinnings. The security apparatus, in particular, became the clearest example of this. Shrouded in secrecy and with an instinct for blocking political divergence, containing dissent, and guarding society, this machinery was reproduced in many forms, industries and partisan spaces to ensure the political longevity of the Presidency.

The following chapter details how the Presidency, operating as a parallel state, used parallel armies, instrumentalised numerous intelligence services, and wielded significant power across society, the economy and other state organs. A group of powerful unelected officials devised policy, helped conduct government affairs, and assisted the President with the country's day-to-day running. They became the shadow government.

3

# THE SHADOW GOVERNMENT

## GUARDING THE GUARDIANS

The one constant institution that retained power, steered policy, replicated control mechanisms, and forged disparate alliances throughout the different political transitions was the Presidency. It revealed itself to be highly adaptable, pragmatic and driven by the need to retain ever more power. With every decade, the Presidency perfected its control over the state, the party, the economy and society. As a party, the MPLA would become a necessary platform for elections, rewarded with ample opportunities for business within the expanding patronage system, a source of counsel and political dependency. Its strength and influence diminished despite the electoral system enacted by the 2010 Constitution that placed the MPLA at the forefront of politics. What upheld this vast structure and provided it with the tools to align interests, control dissent, instrumentalise fear, and manage the affairs of the state was the security apparatus. Controlling the army kept Angola's most prestigious national symbol at bay. Building a complex praetorian guard structure provided the Presidency with assurances of political longevity. The multiple intelligence services expanded the reach of the Presidency in managing society, extending influence over the private sector, the opposition, and the ruling elites. The police and paramilitary units became the face of the securitised state with the population.

The opportunity to consolidate the shadow structures presented itself with the end of the war. The practice of governing in the shadows allowed dos Santos to create an effective parallel machinery outside the formal structures of government, insulated from the scrutiny of parliament and civilian-led structures, civil society, the international community and even the MPLA itself. To govern in the shadows, the Presidency created two supra-structures: the Security Cabinet and the Civil Cabinet. One managed the formal structures of government while the other ran the security apparatus, general state affairs and all strategic portfolios. However, the Security Cabinet of the Presidency (SCP) was far more powerful than the Civil Cabinet. Over the years, the SCP transformed itself into a complex structure that overrode the state.

Within these structures were entire government departments staffed with foreign advisors and technical know-how, well-paid public servants, a parallel army, logistics and communications systems, financial and accounting systems, and the capacity to respond rapidly to any threat. Upheld by a selective group of unelected advisors of military and civilian loyalists, the shadow government existed to serve the President in his need and desire to control the state and the country. The parallel structures provided them with the shadows to enact different policies and steer the country's strategic direction. The shadows allowed for a widespread net of corruption, influence peddling, nepotism and looting that linked personal businesses with the state and state-owned enterprises. The shadows allowed for stabilisation and reconciliation to be enacted by creating a surveillance system of spies, informers, and security agents. The shadows allowed democratic procedure to be hijacked. While the shadow government created some stability and predictability, it became too big to reform.

The shadow government exposed the MPLA and the Presidency to multiple threats, deepening nationwide fault lines and creating an impenetrable barrier to political and economic reform. The centralisation and decommissioning of formal state structures reversed efforts to state-build. It reduced the efficiency and effectiveness of the security sector, putting at risk the government and Presidency's legitimacy. It put at risk the ability of the Presidency to distance itself from governing mishaps, the mismanagement of resources, and the general decay of governance. It weakened the MPLA by influencing its structures and loyalty to suit presidential priorities and strategies. It also indefinitely delayed the creation of much-needed administrative systems that would help strengthen state institutions. This led to the mutation of institutions in how they operated with each other and fed an existing political culture of fear, paranoia, and the social pathology of infiltration and securitisation.

This chapter describes the structures of the SCP, its parallel army, the intelligence service's role, and its interventions during elections. It will describe the many operational connections, contextualising the aggression and dysfunctions of the system using three cases of political repression and social control to illustrate the fears of political dissent.

### The Supra-Structure: Security Cabinet of the Presidency

The SCP allowed President dos Santos to weather the most divisive years of the civil war. It shielded him from unwarranted international scrutiny, economic collapse, opposition politics, and internal MPLA schisms. The system it erected ensured that the leadership of the FAA, the police and the intelligence services, and the members of the executive, parliament and party elites were all beholden to the President. None of these structures was new or unique to Angola. The influence of Soviet procedure and the Cuban modus operandi seeped through the SCP's every action. Russian and Cuban advisors helped strengthen the different units of the security apparatus, direct their activities to contain "subversive" actions effectively, and ensure that command and control was tight, disciplined and patriotic. The SCP employed thousands of men and women, both highly educated and with mere basic literacy, war-hardened commanders and generals and political commissars. Technocrats and local and foreign advisors injected efficiency into some structures while several units operated through sheer force of their budgets. Competing agencies built the apparatus, all broadly aligned around the mandate to keep the President safe, the MPLA neutered but in power, and all interest groups tied to the Presidency through patronage, loyalty, fear or need. Every significant portfolio ran through the SCP—from post-war reconstruction, national elections, regional diplomacy, and defusing political tensions to public health emergencies.

This gradual usurpation of power occurred in tandem with the passing of numerous laws intended to concentrate power further or provide the illusion of a functioning executive and legislature. The 2010 constitution defined the terms and responsibilities of the different security sector units, but made no mention of the supra-structures supporting the Presidency. Instead, these were established in separate Presidential Decrees. Constitutionally the President was advised by the Council of Ministers, the Council of the Republic,[1] and two national councils on security and defence issues. The Superior Military Council (made up of different generals and military chiefs) and the Defence and Security Council (bringing together the Ministers of Defence, Finance and the Interior, among others) existed in theory to provide the overall coordination of the security sector. Both structures were largely overshadowed by the SCP. Oversight was theoretically provided by the Inspector General in the Ministry of Defence and the General Staff Inspector in the armed forces, an Audits Tribunal, and a Parliamentary Committee on Defence, Security and Internal Order.[2] In practice, the rules were unenforceable and oversight mechanisms were weak and functionally and procedurally dependent on overlying power relations.

The SCP was meant to operate as a secretariat for the Presidency regarding military and defence issues when it was created in 1992. According to its statutes,[3] the SCP was meant to assist the President in formulating and executing national security policy. It was meant to provide technical support and advice in matters of defence and state security. It was also in charge of security for the President, his family and the Vice-President's, and was responsible for administrative matters of the Council of National Security. Instead, it became the most powerful organ in Angola, coordinating the strongest apparatus, commanding the largest budget, and extending the President's control to any strategic area. Under the leadership of General Manuel Hélder Vieira Dias "Kopelipa" until 2017, it became a colossal structure. Previously known as the Military Cabinet, the SCP was created by Presidential Decrees 181/10 of August 2010, when Kopelipa's position as state minister was formally confirmed. His ascension began during the war but was fast-tracked in 2001 when the powerful FAA Chief of Staff, General Matos, was dismissed. As communications and intelligence commander, Kopelipa remained relatively anonymous during the war, with notoriety mostly reserved for army generals. His relative obscurity did not reflect his power. For many years he ran the FAA's procurement agenda with state company SIMPORTEX, advised the President on national security, and took a leading role in intelligence. He became dos Santos' "Machiavellian point-man".[4] As SCP head, Kopelipa had a crucial role advising the President on security and defence matters, overseeing interactions between the cabinet and the Presidency, ensuring the coordination of key government portfolios and guaranteeing a clear chain of command that reinforced central decision-making by his office. He was regarded as one of dos Santos' closest confidants and became one of Angola's most powerful politicians. He was regarded as a sophisticated strategist who presented himself as a very balanced and discreet manager.[5]

The President was said to have promoted this vertical alignment to reduce the power and influence of the MPLA and old-guard generals that still carried influence with the rank-and-file membership of the party and the FAA.[6] "Dos Santos needed to trust someone and Kopelipa became instrumental in helping the President manage all the governance dossiers. His power was utilitarian, and he greatly influenced the President. Kopelipa was very persuasive, preferring to always suggest rather than instruct".[7] "The problem became that Kopelipa's role weakened the national defence system because of the diffusion of roles and emasculation of the FAA".[8] The defence and interior ministries, as well as the heads of the three intelligence services, External Intelligence Service (SIE), Internal State Security and Intelligence (SINSE) and Military Intelligence (SISM), reported directly to Kopelipa. Both the FAA Chief of Staff and the National Police Commissioner reported directly to him too, bypassing their respective ministerial line functions. Kopelipa's direct access to dos Santos gave him power beyond his mandate and enabled him to allegedly play a powerful gatekeeping role, filtering the information reaching dos Santos and forcing all the generals to pass through him to reach the President.

Of the many dossiers that Kopelipa helped the President manage was the National Reconstruction Cabinet (GRN), which operated between 2004 and 2010 and became a founding pillar of the President's ability to control the pace and design of the country's post-conflict development. The GRN was responsible for managing Chinese loans to Angola. Through Kopelipa, the President retained direct control of the reconstruction efforts and the funds involved. As much as $15 billion is estimated to have passed through the GRN and little transparency or accountability has ever been provided for how funds were spent or managed. "In Angola the two main avenues for corruption were reconstruction and the oil industry".[9] Reconstruction was necessary to extend state control across the 18 provinces, facilitating the extension of securitisation. Reconstruction was also important for the extraction and reach of economic interests of the elites and foreign investors. Placing the GRN within the Presidency, mainly run by the SCP, was the most poignant illustration of the SCP's power in shadowing the work of several ministries not directly related to national defence issues. The GRN was eventually disbanded after concerns over maladministration, with projects transferred to two other offices directly run under the Presidency—the Gabinete de Obras Publicas (Cabinet of Public Works) and the oil company Sonangol (Gastrow 2016).

The Cabinda file also fell uniquely under the management of the SCP. The oil enclave was the only province that the Presidency managed. However, it still retained a governor on-site and had a standing peace agreement with a Cabindan faction since 2006 meant to devolve authority and revenue to local leaders. "The governor (did) nothing without checking with the Casa militar (SCP). They began fencing off Cabinda from the Congos with Construction Brigades to control the borders. In reality we lived a militarised existence. In the 1990s there were about 40 battalions stationed here but after 2002 flights came in every night into Maiombe with troops. We may have had as many as 50,000 men from the FAA, the Presidential Guard/ PIR/ the *Fuzileiros Navais* (marines) *e commandos caçadores* (special forces)".[10] The SCP managed the enclave by overwhelming it with multiple forces to contain rebel groups that were actively fighting for independence. Although the conflict was a low-level insurgency that hardly threatened the economic interests of Luanda or its national security, the clampdown reflected fears of regional interference, coordinated dissent and the loss of oil revenues (Cabinda supplied Angola with 60% of its oil).

The cost of running such an operation for several decades is difficult to estimate, even when we can identify numerous lines of the national state budget as funds for the security forces. At the peak of government spending in 2013, the Ministry of Defence had a budget of $5.7 billion while the Ministry of Interior had a budget worth $4.7 billion. At his disposal, the President also had $1.8 billion, labelled as discretionary funds "that functioned as a strategic reserve of the state".[11] Of that amount, 81% was set aside for military defence, including the running costs of his praetorian guards. Salaries and the running costs of these structures were the bulk of the spending, but the authorities made a yearly effort to invest in better technology, training, weapons and equipment. This meant that at the peak of defence spending, the SCP, directly and indirectly, influenced almost $12 billion out of a national budget worth $69 billion.These numbers also sharply contrasted with spending in other key sectors. The discretionary budget of the Presidency in 2013 was superior to the budget of the Ministry of Health ($1.5 billion); the funds for one branch of the intelligence service, SINSE ($695 million), was superior to the budget for the Agricultural Ministry ($611 million). The SIE intelligence service had a budget ($340 million) comparable to that of the Foreign Ministry ($380 million).[12] All budgets from 2014 onwards decreased due to the oil crisis, which slashed government revenues, although defence spending remained a priority even during the crippling recession of 2020 (discussed in Chapter 5).

*Praetorian Guard*

To ensure the predominance of security over politics and the military, dos Santos created a parallel army. They became his praetorian guard of elite forces that operated a private secret service and became the visible emergency deployment force against existential threats. As a parallel army within the SCP, it provided assurances against possible dissent within the FAA, the MPLA and the state. It created the idea of an untouchable guard, immune from prosecution, that was subservient to the President and his elite group of generals. Together with the police and the intelligence services, these forces intimidated, spied on and arrested suspected enemies of the state and played a role in keeping the opposition contained. The origins, training and expertise of dos Santos' Presidential Guard have been a source of much speculation and comment. As with other Presidential Guards on the continent, they were sizable military units capable of prolonged operations, akin to specialised units of regular armies, but better equipped. This parallel army could have had as many as 15,000 elite soldiers. In order to ensure allegiance during several critical moments, dos Santos bolstered their ranks with Cuban operatives, including in the run-up to the first post-war elections in 2008, and following the 2015 massacre in Huambo. Many units were also composed of Kwanhama troops (ethnic groups from the south of Angola) not linked to any political group in Luanda. The Kwanhama were known for their ferocity and loyalty. Information on the structures and history of the Presidential Guard was difficult to access. Information remained very general, at times anecdotal, and permeated by some specific examples of structural inefficiency.

The first Presidential Guard unit was created in September 1976 and was called the Unidade Operativa Especial (Special Operational Unit). In May 1977, it became known as the Batalhão da Guarda Presidencial (Presidential Guard Battalion), a restructured unit following the internal MPLA purge. The Presidential Guard only took its current form in 1989 when the President began restructuring to reflect the withdrawal of Cuban troops. There were several layers of protection in the presidential security universe, which included two formal armed formations. The Unidade de Guarda Presidencial (UGP) was the Presidential Guard Unit, commanded by Lt. General Alfredo Tyaunda and comprising between 10,000 and 12,000 men; and the Unidade de Segurança Presidencial (USP), the Presidential Security Unit, commanded by General José João Maua and comprising three battalions. Indicative of the level of paranoia, another layer of close protection security guarded the President at all times. These men were cousins and close family members and were seen around dos Santos in many presidential photos.[13] In addition to these units were the Chacal special forces and the Destacamento de Protecção da Casa de Segurança (DPCS), the Reconstruction Protection Unit that fell within the Presidential Guard. Despite their proximity to power and the key role they played in protecting the President, having better pay, training and equipment, these units neither became cohesive nor sufficiently politicised to deflect lower ranks from protesting over the years. They were meant to guard the guardians, to contain the prospect of reactionary and dissenting military non-elites, but soon absorbed the inefficiencies and corruptibility of the system.

The UGP were elite troops trained by Israel and North Korea, with embedded Russian, Israeli and Cuban advisors. Mirroring the FAA, it had parallel structures dealing with finances, intelligence, human resources, internal affairs, and telecommunications, as well as its own logistics base in Kikolo.[14] UGP troops were deployed to guard the President and carry distinct identification tags to avert infiltration and potential security breaches. When they were spread throughout the capital, following the President's moves around Luanda, they would carry these tags to differentiate from other FAA units positioned in the area. The SCP employed a wide-angled approach to presidential security, suggesting lower levels of trust in the general military command. This trust deficit in the generals of the FAA, those from UNITA and former FAPLA, explained the need to create parallel security structures that were better equipped and resourced.[15] In times of political tension, the UGP were deployed to strategic areas of Luanda and the headquarters of the opposition parties. This happened in October 2013 when dos Santos was rushed to Barcelona for urgent medical care and was away for several weeks while protests erupted in Luanda.[16] Reflecting the influence of the SCP, it was Kopelipa who ran the country in dos Santos' absence, instead of Vice-President Manuel Vicente.[17] Placing Kopelipa in charge indicated continuity and contingency rather than following the civilian constitutional chain of command.

The Presidential Security Unit (USP) was created to provide the first ring of defence for the President. It was previously under national police command, which was under the Department of Presidential security. While the UGP was charged with protecting the president outside the palace, the USP provided close quarter protection within the perimeter of the presidential palace and was responsible for the safety of the first family. They had equivalent and superimposed functions to countercheck and coordinate security. USP personnel travelled with dos Santos both within the country and abroad. Both forces were meant to provide an uninterrupted and incorruptible system of protection for the President. Perceptions of UGP and USP privilege unsurprisingly generated resentment elsewhere in the military, compounded by better pay and conditions.[18] A sergeant in the armed forces was, for example, paid in 2015 on average 150,000 Kz ($170) a month, compared with a UGP sergeant who received 375,000 Kz ($400).[19] At the height of economic growth in 2013, a Presidential Guard earned $1,050 monthly, five times more than a soldier in the FAA.[20] Despite this continued disparity, USP soldiers openly criticised the culture of nepotism and corruption within the unit. In a letter to the Inspector General, dated November 2019, a group denounced the irregularities surrounding their pay and the *base de familiarismo*, the informal and nepotistic system of rank promotions. They also described the precarious work conditions and daily struggles of the lower ranks.[21] The pathologies threatening the entire national security system had permeated the elite units.

In addition to these two forces was the Chacal unit of special operations. They were positioned as the elite of the elite. Every member of the Chacal had been personally invited to join.[22] Created to provide security for the members of the dos Santos family and some members of the inner circle, the unit was trained by Israeli instructors in anti-terrorism, anti-guerrilla warfare and other tactics. It was formally commanded by General Francisco "Lindo" and headquartered at the UGP Instruction Centre in the Benfica neighbourhood of Luanda. Once João Lourenço took over as President, his brother General José Lourenço Serqueira, nominated as deputy head of the SCP, took control of the unit. There were thought to be about 380 men, their operations cloaked in secrecy. Chacal troops were allegedly deployed in both the DRC and Zimbabwe to alleviate political tension.[23] In May 2012, Human Rights Watch reported on coordinated operations between Chacal, FAA and PIR in the abuse and expulsion of Congolese immigrants in the diamond-rich provinces, further pointing to the unit's use in domestic operations.[24] However, this elite unit was also thought to be part of a large bluff by the Presidency, which portrayed a battalion that were effectively bodyguards as an elite crack force.

Growing frustrations within the unit regarding irregular payments contributed to protests in 2013. In a letter addressed to the FAA Chief, staff demanded to be paid via bank transfer so that they could get credit and bank loans, and described how their commanding officers would arbitrarily threaten salary cuts and forced demobilisation.[25] The letter called for the stability of proper procedure and was echoed in demands from other military units. Despite their prominence and elite training, the unit was, like other Presidential Guard units, weakened by the lack of accountability that fed informality, arbitrariness and impunity. The Reconstruction Protection Unit (DPCS) was a special armed unit of over 2,000 men with a mandate to operate until 2025.[26] "The DPCS was part of the Presidential Guard but never appeared in the organogram of the SCP. We cooperated with all units and had a footprint in all 18 provinces".[27] Created in 2004 to provide security for Chinese-funded reconstruction projects, it fell under the GRN Office of National Reconstruction run by Kopelipa,[28] and the DPSC's central command operated from the China International Fund (CIF)'s warehouses on the outskirts of Luanda.[29] This arrangement was unprecedented and reflected the unparalleled influence of Chinese interests in Angola.[30] It also highlighted the opaque nature of the President's security priorities. DPCS became security guards for Chinese capital and was commanded by General Jesus Manuel, who, under Kopelipa's tenure, had been the executive secretary of the SCP.

Dissatisfaction within the DPCS led to several soldiers facing disciplinary action at the military tribunal in September 2012 after they filed a petition against poor working conditions and irregular payment, and questioned the mandate of protecting Chinese interests.[31] DPCS soldiers claimed that while UGP soldiers earned over $1,000 a month, they only received $280–$340, and claimed that their unit's commanders were siphoning off the money intended to pay their salaries to set up their own businesses instead.[32] They also accused the military leadership of using this irregular unit to work on its own private projects.[33] In 2015 the DPCS was allegedly sent to recover an estimated 20,000 army deserters from the provinces. Many had stopped coming to the barracks weekly because they didn't have money for transport. "We had many men out of the army and this was dangerous".[34]

After the fall in oil prices in 2014 and the implementation of austerity measures, the government's threat assessment levels rose exponentially.[35] The Presidency began using overwhelming force to manage the fear that an uprising could occur in Luanda, given the deterioration of conditions in the capital's most crowded neighbourhoods. To preempt any potential social unrest, in February 2015 it reinforced the anti-riot police (PIR), bolstering their ranks with Military Police trained in military tactics.[36] The President also reinforced his security units with Cuban operatives.[37] He also created an anti-coup force of 2,500 men in the southern province of Kuando Kubango. The Forças Especiais de Apoio ao Comandante em Chefe (Special Forces in Support of the Commander-in-Chief, or FEACC) was a special unit created to curb any direct threat to dos Santos. Positioned along the river Kuebe near Menongue in the south of the country, they were able to reach Luanda in two hours to neutralise any threats. In 2015, following police confrontations with a religious sect in Huambo, dos Santos strengthened his praetorian guard with over 1,000 of these troops.[38]

In February 2018, President João Lourenço decided to change the organisation, not the function, of the SCP. He formalised the existing organs that had been left out of the previous bill of 2013, including the Chacal and DPCS units and added a special minesweeping team. He also added a cabinet on psychological action, patriotic, moral and civic education, the Hospital Pedro Maria Tonha "Pedale", and an Office for Special Infrastructure Works. More importantly, this new regulation created a deputy chief of the SCP, a role that fell to the new President's brother, General Serqueira. The deputy chief held a ministerial position and was empowered to co-adjudicate on numerous matters with the head of the SCP. It provided an additional layer of protection for the President.

*Intelligence Services—Internal, External and Military*

The different branches of the intelligence services played a central role in managing rivalries in internal political competition for power within and between the services and various groups that strove for power. The services existed purely to serve the President, a mandate reflected in their behaviour and operations. The motto of the intelligence services, "God in Heaven and State on Earth", revealed the extent to which the authorities created a sense of omnipresence. They extended their reach and developed an intrusive structure of control, repression and infiltration that monitored almost all aspects of the state, private life, civil society, the private sector, government and the military. Their actions became completely insulated from government accountability and they wielded unchecked power. One former advisor to President dos Santos commented that discussing politically sensitive issues like corruption was a risk for him: "here they will kill you".[39]

Their power and mandates were broad and interpreted at will, at times excessively and chaotically. They weren't only there to provide the normal functions of intelligence (the collection of information, analysis, counterintelligence and covert operations) but were an extension of an effective wartime apparatus that in peacetime waged war on the multiple threats to the President. Officially, the services were separated into the military (SISM), external (SIE), and internal (SINSE) structures, although during dos Santos' administration they merged under the command of Generals Antonio José Maria and Kopelipa. Institutional shortcomings were overcome, not through an intent to enhance efficiency but to create fear and sow mistrust among the people. "The Cubans and the Soviets weren't always able to train the service properly, and in the same way as the state lacked qualified administrators, the security agencies lacked skilled cadres, so they had to replace people with fear so that no one would question the competency of the government and their leaders".[40]

After the creation of the Direcção de Informação e Segurança de Angola (Information and Security Directorate of Angola, or DISA) in November 1975, the intelligence services had an embryonic link to the leaders of the country. DISA reported directly to President Agostinho Neto and was one of the first measures implemented to institutionalise the new state after independence. Its objectives were to "defend and consolidate independence and national unity, and protect the revolutionary conquests of the people while promoting the re-education of those elements that might threaten those objectives ... as well as to combat any acts or activities against the Constitutional Law, against the organs of the state and the MPLA".[41] The military ethos deeply influenced DISA. It had its own structures and budget and had provincial branches that were mainly composed of FAPLA elements and MPLA militants. Its first commander, Ludy Kissassunda, was deputised by two commanders who were members of the MPLA leadership and the army. The DISA chief was equivalent to a minister and reported directly to the President but was also a member of the Council of Ministers, the National Security Commission and the Revolutionary

Council (Bonzela Franco 2013). DISA operatives wouldn't just collect and analyse information; they would structure security operations capturing and detaining any subversive elements. Cuban intelligence operatives trained its officials and officers and played a big role in structuring the service. Three years after independence, the government passed a law defining the partisan and police-like character of the DISA.[42] Inspired by and structured following the Soviet model of centralised and militarised security, DISA became a powerful organ but was dismantled in 1979 by the Revolutionary Council. The newly created Ministry of Interior absorbed the DISA operatives.

In 1980, intelligence responsibility fell under the remit of the Ministry of Security (MINSE). It was first headed by General Kundy Paihama, a powerful commander and influential member of the MPLA, who was later deputised by Fernando da Piedade Dias dos Santos "Nando". MINSE remained heavily militarised and centralised. Its primary objective was the "organisation, prevention and defence of the country,"[43] while strictly aligning cooperation with other security organs and syndicated party structures. MINSE had a broader operative action and structure than DISA. Structured around militarised commands, directorates and sections, it advanced intelligence, counter-intelligence, state security operations, and the direct protection of government officials.

The Ministry was also mandated to maintain vigilance over the entire territory and state borders, and to protect critical infrastructures and areas of diamond production, as well as all the offices of the state (Bonzela Franco 2013). MINSE's operations became increasingly complex as UNITA developed its own capacities in intelligence and surveillance, leading to the creation of a special department to collect information on the enemy and support operations of the armed units. Throughout the 1970s and 1980s, security agents would be placed in every sector and institution of the state. "Agents were placed in schools, in cooperatives; they were everywhere. They were placed in the administrations of institutions and became part of the management structures".[44]

MINSE was dissolved in 1991 when the government began restructuring under the Bicesse Peace Agreement. An estimated 50,000 intelligence operatives were also demobilised in 1992, resulting from a change in strategy and the need to cut costs.[45] Many of these would later return to the army when the war restarted. From February 1991 to August 1993, the intelligence capacity of the government was greatly impacted by this restructuring, which split intelligence gathering between the Ministry of the Interior and Military Intelligence of the FAA (Bonzela Franco 2013). Another reorganisation occured in 1994 with line responsibilities separated between three branches.[46] Three new services were created.

At first, the Services for Internal Security (SINFO, later SINSE) fell under the Ministry of the Interior, whilst Military Intelligence (SIM) and External Security (SIE) were under the Ministry of Defence.[47] In December 2002, the new law on national security[48] detached SINFO's link to the Ministry of the Interior and created a direct reporting line to the President. In 2010 the service was renamed SINSE, with the new structure becoming an auxiliary service to the President of the Republic. SINSE, together with SISM and SIE, was mandated to produce and analyse information to preserve the country's internal stability and support the legislative, executive, judiciary, and police.[49] In theory, SISM and SIE were there to support external Angolan diplomatic missions to combat international criminal and terrorist organisations. In reality, these services were instruments for political control. SINSE, in particular, became the support structure for all the decision-making organs of the state, with broad interventions in every aspect from economic planning to diplomacy and national defence. This resulted in a centralised, opaque and largely unaccountable structure.

The three agencies had distinct command structures, budgets and personnel, but shared a cooperative mission that was determined by the SCP's priorities for state security. Their effectiveness was questionable. They operated through personalised command structures, lacked effective training programmes, and depended on favours and clientelism to gather information. Many operatives had only basic literary skills, while some commanding officers could not operate any form of technology.[50] This put the state at risk, given the power they had and their commanders' practice of fabricating threats to seek to bolster budgets.[51] Increasingly embarrassing situations emerged whereby the different services interfered with each other's operations, in state-sponsored killings that were exposed in public.[52]

The SCP ensured the intelligence community primarily served the interest of the President and was deployed to that end, infiltrating and monitoring government members, political elites, opposition parties, and the media. This fed a culture of resentment and paranoia regarding the Presidency. These dynamics contributed to regular intelligence failures, misinformation and weak threat analysis that in turn fed into bad decision-making. All the intelligence agencies competed for budgetary support, which was then funnelled into specific operations defined by the national security threats they encountered, perceived and invented. Operations required manpower and spending on arms acquisitions, communications surveillance, and a budget for informers. The more enemies, plots, and threats there were towards the President, the greater the influence of commanders became. This applied particularly to the tenure of General José Maria of SISM.

The difficulty of dealing with unaccountable services, whose overzealous leaders wanted to gain favour for uncovering national threats, was that the President was fed inaccurate information. Fears that the Arab Spring would reach Angola in 2011 led to over-reactions and the restructuring of the three services. On 7 March 2011, a protest was organised by a diaspora youth in Namibia who half-jokingly called for an uprising. The SINSE spent over $20 million in preventive measures to counter the march that essentially rallied only a few youths in Luanda.[53] SINSE also sought the expertise of Israeli technology specialists in the purchase of electronic surveillance equipment. One of the preventative measures taken by the services in preparation for an uprising that never happened was the use of an Israeli device called "Keched" that detects human movement within a range of 1 kilometre. SINSE acquired four of the Keched devices, each costing $100,000.[54] Civil servants, employees of state companies and school children were bussed to Luanda in a show of support for the MPLA[55] to take part in a 30,000-strong counter-march under the threat of sanctions.[56] State media claimed hundreds of thousands had joined the march. These overreactions by the security services fuelled dissent and empowered a generation of youth activists. This youth group would later produce a manifesto calling for the President's removal, the equitable distribution of wealth, for justice and social equality, and direct presidential polls.

### Domestic Intelligence (SINSE)

The State Security and Internal Intelligence Service (SINSE), previously called Serviços de Informação (SINFO), lay at the heart of

Angola's intelligence capacity. It had one of the most extensive operations and span in the country, operating as a political police force. SINSE's headquarters were one of the city's most impressive buildings and occupied an entire city block. Built by the Chinese in the new city of Kilamba, the HQ's construction is estimated to have cost the state $26 million.[57] SINSE's objectives were to fight against subversive internal and external groups, infiltrate and destabilise political parties, and be the eyes and ears of the Presidency throughout the country in all sectors.[58] It controlled an extensive network of officers and informers where each operative had another intelligence officer who verified their information and scrutinised their activities. They were spies of spies. Agents were placed inside the offices of opposition parties and in the different NGOs and civil society groups. They posed as journalists, activists, and dissenters to get information on all subversive activities. "It was easy to recruit civilians to join SINSE because of the levels of poverty. People were hungry and this gave them money. They would sell themselves for pittance".[59]

SINSE conducted disinformation, intimidation and harassment campaigns, and provided a training ground for politicians who had risen in power after passing through the service's command. The Speaker of Parliament and former Prime Minister Fernando da Piedade Dias dos Santos, or "Nando", was its first head in 1991. General Fernando Miala, later head of the SIE, would replace "Nando" and led the services from 1996 until 1999. From April 2006, Sebastião Martins took over and oversaw its change from SINFO to SINSE. Martins came in to alter its operating procedures, publicly stating that the service was no longer one that assassinated people; he aimed to create professional analysts and intelligence technocrats.[60] The service, in principle, no longer retained police powers to search and detain but was focused on researching, producing and processing the information needed to combat sabotage, organised crime, or any political, social and economic threats to society or the state. SINSE's function was meant to "make government's decisions in the areas of internal and external politics, national defence and public order, more realistic and rational, less based on intuition and more based on evidence and reflection".[61]

Before the 2012 elections, SINSE upgraded their surveillance systems by employing the COMINT (Combined Communications

Intelligence Systems) and HUMNIT (Human Collection and Analysis Intelligence) surveillance systems against UNITA and other opposition movements. The objective was to reduce the ambiguity inherent in collecting and analysing information to minimise inaccuracies. Martins was reforming the system when his tenure ended abruptly in 2013, when the assassinations of activist Isaias Cassule and undercover SINSE operative Alves Kamulingue led to public fallout. His removal as head of the service weakened it and generated internal anger.[62] General Eduardo Octavio, Martins' deputy, who reverted more easily to taking orders from SCP, ran the services until Lourenço took over as President. In 2015, the command made several changes to the directorate structures of SINSE, dismissing several chiefs.[63] These changes were propelled by Octavio, who replaced the directors of the terrorism, organised crime, political and social subversion, state security, technical vigilance, and communication departments. During these years there was little evidence that SINSE's intelligence capabilities were enhanced or had broken with the pattern of reaching erroneous conclusions and pathological inefficiency.

The surveillance ability acquired by SINSE extended to phone tapping and other measures of listening in on conversations, and hacking into email exchanges and text messages.[64] The dos Santos family's control of Angola's leading telecom services—UNITEL and MOVICEL—allowed the intelligence services to operate undetected when placing phone tapping systems.[65] Angola also allegedly tried to use satellites to further this aim[66] and Luanda was expected to obtain its own satellite system from Russia in 2014. The satellite, Angosat, cost more than €286 million and would have a lifespan in orbit of 15 years. It was part of a mass effort to refurbish the country's telecommunications infrastructure, which led the government to partner with Rosoboronexport, a specialised Russian defence company, in 2009. Russian banks would lend the money and RKK Energia, which had pioneered satellite communications for the Soviets in the 1960s, would build the spacecraft.[67] However, within two days of its launch in December 2017, the satellite lost communications. It was lost in space. In early 2020, the government announced that Angosat-2 was being built. A third Angosat satellite was already being commissioned to advance Angola's ambitious development plans. In May 2019, the new President, Lourenço authorised the Minister for Telecommunications and Technology to sign a contract for the Angosat-3 project as it became incorporated into the Spatial Strategy for Angola 2016–25. According to civil society members, one of the objectives of Angosat was the possibility of allowing the government a more comprehensive capacity for surveillance and wiretapping. Regardless of the actual capabilities of the government to use the satellites for widespread surveillance, the perception remained that "the government was always listening".[68] Installing paranoia was undoubtedly part of the strategy.

SINSE also supported the work of the Interior Ministry and the national police. The police increasingly relied on information provided by SINSE and less on their own intelligence-gathering capacity. The capacity of SINSE and its effective power shifted in 2017, under General Fernando Miala, who was installed to lead the gathering of information on MPLA corruption. Essentially, SINSE became an instrument to politically purge the MPLA elites. The President's management of corruption, a way to silence internal critics by mining their moral standing and assuring control through opportunities, had already led dos Santos to create a separate intelligence department inside his office. This department created companies and selected shareholders and kept a log of corrupt practices to blackmail those who became defiant.[69] In May 2019, Miala was given the status of Minister with the corresponding protocol, status, salary and immunity from prosecution. This signalled the prominence of SINSE in the post-dos Santos era as a force used for political reckoning and the war on corruption.

*External Intelligence (SIE)*

The External Intelligence Service (SIE) was created in 1991 with the Bicesse accords. In its previous form, it had been the Service for External Security (SSE). It had functioned as a private service of the President, aiding him in his external priorities and missions. It began as a centre for communications attached to the Presidency that was allegedly run by dos Santos when Agostinho Neto was President (Bernardino 2013). It was known as "Cosse", a service that was controlled by the Defence Ministry when it was the Service of Military Counter-

Intelligence (Contra Inteligência Militar, or CIM) under Minister Henrique Telles "Iko" Carrera. SIE was then transferred to the SCP. As the service for external intelligence, it covered the region, particularly the DRC and the Republic of Congo. SIE's activities during the 1990s were aimed at supporting diplomatic efforts to neutralise UNITA. Their activities on foreign soil generated tensions with several countries, namely an incident in October 1997 when operatives attempted but failed to abduct Savimbi's son, Eloy Sakaita, in Togo. Operatives were based in all of the country's diplomatic missions abroad, with more than one operative in countries of strategic importance. Its remit was to seek out potential Angolan informers abroad, who worked in foreign companies, to seek information that was of interest to the state.[70]

Under its former head General Fernando Miala, the SIE, by force of its commander's personality and efficiency, took the lead in operationalising and connecting all three branches of the intelligence services into the "Intelligence Community". Before he was fired in 2006, Miala effectively ran the Superior Council of Intelligence and dealt directly with the President. The Community had a school in Luanda, the Centro de Formação Especial de Inteligência do Serviço de Informações (CFECIS), and functioned under operating procedures that sought to make it more fluid and able to better share information between services. CFECIS began its operations within the presidential area of Futungo de Belas but was later transferred to the outskirts of the capital in Kilamba. In 2009, the SIE began working from their headquarters in Camana in a new building estimated to have cost $78 million.[71]

Miala's tenure as the head of the SIE and his focus on operational success created friction with other leading officers of the security sector. Miala was and remained an enemy of Kopelipa and General José Maria.[72] He was accused of becoming bigger than the institution, which brought about plots to curtail his influence with the President. One theory pinned the intrigue on racial divides within the MPLA. "The mestiço generals came to the President and alerted him to the power of the Black generals. They said to him: 'we don't want your power but the Black generals will kill you'.[73] A group of generals also convinced the President that Miala was organising a coup, leading to his dismissal in 2006 and subsequent arrest in 2007, after which he spent three years in jail. As a result, the intelligence community collapsed and the service that began to take precedence became the SISM under General

José Maria. After Miala's removal in 2006, SIE underwent some restructuring with the purging of his loyalists and the promotion of other operatives who were awarded military patents. However, the founding trio (Kopelipa, José Maria and Miala) managed to coexist and cooperate for many years, while competing for power and seeking to destroy each other. When Lourenço took office in 2017, Miala used his position as head of SINSE to move to destroy those that had led the conspiracy against him.

André Oliveira Sango, an academic and former director of the CFECIS, which grew within the service branch of military counter-intelligence during the war, ran SIE for many years under dos Santos. He took over from Miala in 2006 but was dismissed by Lourenço in 2018. Sango, unlike Miala, did not report directly to the President but instead followed the other service's procedure of reporting to Kopelipa. He was considered a Shadow Foreign Minister, delivering important personal messages from dos Santos to several of his counterparts in Africa and elsewhere. Under Sango, Angola intervened indirectly in the political outcome of the Ivorian electoral standoff by supporting Gbagbo, who had lost those elections. Sango took a role in mediating a peace agreement in the Central African Republic in 2016, which failed to reconcile the different warring factions. Under Lourenço, the SIE was headed by General José Luís Caetano Higino de Sousa, "Zé Grande", who had previously served as the Deputy Chief of Staff of the FAA for Operations. Zé Grande was considered a close ally of President Lourenço as both men had undergone military training in the former Soviet Union. In 2019 Lourenço created the Academia de Ciências Sociais e Tecnologias to invest in the training of SIE operatives. The cost to the state was around $72.9 million, most of which was funded by China's Eximbank.[74] The Academy's objective was to train operatives of any strategic institution of the state, particularly those connected with foreign deployments. With courses taught in Portuguese, the academy also taught English, French, Lingala and Swahili, pointing to the more regional focus of the services.

## Military Intelligence (SISM)

The Serviço de Inteligência e Segurança Military (Military Intelligence Service) or SISM was the most radical and nationally feared of all the services. It was run for many years by General José Maria (2008–17), a hardliner loyalist to dos Santos who built his career in all branches of the intelligence services and depended entirely on the President for his power. Under the new President, SISM would be headed by General Apolinário José Pereira, who had previously served as a deputy to José Maria, signalling a level of continuity. José Maria became the darkest and most authoritarian face of the Presidency, frequently described as calculating and cruel by people he imprisoned, framed and humiliated. His ascendency was quite linear. In his youth he studied in the Catholic seminary in Huambo alongside some UNITA leaders. This connection led UNITA's Secretary General Alicerces Mango to seek refuge in José Maria's house during the 1992 massacres in Luanda, a miscalculation that cost Mango his life.[75] He had also been a military instructor in the Portuguese army during colonial rule. When dos Santos took over the Presidency following Neto's death in 1978, José Maria was brought in to serve as the President's Secretary for Defence and Security where he would also run the dossier of military counter-intelligence. In 1991 he was promoted to Deputy Chief of Staff for Military Doctrine, and in 2001 took over as Chief of Military Security from General Mario Placido Cirilo de Sá, "Ita". For four decades José Maria was dos Santos' most trustworthy collaborator. He would also be responsible for single-handedly weakening the services of military intelligence. His excessive nature and at times violent disposition created an aura of untouchability and arrogance that came from his proximity to dos Santos.

Military Intelligence had been a crucial service during the civil war. Missions and combat operations depended on information and analysis from military intelligence for their operational success. SISM's predecessor service, SIM, belonged to a universe of departments and autonomous units for the collection and processing of information, such as the Directorate for Operational Military Intelligence (DIMO), the Directorate for Military Counter-Intelligence (DPCIM), which had sub-sections for each of the branches (army, navy and airforce) that coordinated with each military region, and the Grupo Operativo de Inteligência (GOI). Like other military intelligence services, SISM was meant to operate under the command of the FAA and the MOD. This changed in 2008 with the fusion of two services—Military Security and the Reconnaissance Service RETO—that José Maria was nominated to lead. He created an autonomous and untouchable service that reported directly to the President. The Operational Intelligence Group (GOI) was also taken over by José Maria and used to conduct extraction operations of Cabindan rebels in the Congos, and to coordinate the anti-guerrilla activities of the intelligence services in Cabinda.[76]

Upon taking control of the service, José Maria accelerated the retirement of key officers within the SISM, diluting the ability of other more qualified generals and brigadiers to hamper his operational control. "General José Maria's strategy for national defence was to promote intrigue. He began by cleaning out key generals in the SISM (there had been 32 and only four remained), in particular Generals Zé Grande and Massango Pereira, the two heavyweights. He then turned his activities against all the generals that came from UNITA, creating an unsustainable climate of persecution within the service and forcing several to leave, like General Diógenes Malaquías 'Implacável', who defected from UNITA in 2000."[77] The situation became so tense, with SISM operating inside the military hospital, that former UNITA officers began seeking medical assistance either from private doctors or any former UNITA doctors that were still alive. "They were too afraid to get treated at the military hospital because of the large net of agents operating there. People would go for treatment and end up dead".[78] The fear of poisoning continued to haunt security agents, regardless of whether they had affiliations to UNITA. "An intelligence agent either died with a bullet to the head or with poison"[79] if his usefulness expired or he became a liability.

The unofficial objective of the SISM was to abort possible threats inside the FAA and within the country's leadership and elites. Agents were placed in every province and every department and unit of the armed forces and other sectors of the security apparatus.[80] José Maria's insistence on counter-surveilling the FAA made him a much-detested figure of the regime. He made many enemies within the government and security apparatus but operated for decades with impunity. As a result, SISM became a purging service that promoted dissatisfaction against the President within his own elite and armed forces. He was never able to shed the political animosities that had fuelled the war. José Maria deeply despised any UNITA commanders, calling them "*provi*" (*Provenientes*, meaning "those from"), and refused to meet with them in his office. He was credited with the so-called purification of the FAA and used it as a way of purging former UNITA generals and destabilising the armed forces. This partisan plot was aided by General "Disciplina" (then the Deputy Chief of Staff for Patriotic Education and currently Chief of Staff of the FAA under Lourenço's presidency), and General João Antonio Santana "Lungo", who at the time was with the Bureau of Intelligence of the Presidency within the SCP.[81] While this plot failed to create enough friction within the FAA to be successful, it did act as a catalyst for the retirement and side-lining of several former UNITA officers.

SISM took over the surveillance system used during the war in order to track UNITA's communications and movements. BATOPE (Batalhão Técnico Operativo) was the government's surveillance system supported by Israeli technology and the Chinese.[82] While BATOPE was essential to counter and monitor UNITA's activities during the war, it became redundant during peacetime. However, the government chose to maintain and further update the system in Cabo-Ledo, allegedly to spy on the regime.[83] The BATOPE system upgraded its electronic and wiretapping surveillance systems, essentially creating a parallel operation to SINSE, and was run by Coronel Eurico, a close affiliate of José Maria.[84] In 2014, the unit reportedly sought North Korean expertise to block critical websites and limit access to online papers reporting on corruption, human rights violations, and illegal detentions or criticising the government.[85] The government had already begun to impose a clampdown on the internet in 2011 through its Law to Combat Criminality in the areas of information, communication technology and social information services. It criminalised anyone who divulged and diffused information that was prejudicial to the country's integrity or had the effect of destroying and subverting the functioning of the state. This bill also allowed the state to intercept emails and phone calls.[86] In 2016 the government passed another bill that criminalised any opinion that displeased the President, with penalties ranging from two to eight years in prison, and created a new body for oversight. The Angolan Social Communications Regulatory Body was given broad powers to "enforce compliance with professional journalistic ethics and standards" and "verify compliance by radio and television operators".[87]

## Control of Elections

Elections have served many strategic purposes in Angola, beyond the functions of electing a parliament and consolidating democratic procedure. In fact, those two objectives have only been residually important. Instead, elections have served to secure and reinforce the President's hegemony, eliminate the opposition and allow for the consolidation of a securitised government. They became the vehicle to return Angola to a one-party state while at the same time gaining long-elusive national and international legitimacy (Roque 2009). Elections allowed the government to legally appropriate the necessary powers to pass laws, decree orders, structure administrations and direct larger amounts of funds to priority areas. The control over the electoral process was of such strategic importance that it also fell to the SCP to hire, fund, direct and coordinate companies, institutions, budgets and mechanisms involved in the run-up to elections, during the voting, and in the tabulation process. The SCP's intervention in elections began in 2008, possibly one of the most important polls in Angolan history. After the end of the war, the MPLA and President had to ensure that they would retain a majority in parliament to continue steering the direction of reconstruction but also change the constitution. The SCP would also intervene in the 2012 and 2017 polls. From hiring the companies to assist in printing ballots and electoral result sheets, to hiring computer systems engineers to work in the tally centres and advising the government organs responsible for the electoral process, the SCP was the arm of the President that ensured influence over the outcome. In 2008, the MPLA won the elections by 81%, in 2012 it won by 71% and in 2017 it won by 61%. With every poll, the strategies used to interfere with the process and its results became more brazen and sophisticated, in line with the fears of the President of his plummeting popularity.

All four electoral processes (1992, 2008, 2012 and 2017) were characterised by irregularities. The first post-war polls of 2008 were somewhat informed by the 1992 electoral debacle. Many leaders relocated their families abroad and across borders in neighbouring countries fearing that violence could ensue. Expats and elites began stocking up on food ahead of any post-electoral violence. Despite the peaceful manner in which they occurred, the polls were heavily lopsided in favour of the MPLA, which had instrumentalised the organs of the state towards supporting its party machinery. The MPLA proceeded to control the rhetoric of peace, positioning dos Santos as the "architect of peace", led a sophisticated marketing and public relations campaign, and co-opted, corrupted and essentially outmanoeuvred mechanisms meant to supervise the fairness of the polls. While the government dispersed $17 million to opposition parties for their campaigns, the MPLA's electoral campaign cost over $300 million, allegedly funded by state enterprises, private companies and investors.[88]

Several key strategies allowed the MPLA to achieve its desired outcome. One involved weakening the National Electoral Commission (CNE), which gradually had its powers either transferred to other organs of the executive or whose functions were shadowed by parallel organs operating in the Presidency. In 2005, the ruling party began the process of controlling the electoral register through the Council of Ministers' decrees, transferring key responsibilities away from the CNE. Tampering with the electoral roll allowed the ruling party to determine who could and couldn't vote. The work of the CNE was supported by the intelligence services and controlled by the MPLA. It was composed of 11 members, eight of which were from the ruling party. Brigadier Rogerio Saraiva of the SCP, an expert in technology, was inserted as an advisor to the then CNE President, Caetano de Sousa. Saraiva was thought to have been behind the 81% result achieved by the MPLA in 2008 through his intervention in the vote-counting processes.[89]

The MPLA's campaign for the 2008 legislative elections was centred around its slogan "The right path for a better Angola", where the ruling party portrayed itself as a permanent requirement for national stability. During these elections, the MPLA mobilised over 30,000 party committees (*comités de acção*) across the country to campaign and prepare for its victory.[90] These committees were the most basic cell of party organisation. In one municipality of Luanda, Kilamba Kiaxi, over fifty of these committees were created. MPLA specialist committees were also set up and strengthened across different sectors of society to ensure that professionals inside and outside the state bureaucracy and the private sector were informed of the most "patriotic" way to vote. The provinces were structured in a way that allowed for greater control of the vote and the population. Members of the church and civil society drew attention to the government's tactic of conditioning the rural population's vote by inserting them into a "framework" of intimidation and co-optation. Traditional authorities, government officials and MPLA supporters were all mobilised to advise individuals on how to vote.[91] A former Secretary General of the MPLA commented in 2008 that, "in the rural areas people are '*enquadradas*' [meaning they are inserted into a regulating framework] with the directions of the Sobas. We are not worried about the countryside. The great unknown is Luanda".[92] In the rural areas, civil society and the opposition observed how members of SINFO (SINSE) were inserted inside the polling stations and among voters queuing outside polling stations to ensure they would vote for the MPLA. Their presence was an intimidation tactic and some people believed that the government would see how each person voted. A UNITA provincial leader explained that the MPLA chose this strategy because "order without justice is only maintained through force".[93]

Several provinces registered different irregularities. In Cabinda, Congolese citizens were voting for the MPLA, a fact highlighted by an EU electoral mission observer. In Lunda Sul, ballots were distributed to traditional authorities ahead of the vote. In Kwanza Norte, all 156,666 registered voters turned out to vote, while in Lunda Norte the CNE reported that 311,684 people had cast their votes, when final results revealed that only 290,889 had voted (Marques 2008). Intimidation was widespread and people were instructed to "vote for peace", meaning that if the opposition won, there would be war. Inside the army and police barracks, special ballot boxes were installed to allow the security forces to vote "patriotically" so that if there were votes for the opposition the government would know within which unit there was dissent (Roque 2008). In the capital, where control over the population was harder, "chaos" ensued on voting day with polling stations failing to open on time or missing registration lists. This led to 320 polling stations having to schedule a second day of voting. The company Valleysoft, charged with distributing ballots and other materials, was behind the logistical and organisational issues in Luanda. Valleysoft had direct links to the SCP.[94] The company had bought 26 million ballots from the Spanish company INDRA when only 10 million were used.[95] The remainder, UNITA argued, were used in ghost ballot stations, a fact verified during tabulation when results were being counted from 50,195 voting stations when only 37,995 existed. Those extra ghost voting stations were produced by intelligence agents in an operation that was controlled by the SCP.[96] With the MPLA's crushing victory, the opposition became a residual political force with only 40 seats in a national assembly of 220 members. This marked the definitive end of any opposition engagement and dialogue. The Lusaka structures of reconciliation and political accommodation—the unity government and the joint political and military commissions—had been dismantled.

The MPLA's slogan for the 2012 polls was "Angola: continuing to grow to distribute better". It reflected an understanding that inequality and pervasive corruption had weakened their credibility with the population. The CNE was expanded to 17 members that, following the new electoral laws disbanding the Inter-ministerial Commission for Electoral Process (CIPE), became responsible for the entire electoral process. During the 2012 elections the infiltration of counting centres by SINFO and elements of the SCP replicated the system used in 2008. However, an additional structure, a parallel counting centre, was implemented to shadow the CNE within this parallel vote tabulation process.[97] The alleged shadow commission established by the SCP was run by promoted General Rogério Saraiva to observe the polling process.

According to the opposition parties, the results of each of the 18 provinces were pre-determined by the government in Luanda and the result sheets bearing the real numbers were never opened (Roque 2013). General Kopelipa was thought to have been the point person contracting INDRA, the Spanish company accused of printing 13 million ballots when only 6.1 million were used, with little accountability for what happened to the remainder. Other tactics included phantom polling stations, unaudited registration rolls, voter profiling and forced abstention. Over 37% of voters abstained during these polls, which the opposition and civil society argued pointed to a strategy of structured chaos in the cities where voters were turned away from polling stations having been informed that their names were on a list to vote in other provinces. In Luanda alone fewer than 30% managed to vote because of this strategy. Information, leaked from the Presidency to UNITA, revealed how technology experts from China were used to profile voters and disenfranchise them using their ethnicity, names and regional origins to determine if they were potential opposition supporters. UNITA brought criminal charges against General Kopelipa and his counterpart at the Civil Cabinet of the Presidency, Edeltrudes da

Costa, as well as several generals for falsifying electoral documents and fraud. Nothing came of this.

The MPLA's slogan for 2017, "improve what was good and correct what was bad", was a much more tempered campaign, aimed at balancing both continuity and change. The 2017 elections replicated all the previous manoeuvres of election rigging with the SCP at the helm of the strategy. The party was worried about the impact of the 2014 oil crisis that had plunged Angola into a recession. Having experienced two electoral cycles characterised by irregularities, the opposition was better equipped to monitor the results by creating a parallel tabulation process. Although UNITA never officially released its results, it claimed privately to have tallied about 90% of the results where the ruling party's majority had slid down to 54% with a complete loss of the popular vote in the capital, Luanda. At the CNE's national tally centre, no results were being processed: "the phones didn't ring and somehow the CNE was launching preliminary results from the different provinces".[98] Members of the CNE at the provincial, local and national levels confirmed that they did not observe or participate in any tallying of results.[99] Calls for the opposition to stage mass protests in Luanda and other provincial capitals were widespread. The youth in particular expected that UNITA would act with some political courage and take to the streets. However, the threat of a brutal crackdown became clear. Fliers and leaflets were distributed throughout the capital, with some dropped by planes over the informal settlements, advising people to stay home to avoid the level of destruction that had taken place after the 1992 elections. Images of these planes airdropping the leaflets and copies of their text circulated on social media as youth activists understood, incredulous, the fear emanating from the presidency as it resorted to such raw strategies. The threat of war remained the President's go-to. The securitisation of the electoral process that began in 1992 had come full circle in 2017 and is likely to continue in 2022, reflecting the need to contain dissent, protect power and ensure order in the aftermath of the Covid-19 pandemic.

*Police and Phantom Threats*

As the most direct interface between the security apparatus and the population, over the years the police became an instrument of repression,[100] facilitating violence and intimidating marginalised groups and communities. The police force coordinated actions with the intelligence services and unofficial paramilitary groups to patrol the capital and the country. They became instrumental in neutralising any potential focus of instability or social mobilisation demanding services, reform, or recourse for economic hardship. The strategic role they played in ensuring that community concerns would not escalate into coordinated action made them one of the best paid forces, above the military. They became a key component of the state's securitisation infrastructure.

The national police evolved from the Portuguese colonial police and the People's Police Corps of Angola (CPPA), which was the first force established after independence under the Ministry of Defence. Heading the Police Corps was General Santana Andre Pitra "Petroff", one of the country's most important commanders. In 1979, the CPPA was replaced with the National Directorate of the Popular Police, which began to incorporate organisational reforms. In 1985 it integrated all the police organs under the Ministry of Interior. It was only in 1991, however, that the police force was organised around a general command and headed by a police commissioner appointed by the President. Following the end of the war in 2002, a restructuring programme was launched to modernise the force with the aim of enhancing professionalism and increasing educational qualification requirements for new recruits. The 2003 plan created offices where civilians could complain about police conduct, and restructured the provincial command of Luanda into seven divisions to increase public security. Oversight was also provided by the Provedor da Justiça (Ombudsman), a position created in 2005, yet few ever got justice in cases of police brutality.

The provincial commands were under the central command of the police commissioner, subdivided by divisional commands in the capital and municipal commands in the provinces. The police commissioner held the equivalent position of a Deputy Minister. Despite laws determining disciplinary regulations[101] to supplement the roles and responsibilities articulated under the constitution and national police law,[102] the force remained a militarised entity that was increasingly used for partisan and repressive purposes. Different police branches came under the general command of the police: the public security officials, the economic and fiscal police, traffic brigade, the Paramilitary Rapid Response Unit (PIR), diplomatic protection unit, border guards, helicopter squadron, unit for strategic objectives, and the protocol protection unit. The police theoretically fell under the Ministry of the Interior and were responsible for the maintenance of public order. In practice the police commissioner reported directly to General Kopelipa. The interior minister, on the other hand, was merely briefed about operational matters and dealt mainly with administrative issues.[103] Ambrosio de Lemos acted as police commissioner for many years under dos Santos but was retired in November 2017 by the incoming President. Lourenço nominated Alfredo Mingas "Panda" as the new police commissioner replacing Lemos. Commissioner Panda had previously served as a commander of the feared and militarised PIR.

The more violent branches of the police included the PIR and the Directorate for Criminal Investigation (DNIC). From February 2015 the DNIC was taken from the command of the commissioner and began answering directly to the then Interior Minister, Angelo Tavares. The DNIC and the Directorate for Investigation of Economic Activities (DNIIAE) were incorporated into the new Service for Criminal Investigation (SIC) with the intention of streamlining investigative services and giving the interior minister greater power. SIC had been created by a Presidential Decree aimed at forming a judicial police. In 2019, President Lourenço decreed that the police would report directly to his office and formed a new Directorate for the Investigation of Illicit Actions (DIIP). As a result Angola had two investigation services—SIC and DIIP—duplicating roles, obfuscating operations and further burdening the national budget. Their methods remained violent and unaccountable. In 2016–17 a wave of terror was unleashed by the police with the extrajudicial killings of youths in Viana and Cacuaco, two of the most populous neighbourhoods of Luanda. An investigation into nearly 200 summary executions revealed how SIC agents were operating like a death squad.[104] The police were attempting to deal with delinquents and criminals but in several cases killed youths that had no criminal links. The police would also be seen harassing and assaulting street vendors, mainly women, on the streets of the capital because of their unregulated business activities and failure to abide by randomly evoked regulations. Campaigns were launched to tackle the informal market in bids to clear criminals, expel illegal immigrants and shut down small businesses. These and other actions led one opposition intellectual, who had defected from the MPLA, to state that "in Angola it is the poor that are combated not poverty".[105] The actions of these branches were supported by paramilitary groups that fell outside the official organogram. A special Anti-Crime Unit was created in 2012 to deal with further threats emanating from social dissatisfaction and crime in the capital. It was one such group that was suspected of being involved with DNIC agents in several operations that resulted in the deaths and torture of protesters.[106] In 2013 the unit was expanded to the entire country as part of the Police Reserve Force.

Any form of public protest was brutally suppressed. The police would go to great lengths to stop any protests from creating momentum and mobilising the masses. Every demonstration, no matter the size, would become costly for the state: "a protest of four youths meant the police had to mobilise 2,000 men who had to get their 'risk subsidy' of $100 each".[107] The threat of protests and the disproportionate responses were more revealing of the paranoia of a government than the potential for social groups to destabilise the country. Protests began building in the post-war years, signalling a generational shift towards youths who were no longer intimidated by the experience of war or memories of security operations. For this generation, political dissent did not equate to treason or counter-revolutionary activity. It was their right and their duty.

Since 2005, small but peaceful marches of students and activists protesting Angola's social and economic conditions were rapidly stopped by the deployment of police units with dogs. As protests continued in the run-up to the first post-war elections in 2008, the response of the police became more severe. However, it was the global events of 2011, with the Arab Spring, that truly injected fear into the government. "From 2011 onwards spies were everywhere. Inside taxis people couldn't voice opinions because at the next stop they could be detained by police".[108] The likelihood that the government had the capability of mounting operations to detain all their critics was, of course, remote. Nevertheless the idea of infiltration, surveillance and omnipresence permeated many social circles. The government took the potential for an "Angolan Spring" very seriously and began to clamp down brutally whenever more than 40 people gathered in one place. From the first youth protests in March 2011 until late 2014, there were over 50 peaceful anti-government demonstrations, all of which were met with overwhelming force.

The formation of a group of revolutionary youths was atypical. An anonymous call for a revolution in March 2011, circulating on social media through the pseudonym of Agostinho Jonas Roberto dos Santos (an amalgamation of the names of the four leaders of Angola's anti-colonial struggle), led to 17 youths meeting at midnight on 7 March in Luanda's Independence Square. They were swiftly detained by the police and from there onwards the movement of "Revolutionaries" was unexpectedly born. The "Revus", as they became known, included a core group of rappers and activists that years later would be accused of staging a coup. They became the target of sustained government harassment, with militias and police invading their homes before protests and violently beating them. Their families would be threatened and they would fall victim to numerous set-ups, with the security forces bent on framing them for serious crimes. Inspired by their courage, civilians from different informal settlements (Cazenga and Cacuaco) in Luanda would take to the streets. Small protests would be replicated in the provinces of Cabinda, Benguela, Bengo, Kuando Kubango, Lunda Norte and Huila, demanding improved services and denouncing police repression and human rights abuses. In June 2012, thousands of war veterans marched on Luanda demanding their pensions. Many of them had been waiting for 20 years. These protests panicked the government and it rapidly deployed the PIR and Military Police to detain the ex-combatants, but these demands were echoed in Lubango (province of Huila) and Menongue (capital of Kuando Kubango) by former FAPLA veterans marching to demand their retirement packages. Police repression grew as these small protests morphed into what the authorities perceived to be existential threats.

While both of the leading opposition parties, UNITA and CASA-CE, had huge mobilisation capacity, they rarely used it. They were acutely aware that any demonstration would be met with force. The test case of the government's response occurred in November 2013 when UNITA brought over 15,000 people to the streets of Luanda in protest at the killing of a CASA-CE youth leader, Manuel de Carvalho "Ganga", by the Presidential Guard. The security forces' overreaction, with the deployment of the anti-terror units and attack helicopters, sent a message to the opposition to never test their willingness to use disproportionate force again. Ganga had been shot twice in the back, on 22 November 2013, after being detained by members of the USP for posting flyers calling for a demonstration to honour the murdered activists Cassule and Kamulingue. His killer was absolved of involuntary murder by the courts on the grounds that that he had performed his duty to protect the presidential compound, which was near to where the killing happened. The same day, 213 activists from the youth wing of CASA-CE, Angola's third largest party, were arrested.[109] The USP's impunity had already been exposed with the assassination of another youth, Arsénio Sebastião "Cherokee", in November 2003 in the bay of Luanda. He was singing a song by Angolan rapper MCK that was critical of the government while washing a car. UGP officers tied his hands and held his head under water until he drowned. The subversive act of singing led to his death, for which the UGP was never held responsible.[110]

Due to the government's panic over the Arab Spring's contagion factor, the police and intelligence service activities were bolstered by the armed action of the Groups of Political Combat (GCP), an unofficial paramilitary group created in 2011. The GCP originated from the MPLA party structures under the provincial Political Action Committees (CAPs) located in all neighbourhoods of the country. In Luanda alone, there were over 100 CAPs. In addition to these GCP units were groups of plain-clothed 'thugs', also known as *caenches*, that played a vital role in harassing, intimidating and abducting youth protesters.[111] These *caenche* militias worked in tandem with the security forces and were coordinated by a close associate of dos Santos, Bento Kangamba (who later married the President's niece). Kangamba was a controversial and unsavoury figure who owned Kabuscorp Sport Clube do Palanca FC. He was accused by Brazilian authorities of trafficking women from Angola to Brazil to work as prostitutes but was acquitted in June 2014 for lack of evidence. Dos Santos later promoted Kangamba to the rank of a general.

The GCP was deemed an anti-terrorist group that operated outside the legal framework of the police and intelligence services functioning within party structures to neutralise dissent. The MPLA's use of *caenches* was noted in numerous reports and linked to the intimidation of a particular group of activists.[112] On 9 March 2012, members of the *caenche* militia invaded activist Carbono Casimiros' house and beat him and other activists for planning a protest for the following day. On 10 March they assaulted Filomeno Vieira Lopes, the Secretary-General of the opposition party Bloco Democrático, who had tried to help a UNITA supporter, Ermelinda Freitas, who was also being attacked. That morning over 30 activists were beaten on the streets of Luanda. The public broadcaster, Televisão Pública de Angola (TPA), was also used by the MPLA to send the message that those choosing to protest against them would be met with violence.[113]

Three episodes were emblematic of the overreactions of the government and the Presidency's use of its multiple security and intelligence units. The first involved the killing of two youth activists in 2012 by the security apparatus in Luanda. The second involved the highly publicised case of the arrest and trial of "15+2" book club activists in 2015. The third was the 2015 Kalupeteca massacre and the subsequent cover-up. All of these episodes shared the mass deployment of different security forces, the unaccountability of those giving orders, and the undertone of deep repression.

The first event occurred in May 2012, when Alves Kamulingue and Isaías Cassule were kidnapped in Luanda for allegedly trying to organise a protest of UGP veterans and ex-combatants demanding their pensions. It later became known that while Cassule was the leader of the United Patriotic Movement (MPU) that had called for the protests, Kamulingue was a SINSE agent embedded inside the movement. Kamulingue had been recruited in 2010 by the intelligence services and was placed inside UNITA offices in 2011 with the objective of reporting on any signs of the opposition joining in youth protests.[114] When MPU sent a letter to the provincial government requesting permission (as per the law) to stage a protest, the security agencies were alerted to the fact that former UNITA combatants and UGP soldiers were joining the dissidence. Both Kamulingue and Cassule were kidnapped and killed in May 2012, their bodies disposed of by a hybrid group of agents sent to silence them.

Angolan investigative journalists and human rights activists gradually began discovering the truth behind the assassinations and what they revealed about the intricate connections among the state's security services. No one knows who gave the kill orders, although a meeting was held the day before at the SCP where SISM, SINSE and police officials discussed how best to deal with the organisers of the protest.[115] Kamulingue was detained by UGP soldiers on 27 May, after being lured to a meeting with a SINSE agent Benilson Pereira "Tucayano", and taken to a police station where he was tortured and then shot in the head. His body was disposed of in a wooded area outside of Luanda.[116] Tucayano, it was later reported, had also infiltrated himself into the youth's revolutionary movement and became close to their leadership. Tucayano belonged to the family of the then Attorney General José Maria de Sousa, a much-detested figure of the judiciary who aided in the persecution of activists. Cassule began denouncing and spreading the word of the detention of his friend Kamulingue on the only independent radio station in Luanda, Ecclesia. He was, however, also lured to a meeting with Tucayano, who told him he had information about Kamulingue.[117] On the night of 29 May, Cassule was kidnapped by five undercover agents and was beaten to death two days later. His body was disposed of in the Dande river in neighbouring Bengo province. The outcry in Luanda among activists, the independent press and the opposition countered the efforts to bury these killings and led to an investigation by state prosecutors.

Seven people were put on trial for these murders. Two belonged to SINSE, four were police officers and one belonged to the provincial committee of the MPLA. One of the accused was António Manuel Gamboa Vieira Lopes, at the time a SINSE agent, who was sentenced to 20 years by the Supreme Court in February 2016. He was later acquitted by the Constitutional Court due to lack of evidence.[118] In March 2015, during the murder trials, details of Death Squadrons came to light. One defendant, Junior Mauricio "Cheu", who at the time was the head of the technical cabinet of the MPLA provincial secretariat in Luanda, and his co-defendant João Luis Fragoso revealed details of the existence of an underground intelligence service inside the party committee in Luanda that was directly coordinated by First Provincial Secretary Bento Bento, former Governor of Luanda. This shadow intelligence service was financed by General Filó, then the deputy head of the SISM under José Maria. It became clear that "Cheu" was a subordinate of João Francisco Kinguengo "Luta", who established the link with SINSE and SISM, and was instructed to kidnap and beat (not to kill) Cassule.[119] Details of GAP activities also became known, confirming that these MPLA organs were purposefully created to neutralise political activists and protesters.

The second episode became known as the "15+2" case and caught the attention of activists globally. In June 2015, 17 activists were arrested and charged with staging a coup. The threat was posited as a call to insurrection on the basis that these youths had organised a session to discuss Gene Sharp's book *From Dictatorship to Democracy: A Conceptual Framework for Liberation*. The book describes strategies for nonviolent resistance towards repressive regimes and was interpreted by the authorities as promoting a violent revolution. The 17 activists arrested included the rapper Luaty Beirao who, while awaiting trial, and having spent over four months in police custody, went on hunger strike. His hunger strike led to global condemnation of the Angolan authorities. The other book club members were: academic Domingos da Cruz, Nuno Dala, Manuel Baptista Nito Alves, Sedrick de Carvalho, Inocêncio de Brito, Fernando António Tomás "Nicola", Afonso Matias "Mbanza Hamza", air force officer Osvaldo Caholo, Arante Kivuvu, Albano Evaristo Bingobingo, Nelson Dibango, Hitler Jessy Samussuku, José Gomes Hata, Jeremias Benedito, Laurinda Gouveia and Rosa Conde. This group became the face of the resistance to dos Santos and rallied support across Angola. These youths endured months of deprivation and psychological strain under inhumane conditions. Despite the case's publicity, one fact is less well-known: Captain Zenobio Zumba of Military Intelligence was tried in a military court and later fully acquitted. His involvement was fabricated to make it seem like the youths were liaising with the military. His case never received the same level of international attention. SISM had tried to show evidence that Zumba and the air force Lieutenant Osvaldo Caholo (who had studied together) were conspiring and sharing military secrets.

Addressing the nation after their arrest, President dos Santos spoke of the MPLA's internal purge of 1977, indirectly establishing parallels between the alleged coup against Agostinho Neto and this fabricated coup against his government. The historical reference to the 27 May purge hinted at the need to secure the state and swiftly act against signs of insurrection. The illocutionary act of securitisation was repeated. The youths were sentenced in April 2016 to between two and eight years in jail, then provisionally released in June pending the outcome of an appeal. They later had all charges dropped.

General José Maria was believed to have been the architect of the fabricated book club coup, having provided the "evidence" with which to charge the youths. The entire court case and trial were a farce. A whiteboard used by the group to collate notes on the book, a list of names they came up with of opposition and dissident intellectuals to create a government of national salvation, and videos of the youths criticising the President were all presented as evidence of violent intent. SINSE officers lined the courtroom waiting to detect any supporters of the youths entering the courtroom. An interview with a SISM officer during that period warned that any person seen going into that courtroom would never be allowed back into the country. The 15+2 case epitomised the fragility of "a giant with clay feet." A securitised state, present in every aspect of its citizens' lives, was unable to detect the instrumentalisation of power by the intelligence services to retain favour with the President. It was also unable to understand how making an example of a group of relentless revolutionary youths, who had been at the forefront of anti-government demonstrations since 2011, would not dissuade dissent. Instead it portrayed the government as hiding from the shadows it had created. The fabricated coup was politically damaging to the President who was publicly outmanoeuvred by the youths who remained defiant until the end.

Luaty Beirao's 36-day hunger strike—a day for every year dos Santos had been in power—signalled, like the hunger strikes of political critics before him, the unravelling of the image of "the architect of peace". Dos Santos' inability to steer his way gracefully out of the situation only further eroded his image, especially with reports of torture and solitary confinement, and devolved some power to the youth and the streets. The book club case generated so much publicity, both inside Angola and globally, that it became impossible to hide the truth of repression and the paranoia of the Presidency. Even the church did not escape police interference. Several vigils were held in Luanda after the youths were charged, which resulted in the PIR forcibly disbanding 400 civilians gathered inside and outside the Sagrada Familia church.

The third episode was the least reported but certainly the most violent. On 16 April 2015, police officers were sent to arrest the leader of the Seventh Day Adventist Light of the World Church, Pastor José Julino Kalupeteka, who was leading a congregation of over 6,000 members in his main camp of Mount Sumi in Huambo province. The warrant was a desperate attempt by the provincial government to bring this church under its control, having attempted on several occasions to co-opt the pastor. "The government feared Kalupeteka's mobilisation capacity. ... Since 2002 the church had grown to over a million followers ... and the state needed this group to pledge vertical allegiance to the political power yet Kalupeteka resisted and his position was 'give to Caesar what is Caesar's and to God what is God's'.[120] Testimonies and events leading to the Mount Sumi massacre point to a premeditated clampdown that was allegedly authorised by the President who gave orders to "completely dismantle the church".[121]

The clampdown began days before on 11 April in the province of Benguela, when the police attacked a gathering of the sect and killed 28 and wounded 40; it continued into the province of Bie and resulted in clashes. These attacks lasted for two days. The wounded were then transported to Mount Sumi to receive medical assistance. It was on the basis of events in Bie that the arrest warrant was served on Kalupeteka. General Kundy Paihama, governor of Huambo and former defence minister, allegedly ordered a police contingent to set up camp 500 metres from Mount Sumi, ostensibly in the event that there was unrest. Two PIR teams of anti-terror specialists were deployed. These specialists were trained to kill, with their motto being "the enemy should never be allowed to retaliate".[122]

The police were sent to arrest Kalupeteka on 16 April at his camp in Mount Sumi. Clashes occurred during the arrest, resulting in the deaths of nine officers.[123] This triggered the disproportionate response that resulted in a massacre of unarmed civilians. The number of dead and injured was heavily disputed—the police admitted that 13 were killed, claiming self-defence against 'marksmen'—but early reports from the opposition put the numbers at around 1,080 dead. As the PIR entered the camp and began shooting, members of the congregation kept singing and held their ground even as the attack continued. "Their faith was so strong that they kept singing even as people were being mowed down by bullets. Their voices were becoming fainter as they were being killed but they kept on singing".[124] The FAA was called in to assist. Testimony from an army officer reported that "the mountain was surrounded and we first started shooting in all directions using 82mm mortars and RPG-7 launchers"; attack helicopters were also dispatched.[125] Videos filmed by the police of officers killing wounded civilians inside their homes and looting their properties circulated on social media. Activists claim that the security forces' actions were more systematic on 17 April as they went from village to village in the surrounding municipalities, killing the wounded and the followers that had escaped. This execution raid lasted until 2 May.

Over 3,000 followers disappeared after the attack. Surviving family members claimed most were dead. Local human rights activists began compiling a list of the dead and the testimonies of the security forces, survivors and witnesses into a report. These activists were threatened with death. Testimonies from police and military officers backed the assertion there was a massacre, and a subsequent clean-up operation. Angolan police shut down the town, preventing aid, human rights organisations, and opposition party representatives from coming into the area. Access was subsequently granted once the bodies had been disposed of, although the area had officially been transformed into army barracks to avoid any further access. "One policeman told us that he had spent the entire night transporting 828 bodies from a mass grave to the municipality of Longonjo. ... Others told us that the remaining bodies were sent to the province of Kuando Kubango".[126] Some claim bodies were burnt, while others were buried in graves containing three to five bodies each, to avoid mass graves being found. Information was forthcoming because several police officers were supporters of Kalupeteka.[127] The police were allegedly instructed to carry out searches in hospitals and medical centres to locate the injured and kill them. They were told to identify supporters and their family members by following funeral services and then to kill them. A civil society report sent to the UN Human Rights Commission and its counterpart in the African Union described how new directives were drafted to improve the response of the police seeing that they failed to control the crowd and had to call in the military.[128] This report stated that the police force entered a new era of militarised operations as they were instructed to undergo training in new techniques used by the PIR and FAA and their respective anti-terror units and delta force.

UNITA and civil society groups called for accountability and an international inquiry. The UN High Commissioner for Human Rights suggested, in a standard response, that Angola ensure that an independent and thorough inquiry be conducted into the Mount Sumi massacre to clarify contradictory versions of events. The government refused to cooperate and demanded that the UN apologise for meddling.[129] President dos Santos issued a statement declaring the sect a threat to peace and stability, comparing them to Boko Haram. He recommended that the Interior Ministry and the National Police take "the appropriate measures to put an end to these illegal activities." The government portrayed the security intervention as necessary and justified but was seen by many as a desperate attempt to justify the mass killings of civilians in an opposition stronghold. Kalupctcka was transferred to Luanda and remained in detention until his trial. On 5 April 2016 he was sentenced to 28 years in jail. The government subsequently began cracking down on several other religious organisations including closing the majority of mosques, and the Brazilian Church of the Kingdom of God, amongst others. It proscribed eight evangelical churches, and introduced conditions for registration that were designed to enhance intelligence about those involved.[130]

These three cases revealed two dynamics. Firstly the need to control, through infiltration, intimidation and violence, social voices and any form of dissent. Secondly the need to enhance the dangers of certain groups to secure favour with the President and secure a budget for operations. General José Maria of SISM in particular was thought to be behind the need to inflate the dangers associated with any form of social or political gathering. By exposing plots or alleged coups the general was able to justify the requests for budget support and the prominence of his service above the others. It wasn't just the fear of revolts that contributed to overreactions and costs to the state, it was a lack of technical ability to seek accurate information and process it analytically. Many civil society activists questioned how informed President dos Santos was of these events and if he had any sense of the "social pulse" of the country. His security forces acted within a framework of self-imposed fear when there was little appetite for violence and insurrection within society. While anger was certainly rising amongst the youth and the urban poor because of heightened inequality and entrenched poverty, the memory of extreme suffering during the war kept at bay any intentions for violent regime change. The brutal response of the police and FAA during the Kalupeteka clampdown also revealed the level of impunity and complete disregard for human life. This would continue to inform some operations of the police in the years that followed.

This chapter has detailed the security structures supporting the shadow governance of the Presidency. The services used security concerns or threats to uphold unequal power relations. The state's functions, coordinated by the SCP leadership, became subservient to the President's whims and priorities. The public and society more broadly were perceived as drivers of insecurity because of their unaddressed needs for employment, services, and dignity. This led the police and intelligence services to widen operations. The opposition were aware that their political actions were ignored as long as they did not mobilise people in protests.

As 'enemies' emerged in the post-war years, more institutions responded to these threats. The instruments used to protect dos Santos in the 1990s increased in prominence and strength after UNITA's military defeat. They revealed the state of mind of a President besieged by threats. Most of these were exaggerated or imaginary. The President shielded himself and his government but weakened the MPLA's political reach and its support base, which became increasingly disenchanted by decades of bad governance. The next chapter discusses the role of the armed forces and highlights the processes that weakened the only remaining institution able to bridge the partisan divide.

4

# THE ANGOLAN ARMED FORCES

## A STRAINED NATIONAL PILLAR

Two decades of peace left the FAA without a designated national role. It was a founding pillar of an integrated national security system, but the size of its contribution to the political survival of the MPLA did not reflect efforts to streamline its organisation in line with defence transformation programmes. The FAA became a relatively idle combat-hardened force, primarily operating outside democratic oversight. An ambitious post-war reform programme to re-edify the FAA (2007–25) aimed to modernise, upgrade and expand Angola's military. Nevertheless, the FAA's national importance diminished, as it encountered several difficulties. Domestically, the FAA's actions, namely its deployment over the years to Cabinda and other provinces to restore order in conflicts that could have been resolved politically, damaged its image as a pillar of regional balance and integration. Forces were used internally to "stabilise" areas of economic importance to the governing elites, which placed the military at odds with the population. Despite the many differences separating the military from society, the FAA was also the most representative institution because of its composition and history. In its ranks, it mixed ethnic and racial groups and social classes and represented regional differences. It was the only remaining institution to uphold the spirit of the

Lusaka Accords, aggregating different political rivals into a cohesive and unified unit of national symbolism and stature. The integration and promotion of former UNITA generals retained critical import and remained a valuable move to promote accommodation.

The pathologies that came to haunt the FAA's operations, leadership and future preparedness also damaged its role as a political bridge between diverse communities. Its societal imperative, which arose from the "social forces, ideologies, and institutions dominant within the society" (Huntington 1957: 2), meant that the security needs of the Presidency overshadowed the needs of society. Viewing events through the prism of security had placed society in opposition to the President's security forces and to his capacity to retain a hegemonic grip on politics. Three elements, in particular, threatened the integrity and capacity of the FAA: the delinking of comradery and hierarchical respect between officers and soldiers due to corruption and business interests; the burden of an inflated army, which absorbed large amounts of the national budget but did not translate into continued effectiveness, and its constant demands for the upkeep and maintenance of equipment; and lastly, the politicisation of retirement and demobilisation which created tensions between the FAA and its leadership, as efforts to introduce divisionary tactics to politically "purify" its leadership increased in recent years. This chapter broadly introduces the Angolan armed forces and their post-war state to highlight the current pathologies experienced and the dangers of the President's shadowing strategy. It also highlights the FAA's domestic role in operations in Cabinda and the Lunda Norte and Sul provinces and the foreign dimension of FAA's interventions in Africa.

*Structure, Composition and Command*

The FAA was one of Africa's premier armies. In the post-war era, it remained a highly trained force of over 120,000 men.[1] The majority were in the army, while the navy had fewer than 1,000 men and the air force around 7,000 personnel. The armed forces essentially maintained their wartime levels during two decades of peace. Military service was still mandatory in Angola. Out of a population of 31.8 million, over 6 million people across the country were eligible for service. Tens of thousands yearly reached the age for mandatory military service, placing a significant burden on the state to incorporate some and leave others in reserve.[2] Military service was divided among permanent staff, non-commissioned officers, compulsory and reserve military service.

The FAA's formal command chain began with the President as the Commander in Chief, followed by the National Assembly, the cabinet, the superior command of the FAA, the National Defence Council, the Superior Military Council, the Chief of Staff's office, followed by the respective service chiefs.[3] In practice, the SCP controlled every aspect of the FAA, from procurement to policy development, rendering the formal command structure redundant, underscoring the impression it existed only to promote a veneer of efficiency and democratic control. As commander in chief, the President, in coordination with the National Security Council, had the power to nominate all the security chiefs, demote or promote generals, and take over the command of the FAA in times of war. Nevertheless, and despite SCP pervasiveness, a measure of operational autonomy had been retained. The FAA was headed by a Chief of General Staff (CEMG) deputised by staff chiefs responsible for Logistics and Infrastructure, Operations, Patriotic Education, Administration and Finances, Training and Personnel. Strategically the CEMG was still consulted on matters of the FAA's reform and role internationally. The CEMG also benefited from an advisory team of different generals that brought different military doctrines and areas of expertise. Each of the branches—navy, army and airforce—had its own chief. In addition, the CEMG commanded three strategic units: a tank brigade, an intelligence battalion in Kangombe, and a special forces brigade based in Cabo Ledo (150 kilometres from Luanda) that was trained for peacekeeping duties.

All Chiefs of General Staff of the FAA were well regarded and respected commanders. Each supervised and witnessed changes within the armed forces during wartime and peacetime. General João de Matos was the first CEMG, operating from 1992 until 2001. His tactical acumen was credited with having turned the military situation around in 1994 after government forces faced heavy defeats from UNITA. Matos reorganised the FAA and changed strategy, focusing on sustainability rather than the ferocity of military operations. He was replaced by General Armando da Cruz Neto, who was succeeded by General Agostinho Nelumba "Sanjar", followed by General Francisco Furtado. Neto's strategy of encirclement and his unrelenting pursuit of UNITA's top leadership, coupled with the FAA's scorched earth policy, was credited with ending the war. In 2010, General Geraldo Sachipengo Nunda, who from 1998 had been deputy CEMG to all four CEMGs, became the new Chief of Staff and held that post until 2018. An intellectual who defected from UNITA's top command in 1993, he earned the respect of dos Santos after years of proven loyalty and service. He was replaced by General Egídio de Sousa Santos "Disciplina", who was rapidly becoming the most controversial and divisive of all the chiefs of staff. He was thought to be actively breaking the unity of spirit of the armed forces and politicising the command structures.

The Soviets and Cubans greatly informed the military ethos of the FAA through the support they had given to the FAPLA. Russia and Cuba retained instrumental influence within the FAA command. Although the FAA no longer used the Soviet designation of divisions and regiments, most of its weapons systems and equipment reflected the Cold War stocks from the Soviet Union. During my research, numerous references were made to Russia's modern-day influence on the military. Throughout the first war (until 1991), the Soviets provided training, advisors and armaments while Cuba provided training and a massive contingent of combat troops and civilian cadres. Together, the missions from Moscow and Havana trained tens of thousands of FAPLA troops, acted as advisors in combat operations, and provided advice to the military high command and an ample supply of weaponry. While the two allies operated with a division of labour, with Soviets attached to regular forces and Cubans occupied with the light infantry brigades, the units of the People's Defence Organisation, and their own combat units (Shubin 2008), their strategies differed. The Soviets focused on supporting FAPLA training and operations for conventional warfare, creating an army reflecting its own experience. The Cubans tended towards a counter-insurgency approach, pushing the FAPLA to operate in smaller anti-guerrilla units. These differing strategies served the FAA well in their operations against UNITA in the last decade of war (1992–2002).

The Soviets had begun to help the MPLA as early as 1961, yet massive military support and supplies would only arrive in late 1975. In the 1980s, the Soviet military mission had grown to 1,500 advisors that served as instructors in the use of weapons supplied by Moscow, helped maintain equipment, and were placed within the academies (Gleijeses 2013). Between 1982 and 1986, Angola received over $4.9 billion in military equipment from the Soviet Union.[4] By the end of the war, the total tally of support was unquantifiable. Russia remained the FAA's most trusted ally and arms supplier in the 1990s and thereafter.

The FAA continued to operate with the Russian model of 'mass of men and means', with its post-war re-edification programme aiming to bolster troop numbers in peacetime further. Moscow's continued influence on the Angolan military challenged any prospects of reform that embraced models of democratic oversight. From a domestic standpoint, Russian military doctrine identified internal threats as military threats requiring military responses.[5] Russia's influence spread through the strategic thinking of the leadership of the security apparatus. However, the FAA's historical reliance on Russian equipment, much of which was obsolete and in disrepair, generated prospects for procurement from others, including Western sources.[6] With it came other training opportunities and military mentalities.

Like Russia, Cuba's influence on Angola's military establishment and the MPLA's political elites was far-reaching and comprehensive. Cuba's military mission began before independence. The Centros de Instrução Revolucionária (CIR) (Centres for Revolutionary Instruction) established in Cabinda, Saurimo, N'dalatando and Benguela were key in organising the FAPLA in the first wave of Cuban assistance in 1975 (Villegas 2017). Between 1975 and 1991, the Cuban presence would see over 425,000 volunteers serving in Angola. The majority were combatants serving in the internationalist mission, but they also included 50,000 civilian workers placed throughout the country as teachers, medical personnel, agricultural specialists, and construction workers.[7] Fidel Castro asserted that Cubans had saved Angola "from mortal danger" at least three times in 1975, 1976, and during the Nito Alves "coup" in 1977 (Shubin 2008), although that number was likely higher.

Until their integration in 1991, the FAPLA and FALA armies had different levels of training, expertise, discipline, ideology, doctrine, and capacity. Both UNITA and the MPLA trained their troops using foreign models, tactics and philosophies. At differing times and levels of influence, the integrating elements of the FAA had at one point or another received training from Russia, China, Cuba, South Africa, Portugal, the UK, France, Brazil, the US and others. Political commissars were used for both forces as a way to ensure ideological purity, continuity and loyalty. When the FALA and FAPLA came together to form a unified army, there was mistrust, division, and culture shock. Despite this, the officers on both sides who were involved in the formation of the FAA describe how they overcame this to build a solid foundation that allowed former enemies to unite into a single organisation governed by national rather than partisan imperatives. While the FALA and FAPLA were certainly affected by the divisive allegiances of their parties during the war, the FAA's founders placed great effort on making the army a national institution that would be immune to these divisions. The FAA was edified based on multiparty politics and national unity, stemming from the 1992 transition and peace process, but it retained its core quality of obedience to the Presidency's political imperatives and not the state or nation.

The Russian and Cuban influence would remain of key import for the FAA. The continued presence of foreign advisors to the FAA post-2002 highlighted the different areas of influence and expertise. The Chief of Staff had a permanent Russian advisor assigned to him, and the majority of the senior FAA officers were trained and educated in the former Soviet Union. Anecdotally, in 2014 a training programme for the 30 most senior generals of the FAA was conducted in Russian with only four requiring translators.[8] There were also Cuban advisors that assisted in strategic issues in different departments. While they were present in the directorates for logistics, operations, special units, and training, they were not used in the less important finance and personnel departments. Different advisors were likely continuations of former training arrangements for the companies under the direct command of the CEMG. There were Portuguese advisors for the Special Forces and the Marines and Serbian advisors for the Mechanised Brigade.[9]

## Organisational Structure

Since 2002, the FAA has retained the same organisational structure it had during the war, using Angola's 18 provinces as designated military regions (RM), subdivided where necessary into military zones. The

THE ANGOLAN ARMED FORCES

FAA was structured by unit (five men), section (15 men), platoon (30 to 40 men) company (105 to 120 men), battalions (300 to 400 men), brigades (over 1,000 men), divisions (over 3,000), and an army corps, comprising three divisions. It operated using six military regions: Cabinda, Luanda, Centre, East, South and North. Competing information over which units and how many men were stationed in each RM made it difficult to describe with precision. Nevertheless, the following description makes an attempt.

The RM Cabinda, where several Frente de Libertação do Enclave de Cabinda (FLEC) groups continued to operate, included several military zones. The Northern RM was supported by an infantry division, three motorised infantry brigades, an artillery army corp (guarding the hydroelectric dam of the Kwanza river), an engineering brigade and a Military Artillery School. The Eastern RM, which bordered the DRC and incorporated strategic diamond areas, had two army corps, an anti-aerial defence group, and five light infantry brigades. The Southern RM had two army corps and two light infantry brigades.[10] The Centre RM, which covered the provinces of Huambo, Bie, Kwanza Sul and Benguela, had an infantry division, several motorised infantry brigades, and a tank brigade, and it was where the Army Military Academy resided.[11] The military region of Luanda was where the top command of the FAA, the Superior Academy for War and the Technical Military Institute were based. In Luanda's RM were the Grafanil military base and a military police regiment, a regiment for logistical transport, an artillery brigade, and other support units.[12] The command of each RM was responsible for all the units integrated into its territory. It was expected to manage all military issues, including the mobilisation and preparedness of reservists.

The three branches of the FAA—army, navy and air force—began a restructuring under a re-edification programme intended to reconfigure, re-equip and resize the armed forces.[13] Initiated in 2007 under Defence Minister General Kundy Paihama (1999–2010), the programme set out an ambitious reform agenda but lacked a clear framework for implementation. The principles behind the intended military reform emphasised the need to restructure the Joint Chiefs of Staff towards greater focus on improving military administration and logistics, adapting the system of forces, and improving teaching, technical maintenance and repair. It focused on patriotic education and psychological action, and on improving discipline and control (Junior 2019b: 49). It also aimed to increase the FAA's size and capacity, building a military enterprise larger and more equipped during peacetime and enhancing their status as a symbol of national pride, projection of strength, and the image of an effective state. The programme was expected to run until 2025.

The first stage of the reform programme (August to December 2007) laid the administrative and legal foundations for implementing the plan. The second phase (January 2008 to December 2012) focused on reforming personnel and restoring the FAA's arsenal. Consolidating cooperation with key allies—including Russia, Israel, Brazil, China, and the DRC—was presented as a core objective. The arms and services components of the FAA were also identified for restructuring. Services included military intelligence, patriotic education, logistics and infrastructure, armament and technical expertise, health, military police, psychological warfare, cryptography, information technology, military justice, international cooperation and public relations. Arms components included infantry, tanks, artillery and rockets, aerial defence, engineering, nuclear, chemical and biological defence, aviation, radar units, coastal defence and navy forces. However, modernising the FAA would be constrained by the ability and capacity to absorb new weapons and skills given the lack of articulation between training, weapons procurement, and professionalisation programmes. The FAA was operationally hampered by equipment in disrepair, poor maintenance and storage conditions.[14] Operational capacity was uneven, although it appeared capable of responding to internal as well as projected external threats. Whilst the army retained a formidable infantry, with considerable battle experience and the benefits of intensive training and investment, the capacities of the air force and the navy to accompany any operations were constrained. The air force and the navy had to be re-equipped and restructured to strengthen Angola's military capacity. A strong ground force and infantry alone were insufficient for the evolution of warfare and weapons systems.

The Força Aerea Angolana (FAN), the national air force, was organised into six aviation regiments with a corresponding air base. It comprised two combat, two transport, one training, and a helicopter regiment.[15] In the 1980s and 1990s, the FAN mounted a formidable operation against UNITA. Officially established in January 1976, it was the largest air force in Sub-Saharan Africa,[16] with over 7,000 members. The FAN had 180 fixed-wing combat attack and interceptor aircraft, the same number of helicopters, five air defence battalions, ten SAM battalions, and maritime patrol, reconnaissance and transport aircraft.[17] Russia and Cuba assisted with pilots and technicians, who developed a pool of local Angolan combat pilots. A National Institute of Military Aviation was established in the Negage base in 1981, and in 1985, a facility in Lobito was set up for technical instruction.[18] By the late 1980s, the air force was using MiG-23 jets and Sukhoi fighter bombers, Mi-24/25 helicopters, and Mi-8/17 transport helicopters, all supplied by the Soviet Union, and operated Aviocar 212 aircraft to transport troops. During the war, two aerial regions were established—the Northern Aerial Defence Region (RADAN) and the southern Areal Defence Region (RADS). A Training and Psychology Centre was inaugurated in 1991 and used to conduct psychometric tests to select fighter pilots to send for training in Russia.[19] In 2014, 25 pilots completed a three-year training course in Russia,[20] but technological constraints within the air force meant that several of the highly-trained army officers were unable to operate outdated weapons systems they were faced with on their return.

Angola's war experience developed the structures and procedures to perfect the airlift capacity needed to transport troops rapidly into the field. There were major air bases in Lobito, Huambo, Kuito, Luena, Menongue, Moçâmedes and Luanda. In the late 1980s, Luanda could move 3,000 troops from Kuando Kubango in the south to Luanda within three days.[21] In peacetime, Angola retained its airlift capacity to transport troops and equipment quickly to respond to humanitarian or peacekeeping tasks. Its fleet of Russian IL-76 aircraft and its war experience of rapidly deploying troops and hardware into different war zones remained a vital selling point for peacekeeping operations.

The re-edification programme expected the FAN to reach over 12,000 men with the capability to operationalise fighter jets, anti-submarine planes, reconnaissance aviation, radio technological warfare, anti-aerial defence, radar control systems and investments to improve its airlift capacity.

It began procuring new aircraft. A procurement deal with Israel worth $1 billion to buy combat helicopters, UAVs and other hi-tech equipment was reported in 2012.[22] In January 2013, three A-29 Super Tucanos were delivered from Brazil. Angola secured another billion-dollar contract with Russia to deliver 12 Su-30 fighter jets and cargo planes and to construct a munitions factory in 2013.[23] This deal with Rosoboronexport, Russia's state arms dealer, generated some controversy given that Angola was going to be supplied with outdated equipment. The aircraft, meant to form the backbone of the FAN's fighting capability, was second-hand equipment being offloaded by Russia. Details on arms purchases were limited. In 2017 Angola began receiving the first batch of the 12 secondhand Su-30 Flanker fighter aircraft.[24]

The existing state of disrepair of many FAN aircraft underscored the need for new equipment and maintenance capacity. Serbian technicians maintained the equipment, despite an aviation maintenance brigade ostensibly equipped to repair different types of helicopters, transport planes and fighter jets.[25] Several accidents exposed the brigade's inadequacies. September 2011 saw the worst air force accidents when an Embraer-120 crashed and killed 19 senior officers (including three generals and three coronels); in a different incident, a Su-22 crashed in Lubango, killing another general. In March 2012, an Alouette III helicopter crashed on a mission from Huambo to Bie. On the 39th anniversary celebrations of the air force, in January 2015, another Alouette III broke apart in mid-air and crashed. While the air force's helicopters were in disrepair, the national police began to re-equip its airwing in mid-2014.[26]

Angola's navy, Marinha de Guerra (MG), was the weakest and least equipped of the services. It was organised into two naval zones with three naval bases along 1,600 kilometres of coastline and included a marines brigade (*fuzileiros navais*) and a marines academy in Ambriz. Before the 1992 DDR process, the navy had over 10,000 men, but this number was substantially reduced, bringing force levels down to between 1,000 and 2,000.[27] In the 1980s, the Angolan navy was a powerful force equipped to neutralise any potential invasion from South Africa. Attack craft, patrol boats and landing crafts provided a defence against sabotage, attacks or the illegal supply of weapons to

UNITA. By the late 1980s, the navy was estimated to have over 50 vessels that included guided-missile patrol boats, torpedo boats, mine warfare craft, amphibious landing craft and other patrol boats.[28] A quarter of a century later, this fleet was largely obsolete, with little investment in new equipment. With bases in Lobito, Luanda, and Namibe, the navy could not defend the country's coastline effectively. The challenge was magnified by rising maritime insecurity off the Gulf of Guinea, which posed an ever-present threat to Angola's offshore interests.[29] The piracy attack of February 2014, where a Sonangol oil tanker was hijacked off the coast of Luanda carrying 12,000 tons of diesel fuel (worth $8 million), was viewed by authorities as an example of the growing threat.[30] A Maritime Surveillance System (SINAVIM) was reportedly implemented in 2010 to monitor and control maritime traffic and territorial waters against illicit activities.[31] It was meant to be a collaborative effort between the Defence, Interior, Transport and Oil Ministries but it was unclear if this system ever became operational. As part of the system, five centres of regional coordination were to be created in Cabinda, Soyo, Luanda, Lobito and Namibe. In 2019, Angolan state media was still reporting that SINAVIM was being created.[32]

As part of the reform programme the navy was expected to reach the capacity of 13,000 men operating in the naval region of the North (with naval bases in Soyo and Luanda) and the naval region of the South (with naval bases of Namibe and Lobito). The navy intended to purchase destroyers, frigates, and anti-submarine crafts, patrol ships and even submarines while enhancing its coastal and air defence systems. Angola's Naval Academy and Naval War Institute coordinated activities closely with their Portuguese counterparts and its Technical Military Cooperation programme. Brazil and Spain were also assisting the development of Angola's nascent maritime security strategy. Angola's 2010 Defence Cooperation Agreement resulted in the procurement of seven Brazilian Macae patrol ships. Detail on the kind of equipment being procured for the navy and related maintenance and sustainability specifications were scarce. In 2015 the navy was in the process of procuring a frigate, three corvettes, three offshore patrol vessels and several fast patrol boats.[33] There were ambitious projects to rehabilitate several ports, including the country's second largest port of Lobito in land, sea and air capabilities.[34] In 2016, while João Lourenço was Defence Minister, Angola signed a deal with the Middle Eastern company Privinvest for a shipbuilding and maritime economy programme. The deal, worth $565 million, included the purchase of 17 vessels, six of which were delivered in February 2019.[35] Privinvest was one of the companies involved in Mozambique's politically damaging hidden debt scandal (over $2 billion) and had been indicted by Mozambican courts.[36]

## Pathologies and Threats

As the FAA was attempting but failing to reform itself into a modern, technologically equipped, and highly organised force, generals benefited from the spoils of peace. They were making money from the military enterprise and across the extractive industry and other business opportunities. The FAA became one of the vehicles for mismanagement of funds, albeit not the most scandalous one, as it allowed for large-scale theft in military procurement to lower-level loot of operating budgets. The diversion of military spending and corruption with procurement deals benefited private interests rather than operational and strategic priorities and became the largest systemic threat to reform of the military. Other threats included the instrumentalisation of ethnic tensions at the command levels and the badly managed demobilisation and retirement of soldiers and officers which threatened its cohesion and affected its morale.

Scrutinising the military's expenditure and the management of dispersed funds should have prevented the military from having independent access to financial activities or having their leaders involved in business activities. Budgetary oversight by the legislative and executive branches was key to the capacity of the armed forces to maintain their levels of preparedness, civilian control, and democratic supervision. However, details on defence spending mostly remained secret and outside the scrutiny of parliament, the opposition and civil society. Instead, the military, in continuation with the modus operandi of the Presidency and the opaqueness of the SCP, became increasingly weakened by unstructured disbursement of funds, procurement deals that reflected personal rather than institutional priorities, and the continuation of off-budget expenditure.

Legal provisions for oversight remained weak. The 2010 Public Procurement Laws regulated defence procurement, but there was little evidence that the legislation was applied. The constitution made no specific reference to budgetary oversight and the government was not required to submit general state accounts, despite the fact that the Accounts Tribunal had improved its operations.[37] State security laws and others created a barrier for the disclosure of "sensitive" information. Modalities of current arms deals remained opaque, which in turn fed opportunities for corruption. Commissions on these purchases remained a major source of opportunity for personal enrichment. SIMPORTEX was the state's primary procurement vehicle, owned jointly by the FAA and the Defence Ministry. It was responsible for importing all required materials, including food and uniforms. Inefficiencies led to allegations of mismanagement that reflected profound dissatisfaction. In 2010, dos Santos set up an assessment commission into the activities of SIMPORTEX but no findings were ever made public. Given the secrecy surrounding defence procurement, compliance programmes and business conduct standards were not priorities. No needs assessments were published, and procurement of weapons was not publicly justified on the grounds of strategic and clear objectives.

The amounts spent on supporting the security apparatus reflected the country's history, government priorities, and structural needs. The end of the war should have enabled a diversion of military spending towards service delivery and development needs. Yet from 2002, military expenditure increased, further reiterating the rate and level of securitisation. Reports by the Stockholm International Peace Research Institute pegged the 2014 defence budget at $6.5 billion, second on the continent to Algeria, and with a projected increase to $13 billion by 2019.[38] Between 2002 and 2013, abundant oil revenues enabled the security apparatus to consume an enormous share of the national wealth. In these years, Angola spent $40 billion on defence, with only half going to the FAA, the remainder most likely invested in the presidential security units, police force and intelligence services.[39] Spending continued despite the oil crisis of 2014, increasing pressure on public accounts and further impairing options for investing in economic diversification. As with all government spending during the oil bonanza years, it was positioned for immediate and short-term gains. The 2014 oil crisis forced the government to slash the 2015 national budget in half, resulting in a sharp rise in external debt. In 2017, Angola still managed to spend $3.06 billion on defence, up from $2.7 billion in 2016. By 2018 defence spending had decreased to $1.98 billion, although other national security agencies and the Presidency's discretionary funds still maintained unnecessarily high levels of outlay.

Military spending was characterised by obscurity and unavailable detail on disbursements. Allocations were made through the Presidency and the defence budget, but the President's account was not subject to public or parliamentary scrutiny. Percentages of what was allocated to each of the services were impossible to verify.[40] The defence budget for 2020, worth 650 billion Kz, was meant, in its majority to be channelled into paying for salaries and running costs. There were over 500 generals, and the budget had to support their salaries and complementary subsidies of other officers. The Finance Ministry constantly blocked payment orders that came from the chief of staff's office,[41] a reflection of a much broader problem of political governance in the security sector and the political instrumentalisation of the Treasury and the Finance Ministry. "Money from the *fundo de maneio* [operating funds] was taken all the time … they would withdraw around 5 billion Kz in cash from the BPC bank (owned by the state and the social security agency of the FAA), and distribute funds in hand which allowed them to rapidly disappear".[42] The alleged mismanagement of the *fundo de maneio* was at the heart of the opaqueness of military spending and the result of lack of military upkeep, unpaid salaries, poor conditions in the barracks, and several other logistical failings.

Other schemes allowed for commanders to benefit, albeit in smaller dimensions. An estimated 26,000 "ghost" soldiers within the FAA were set up so that different units could receive their salaries. On many occasions, funds were sent in cash to the different units to pay soldiers' salaries, which provided ample opportunity for corruption. Chains of command were also unlikely to be separated from chains of payments, although there wasn't enough evidence that commanders could arbitrarily change the salaries of their soldiers even in the absence of safeguards to stop this from happening. Passing through the military infrastructure were large amounts of money that came from within the military. "In the Caixa de Segurança Social a general would deduct around 3,000 Kz ($50 in 2015) from his salary every month. Multiply this by hundreds of generals and other officers (only from the rank of sergeant upwards) and we are talking about a lot of money".[43]

The strategy to ensure military loyalty was old and tested. It has been applied across Africa, Asia and Latin America with notable similarities in a securitised country like oil-rich Venezuela. It also resulted in a major military decline. Military elites were allowed to profit from their country's resources and were extended business opportunities through partnerships that involved multinational corporations, Western companies, and shady offshore entities. The extension of political patronage facilitated endemic corruption, aggravated by the manipulation of promotions and deployments, which in turn constrained effective leadership. By 2017, Angola had registered 320 multimillionaires, with an average personal wealth of over $10 million, an increase of 82% in only a decade.[44] Not all of these were military elites. "Of the 500 or so generals in the FAA, only about 50 were benefiting from the new economic growth".[45] By 2020 those numbers could have been substantially higher. Those generals' actions were, however, hugely detrimental to the morale of the armed forces and damaged the cohesion of the security sector, the separation of powers, and the possibility of reform and defence transformation. Insiders reflected on the burgeoning income-generating opportunities for military business: "The army was a company and everything was business."[46] The crossover of interests, shareholding structures, and vehicles used became increasingly complex and at times incestuous. Multinational companies, leaders in their fields of operations, would, through subsidiaries, partner in joint ventures with Angolan companies owned by politically connected elites—generals and civilians alike. The funds for such dealings came from the state. Contracts were authorised by dos Santos and top advisors made billions over the course of a decade. For many, their profiting and looting windfall would end under the presidency of Lourenço, discussed in the next chapter, but the recovery of assets would be difficult to secure.

The worst offenders, who accumulated hundreds of millions of dollars in personal wealth, involved close advisors of the President, family members, and MPLA oligarchs. The cases of corruption and misappropriation of Angolan public funds are widely known and are not covered in this chapter. The veil of secrecy was partially lifted by the mass leaks of the Panama Papers, Paradise Papers, and Mauritius Leaks, linking hundreds of subsidiaries in over 40 jurisdictions to the Angolan elites. Corruption crossed from the military into business dealings of civilian leaders, creating an even more promiscuous political link deflecting any attempts at accountability. During the dos Santos era, three top presidential advisors, General Kopelipa, General Dino and former vice-president Manuel Vicente, became known as the business trio with deals in all sectors of the economy bypassing scrutiny through a series of holding companies.[47] The triumvirate owned Nazaki Oil and Gas in partnership with Cobalt International Energy. All three admitted to holding shares in Cobalt, the Texas-based oil company that filed for bankruptcy in 2017 after a deal to sell concessions to Sonangol fell through.[48] They allegedly pocketed €1.3 billion when they sold Nazaki Oil and Gas. Like many other companies, Cobalt had linked itself closely to the power elites in Luanda to further its business interests (Burgis 2015).[49] The asset portfolios of this trio included interests in banks, telecommunications, real estate, oil and energy, construction, and agro-industry, among other sectors. Their empire would begin to slowly crumble in 2020 when Generals Dino and Kopelipa were forced to return assets in cash and shares to the state.

The category of "business generals" emerged post-war as a commonly used term within the rank and file of the FAA.[50] It referred to senior military personnel (active and retired) who benefited from commercial deals involving the armed forces and other state-endorsed businesses. Some were shareholders and directors of state-owned enterprises, while others owned lucrative private security companies deployed to secure the diamond fields[51] and other strategic areas. FAA generals were allowed to access diamonds in the Lundas provinces during the war and gained financial and strategic autonomy in the process. Several generals were awarded diamond concessions after many of these areas were recaptured from UNITA in the 1990s. At the time, UNITA had been making between $300 and $600 million annually from its diamond revenues. The emergence of private security companies in the second war (1992–4) began a more visible trend of Angolan military officials' involvement in business deals. Two in particular—Teleservice and Alpha 5—were key in providing security in diamond areas and providing protection services to oil installations in Soyo. By 2004, over 200 private security companies employed approximately 36,000 people operating in Luanda and the diamond areas.[52] Within a few years, this number had doubled. "There were over 400 private security firms in Angola—the biggest being Teleservice, KPL and Alfa-5, which jointly employed 20,000 men—and had a force … total[ling] 50,000 men".[53]

In 2010 the Defence Ministry launched an anti-fraud service to bolster the Military Inspector's Office (only created in April 2006) for the FAA. The initiative meant to provide technical support in inspecting and auditing the armed forces. However, the inspector general of the FAA who held the title in 2011, General Carlos Hendrick Vaal da Silva, was himself accused of violating the law on Crimes Committed by Public Officials[54] that forbade any public servants from having economic interests in businesses involving the state; as well as the law on public probity. Vaal da Silva was a partner in the Lumanhe company, who, together with Kopelipa and General Adriano Makevela MacKenzie (former UNITA), had a 21% stake in the Sociedade Mineira do Cuango (SMC), a leading diamond company accused of perpetrating human rights violations.[55] Other partners in the Lumanhe company included two former chiefs of staff, Generals Armando da Cruz Neto and João de Matos, and Generals Luís Pareira Faceira and António Emílio Faceira, commanders of the army and the special forces. Lumanhe was founded in 1995 after the FAA recaptured several diamond areas of the east from UNITA. Between 1997 and 2007, the generals behind Lumanhe accumulated a net income after taxes of $120 million each.[56]

In peacetime, many generals began venturing into other areas, creating companies and then hiring them to provide logistical support and services to the security sector.[57] For example, Sadissa, a company owned by Manuel Vicente when he was Chairman of Sonangol, reportedly secured multi-billion-euro deals to supply communications equipment to the military.[58] One of these deals involved a joint venture with the French conglomerate Thales and was undersigned by SIMPORTEX. Companies were also created to run the maintenance and servicing of military equipment.[59] Commercial opportunism manifested in varying guises, from operating car dealerships within military barracks to selling land that ostensibly belonged to the army.[60] Some operations merely involved the transfer of public lands into private ownership through the misuse of positions of power. "One general sold land that belonged to the army to BIC bank. The worst branch of the FAA was the army where there was more money involved".[61] General Eusébio de Brito Teixeira, for example, awarded himself over 300 square kilometres of land in 2014 when he was governor of the Kwanza Sul province for business development purposes. Brito had previously occupied the post of representative of the Intelligence Bureau of the Presidency.[62]

The extravagances of commanding officers did not go unnoticed, creating resentment within elements of the military. Basic conditions in barracks countrywide were poor and contributed to an alarming number of desertions. Military corruption was problematic on many fronts notwithstanding its ability to affect the professional integrity of the armed forces but also its cohesion as an institution. The special access given to commanders of the FAA, and the abuse of power that came with their business interests, damaged the reputation of the military and its relationship with society. The damage done to development prospects and the economy was well known too. An additional problem was the overall spending on defence that the country supported when military-owned companies secured large amounts of revenue. These enterprises were generating sufficient income to help support some of the shortcomings in operations and material. The issue remained that allowing members of the armed forces to profit from the economy with guaranteed privileged access made it much harder to conduct any kind of reform, but ending such practices would have serious political ramifications and security repercussions. While the new President began cleaning up government corruption in 2017, many in the top echelons of his administration had long histories of promiscuous dealings. A level of continuity was guaranteed to ensure stability.

As the "business generals" category emerged, many of the "real" generals found themselves sidelined. These commanders held the respect of the rank and file, yet many, like General Mateus Miguel Angelo "Vietnam", were not in places of command. General Vietnam, a former army chief and FAPLA legend, left dos Santos' government in 2015 after spending a decade being passed over for promotions. His integrity, discipline and intransigence were deemed as having been ill-suited to the military cliques inside the security apparatus that needed their business interests untouched. The problem remained that as of 2017 several of these respected commanders were either pushed into retirement by the President or voluntarily sought to retire.

The retirement of several other generals occurred for more political and divisive reasons. Politicising and ethnicising the FAA's composition threatened its unity and national character. Although the policy of "purifying" the FAA was not a presidential priority or even a strategic objective of the SCP, it was allowed to happen over time. Former UNITA officers were slowly disenfranchised and marginalised even as the Chief of General Staff General Sachipengo Geraldo Nunda, who had belonged to UNITA, led the army from 2010 to 2018. In 2012, two years after General Nunda had become CEMG, "there was a rise in the tribal tone to the extent that it was suggested that only Umbundu was spoken on the patio of the high command of the FAA".[63] Such comments from the security chiefs began causing tensions within the Chief of Staff's office. The perception was that too many Ovimbundu were in leading positions within the FAA, although the reality was quite different.[64] "People began referring to the tribalist quartet of Ovimbundu—Generals Nunda, Lucio Amaral (Army Chief), Geraldo Abreu Ukwatchitembo Kamorteiro (deputy CEMG for Logistics and Infrastructure), and Adriano Mackevela Mackenzie (Chief Director of Troop Training and Education)".[65]

One of the fears of key SCP operatives and a handful of generals was having too many "southern" or Ovimbundu soldiers and officers in the FAA. They were seen as potential UNITA supporters or integrated FALA combatants and, as such, posed a risk to the FAA's ability to secure loyalty. No specific study was conducted to determine the ethnic composition of each region to ascertain percentages. FAA recruitment had been under the same director for personnel since 1992, (Admiral Emilio de Carvalho "Bibi"). It was done across the 18 provinces and was also conducted at a municipal level. De Carvalho happened to be a Kimbundu from Kwanza-Sul, although this was never a relevant factor. "The message that came to us was that there were many descendants and sons of UNITA that would become the next generation of generals. They had studied and were in the intermediary structures, so they had to be stopped and this became the agenda of General Disciplina".[66] Accusations were made that only cadets from the Ovimbundo ethnic group were being sent to military academies. Politicising ethnicity within the FAA began a dangerous process of deconstructing the only remaining pillar of national reconciliation, and a key factor of national stability.

Removing UNITA personnel from the FAA, sidelining their officers from any real positions of power, and overtly surveilling them had been a strategy used by General José Maria of SISM for many years, as explained in the previous chapter. Dividing the FAA was an unnecessary move by elements of the SCP. In fact it rather weakened the Presidency by potentially creating disaffected groups that had otherwise integrated into the armed forces and served the commander in chief regardless of partisan, regional or ethnic backgrounds. The situation deteriorated under João Lourenço, explained in the following chapter, when former FAPLA political commissars were brought in to exert an additional level of control and political interference in the FAA. Two remaining UNITA generals from the Bicesse structures—Peregrino Chindondo Wambu and Adriano Makevele "Mackenzie"—both working within the Chief of Staff's office—resigned from their posts between 2018 and 2019, due to consecutive humiliations.

Another issue undermining morale was the mismanagement of retirement processes. In early 2014, a comprehensive programme to retire generals from the army began without a regulatory framework in place. Over 75 generals and brigadiers were subsequently retired, without clarity on the provision of pensions and other benefits. Others were allegedly summarily dismissed.[67] The process appeared arbitrary and conflicted with the experience of others, including politicians who had been retired with the rank of general in order to benefit from comfortable retirement packages.[68] From 2017, the retirement of senior military personnel increased exponentially, with the new President retiring hundreds of generals and promoting many more. In May 2018, 22 generals were dismissed from their functions in the FAA and the SCP and 62 generals and admirals nominated for leadership positions. According to an MOD document establishing pensions, the

FAA generals should have received between $7,000 and $5,000 a month as part of their retirement in addition to other subsidies.[69] However, the high levels of inflation, currency devaluation and the compounding impact of the economic recession in Angola since 2014 meant that a 3-star general's retirement funds plummeted to $1,000 dollars a month. In 2019, the Caixa de Segurança Social das Forças Armadas Angolanas (the FAA Social Security Bureau) still owed 49,000 million Kz (€138 million) to 350 retired senior officers who had their pensions arbitrarily slashed in 2008.[70] In November 2019, the Ministry of Defence guaranteed that 9,108 officers (retired between 2014 and 2018) would begin receiving their pension.[71] Three months later the country would shut down because of the coronavirus and its oil revenues would plummet, severely constraining government finances.

The retirement of military commanders was part of a broader problem. The total number of ex-combatants in Angola could have been as high as 500,000, given the different rounds of demobilisation and personnel decommissioning from other security apparatus areas. The demobilisation processes left thousands of ex-combatants without support or financial compensation, unemployed and unintegrated. This presented a major security challenge compounded by limited economic opportunities, a rising cost of living and mitigating state support. Socioeconomic hardship amplified the psychological scars of ostracism and disenfranchisement that accompanied the perception that these processes favoured MPLA combatants. The director of the state's Institute for Social and Professional Reintegration of Ex-soldiers (IRSEM) acknowledged in 2019 that to integrate 117,000 ex-combatants (from the DDR processes of 1991, 1994, 2002 and 2006) the state would require €108 million.[72] Of those 117,000 ex-combatants, 80,000 were soldiers, 24,000 were widows and orphans and 13,000 were wounded veterans. Of those 80,000, only 6,000 belonged to UNITA's former army FALA, when UNITA, because it lost the war, underwent the complete demobilisation of its army. In 2002 alone, over half a million UNITA soldiers (100,000 soldiers and their dependents) went into quartering areas. Any effort to politicise this issue and differentiate between those that fought for the government or in the opposition's armies would create serious tensions across the country.

Discontent was increasing, and as many as 60,000 combatants (formally processed in official DDR programmes) were thought to have remained outside the system without receiving any form of remuneration or assistance.[73] The lower the ranks, the more desperate the situation was.[74] In 2019 the government claimed it spent €293 million on pensions for 72,000 ex-combatants (half were for retirement), with the remaining 24,000 pensioners being inserted into the 2019 payments system. Included in these numbers were the combatants from the Bicesse, Lusaka, Luena and the 2006 Cabinda DDR processes. This, the government claimed, closed the reintegration and pensions process, adding that any others claiming compensation were opportunists trying to misinform citizens.[75] For many ex-combatants surviving on the bare minimum, the official closure of the DDR process confirmed their dispensability and provided a demoralising example for any future demobilisations. The government subsequently announced its plan to retire 141,000 FAA members by 2026.[76]

*Foreign Deployments*

As with all ambitious foreign policies, the governments enacting them attempt to export their principles and operations across borders to extend influence, secure political and economic access, and reaffirm the efficiency and nobility of their own systems. Dos Santos attempted to export a version of his securitised state strategy to countries in which Angola intervened. He exported the systems that had kept him in power: a strong and loyal Presidential Guard, the comprehensive and intrusive use of intelligence services, an economic stranglehold on resources and business opportunities, a well-trained army with beholden generals, and an infiltrated and divided opposition. Luanda did not always manage to implement all these aspects in the countries where it intervened, but its operations certainly pointed to the objective of exporting its own system abroad. The FAA became a key foreign policy tool, a consequence of its internationalised war and the role played by neighbouring countries. To extend influence it also tied military and political support for friendly governments to economic interests. Luanda sought to develop a network of strategically positioned client states in Africa. As client states, governments in different African countries owed a debt of gratitude to Luanda for their political and military support, which translated into direct influence and/or economic access (Roque 2017a). These countries were identified for their comparative advantages and fell under the principle of convergence of purpose. Some deployments had greater symbolism and were informed by ideological solidarity while others were based on survivalist imperatives and strategic priorities. At the heart of each of these deployments was the carefully crafted foreign policy that dos Santos designed and commanded over decades from the Presidency. It viewed the two Congos through the national security prism but saw Guinea Bissau, Côte d'Ivoire, Central African Republic and other countries as springboards into different regions and economic investments (Roque 2017a).

The FAPLA's first alleged international deployment was in 1977 when it sent between 1,000 and 1,500 troops to São Tomé and Príncipe to bolster the government of Manuel Pinto da Costa.[77] Support for regional allies would continue in the coming years. Some of these deployments were in the context of bilateral mutual defence pacts signed in the 1990s. In Southern Africa, security and financial relations with Mozambique and Zimbabwe were based on historical and ideological alliances. Angola allegedly sent 'advisors' and police contingents to support the Zimbabwe African National Union—Patriotic Front (ZANU-PF) and the Mozambique Liberation Front (Frente de Libertação de Moçambique or FRELIMO) in stabilising their own political crises. Although the government vehemently denied doing so, in 2007, Luanda provided Harare with as many as 2,500 special paramilitary police as part of the "training exchange" agreement between the two countries.[78] The timing of the deployment was largely coincidental with the post-electoral crisis that led to violent protests.

The large-scale military interventions in the two Congos in 1997 and 1998 were by far the most visible deployments that significantly altered the political design of the region. Angolan relations with the Democratic Republic of Congo and the Republic of Congo were based on security concerns and national stability, driven by the need to control the leadership in both. Luanda supported the rebellions of Dennis Sassou Nguesso and Laurent Kabila and helped both leaders define their strategic priorities whilst in power. In both cases, Angola's military, technical, financial and troop support for the insurrections secured their victories over long-standing incumbents. The driving force at the time was to prevent

UNITA from using the Congos as rear bases, logistics channels, and alternative markets in which to sell their diamonds.

In 1997, Angola deployed troops to the DRC to help remove Mobutu Sese Seko from the Presidency, bringing to an end the mass support Kinshasa had provided for UNITA. In 1998 it once again deployed 1,500 men, together with Zimbabwean and Namibian troops. This second intervention was to secure Kabila's survival, which pitted Luanda against Uganda and Rwanda. By 2001, Luanda was fully committed to guaranteeing a more malleable and dependable presidency under Joseph Kabila. Although unproven, Angola is thought to have played a role in the assassination of Laurent Kabila for having failed to secure the terms of their political agreements.[79] Angola remained a key ally in maintaining Kabila in power. For decades, FAA forces were covertly placed inside the DRC as well as officially proceeding with training programmes. Angola trained over 20,000 Congolese soldiers and an estimated 15,000 police, while it also allegedly maintained the deployment of the FAA brigade. Positioned with military intelligence capacity, they were used to support the Presidential Guard in Kinshasa and to control the level of internal dissidence within the Congolese governing alliance (Roque 2017a). Angolan military intelligence (SISM) helped to collect information and control emerging threats to Kinshasa. In 2006, Luanda helped Kabila defeat fighters loyal to Jean-Pierre Bemba; in 2008, Angola was accused of deploying troops against Laurent Nkunda. Luanda continued to view the DRC as a major national security threat, despite the controversial election of Felix Tshisekedi in 2018. The instinct to continuously interfere and advise politicians in Kinshasa continued under President Lourenço.

In the Republic of Congo, dos Santos helped remove the elected President Pascal Lissouba, bringing Denis Sassou Nguesso to power in 1997. Angola's intervention was once again aimed at denying UNITA access to rear bases and ensuring that Brazzaville's political loyalty would close off the Congo to any other rebel groups, particularly the Cabindan separatists. Luanda's security forces were reported to have maintained a presence in Brazzaville as guarantors of Sassou Nguesso's security, despite Luanda's announcement that it was withdrawing 1,000 troops from Brazzaville in December 2002. This withdrawal coincided with the mass deployments of troops into Cabinda to summarily end the FLEC insurgency. In 2006, as Luanda was trying to secure a peace agreement with a FLEC faction, it was also signing a cooperation agreement with Brazzaville to train Congolese special forces. Relations oscillated between close and cooperative to distant and problematic. Dos Santos and Sassou's foreign policies collided in the Central African Republic when both attempted to find political solutions to the crisis through mediation efforts but undermined each other. Angola had provided Bangui with $10 million in humanitarian aid and support for the new government of Catherine Samba Panza and had hoped to secure privileged positions vis-à vis other regional actors. In an attempt to strengthen bilateral relations with Samba-Panza, Angola was getting ready to provide a protection force for her and the government[80] but stopped the deployment when it realised that it would face resistance from international partners. Luanda's interests in the CAR were tied to its fear of the expansion of militant Islam into the region; its mediating and stabilisation role vis-à-vis the UN and the AU; and the underreported financial interests in the diamond sector (Roque 2017a). Tensions between Luanda and Brazzaville would continue with dos Santos' successor. President Lourenço allegedly sent medical help to Sassou Nguesso's main political opponent, General Joan Marie Michel Mokoko, after he tested positive for Covid-19 in July 2020.[81] Luandan politics would not normally include humanitarian gestures that weren't underpinned by other strategic calculations.

Angola's experience in West Africa was not as successful. Two bilateral miscalculations—in Côte d'Ivoire and in Guinea Bissau—brought Luanda great embarrassment and exposed the level of misdiagnosed support and regional groundwork necessary to appease competing hegemons. In 2010 Luanda's support for Ivorian President Laurent Gbagbo, as a continuation of existing political support, left Angola isolated when Alassane Ouattara was recognised as the legitimate victor of the presidential elections. Angola's first reaction was to send a military contingent of 300 men to protect Gbagbo in addition to shipments of arms.[82] Gbagbo was another key ally, who, unlike his predecessor Felix Houphouët-Boigny, denied UNITA a regional base. When the AU, ECOWAS, and the international community declared their support for Ouattara, dos Santos began to reconsider his diplomatic position by creating a task force within the Presidency and the Foreign Ministry in Luanda to address the situation. Gbagbo was captured before any real reversal of policy could occur. This cost Luanda its privileged relationship with Abidjan and the economic interests that came with this relationship. Angola was heavily committed in the development of the country's extractive industry. Sonangol had signed a deal worth $100 million to increase the Société Ivoirienne de Raffinage's (SIR) capacity and since 2000 had retained a 20% stake in SIR. Angola tried through different means to improve relations with Abidjan although dos Santos strongly disapproved of Ouattara's decisions to send Gbagbo to be tried at the International Criminal Court (Roque 2017a).

Angola would send troops to Guinea Bissau in 2010 to begin a much-needed security sector reform (SSR) programme but would also be overtaken by political miscalculations and a military coup there in 2011. The SSR mission to Guinea-Bissau (Missão de Cooperação Técnico-Militar a Guiné-Bissau or MISSANG) was an important first step in Luanda's exposure in a region that it did not dominate. It was aimed at protecting economic interests but also had geostrategic objectives. In stabilising Guinea-Bissau, Angola was also able to advance economic development priorities, in particular the Port of Buba project. In 2010, the two countries signed a contract for the construction of the Buba port, which would cost US$500–700 million.[83] The port would be linked to Angola's other financial interests in the extraction of bauxite in the Boe region, with a railway and road linking Boe to Buba. MISSANG was the first time Angola took on the responsibility of an SSR exercise with the mandate to institute wide-ranging reforms. The objective was to reduce the army to a mere 3,000 troops, while demobilising the remaining forces and guaranteeing their reintegration with a pension fund worth $45 million (contributed by Angola, Brazil and Portugal). It committed over $100 million to the reform of the Guinean armed forces. All its efforts were reversed when the military staged a coup in 2011, leaving Luanda isolated and unable to protect an elected President. Although it considered launching a full-force invasion with 2,500 troops ready for deployment, it reconsidered any further involvement based on the logistical, operational and political considerations of a military intervention.[84] In 2015, Angola reopened its embassy and began reengaging Bissau on economic matters.

The failed interventions in Côte d'Ivoire and Guinea Bissau informed Luanda's thinking on multilateral engagements that would shield it from outright embarrassment and political fallout. Angola began preparations for peacekeeping operations in 2002 with the establishment of the battalion for support of peace operations at the Cabo Ledo training facility. In 2006, two centres were created to support peacekeeping training: a strategic one at the Higher Institute for Military Training and a tactical one with the 70th Brigade in Vale do Paraíso. Two years later, these centres were joined to create the "Centre for Instruction to Peace Support Operations". It was estimated that over 4,000 officers had been trained since 2008.[85] The Group of Special FAA Forces (GAE) in Cabo Ledo was composed of two battalions of special commando forces, two companies of special operation forces, one battalion of rocket launchers, one logistics unit and a group of special ops. The selection process was very rigorous; recruits received training from Portuguese special commando forces. Angola claimed to have the largest airlift capacity in the region, reflecting its long war experience. With its fleet of IL-76 aircraft, this became another selling point for its contribution to peacekeeping operations.[86]

From 2010 Luanda actively participated and contributed large troop contingents to the Southern Africa Development Community (SADC) and Economic Community of Central African States (ECCAS) brigades and participated in joint training exercises with CPLP that created the expectation that Luanda would join in peacekeeping and humanitarian missions. The Community of Portuguese Speaking Countries (CPLP) "Felino exercises" were held annually from 2000 and aimed to strengthen the interoperability of the armed forces of Angola, Brazil, Portugal, Mozambique, Cape Verde, Guinea Bissau, São Tomé and Príncipe and Timor Leste. After joining the SADC mutual defence pact, Angola played an active role in preparing the SADC Standby Force Brigade (SADCBRIG). The so-called "Dolphin" military exercises had already contributed to the brigade's readiness. In 2009, Angola sent 500 troops.[87] The 2014 "Lohango" exercise integrated the Angolan army, air force, navy and the Rapid Response Police (PIR) elements. Angola also participated in ECCAS military exercises, from the 2003 Biyongo exercise, the Bahr-El Ghazal exercise (2005) and the 2010 Kwanza exercise that launched the CAR mission, FOMAC.[88] They also trained with the US and others in activities like the Obangame Express 2017 and the Utulivu Africa II, part of the AU's African Capacity to Immediate Reaction to Crisis (ACIRC) programme.

In 2014, Angola announced that it would send one battalion of motorised infantry, a company of special forces and a field hospital to the UN Multidimensional Integrated Stabilisation Mission in the Central African Republic (MINUSCA), but subsequently withdrew the offer.[89] The Angolan military highlighted its disagreement over the mandate and the means being given to their troops if they were to be deployed in northern CAR. "There were limitations at all levels—from the water cisterns to the amount of fuel we would be given—(which) meant we would have serious logistical limitations".[90] The financial costs and logistical concerns may have factored into Luanda's reasoning, but given the FAA's level of preparedness the failure to deploy would have been a political decision. To date Angola has only sent 162 troops to Lesotho, part of a SADC intervention in 2017 that was considered a relatively safe and uneventful deployment.

*Political Instruments for National Defence*

Domestically, interventions of the FAA became polarising. Operations in two of Angola's resource-rich and socially unintegrated regions—Cabinda and the Lunda Norte and Lunda Sul provinces—became examples of the militarised nature of social and political control. While Cabinda experienced a low-level insurgency for decades in spite of a peace agreement in 2006, the Lunda Norte and Lunda Sul provinces had no militarily active group. Instead, the Lunda-Chokwe communities rallied behind a community-based organisation to provide a form of resistance to the central state. The two regions provided the government with a significant portion of its revenue—oil, gas and diamonds—and had very distinct group/ethnic and social identities providing a layer of disengagement with Luanda. Both areas were the poorest and least developed in Angola. They were also examples of securitised responses to political and socio-economic concerns of citizens that required a state interlocutor to dialogue with. In the absence of a representative of the state, these communities fended for themselves in precarious and violent circumstances.

# THE ANGOLAN ARMED FORCES

*Cabinda: Struggle for Independence or Autonomy*

The oil-rich enclave of Cabinda has remained a militarised and unresolved low-intensity conflict since the 1960s. It is a military as well as a political, governance and identity-based conflict, with the Frente de Libertação de Cabinda (FLEC) factions and the population continuing to demand independence or a form of autonomy. Cabinda was always important for Luanda. During the war, the role played by US companies (in particular Texaco/Chevron operating under its subsidiary, Cabinda Gulf Oil Company) was of such importance that pragmatic economic considerations easily overcame ideological contradictions. While the US government didn't recognise the MPLA and supported UNITA, US oil interests were maintained and even protected by the most unlikely guard of Cuban internationalist troops.[91] Referred to as the 'African Kuwait', Cabinda produced most of Angola's oil and was controlled by the SCP. In the last two decades, the government's strategy had been to over-militarise and repress the enclave, instigate discord among civil society and activists, and maintain the population in economically subdued conditions.

Cabindans never felt part of Angola and built a robust Cabindan identity. From their perspective, the government ruled the enclave like a feudal colony, systematically exploiting its natural resources. On the other hand, the government saw Cabinda as an integral and inalienable part of its territory. Cabindans based their claim for independence on the 1885 Simulambuco treaty with the Portuguese, which placed the territory as a protectorate of Portugal in the run-up to the Berlin Conference. The Cabindans allegedly asked the Portuguese for their protection from the colonial ambitions of Belgium, Britain and France. The territory subsequently became known as the Portuguese Congo— integrating the three Cabindan kingdoms of N'Goyo, Loango and Kacongo. As a result, they argued that Cabinda was never a Portuguese colony, unlike Angola, which experienced 500 years of Portuguese rule. As the independence movements began to rally against Portuguese imperialism in Angola, so did the Cabindan movements in the 1960s. But just like the MPLA, UNITA and the FNLA, their military strength was limited. However, unlike the other three movements, the FLEC had an overriding political identity force that could have kept it united and with a coherent command. Instead, it fragmented and morphed over the years while never abandoning a cause that remained one of the world's forgotten conflicts. For over 60 years the enclave experienced some form of armed conflict.

The armed resistance has suffered many fragmentations since its inception in 1963. The first occurred with a disagreement over strategy. While one faction, headed by Luis Ranque Franque, wanted to continue pursuing the diplomatic route and had proclaimed Cabinda's independence in Kinshasa, Henrique Nzita Tiago believed that the struggle needed to take on a military form. FLEC-FAC (Forças Armadas de Cabinda) was created and the war launched in 1963. Supported by Zaire, the Congo and Gabon, FLEC controlled over 70% of Cabinda in the 1980s. However, Nzita Tiago's leadership was also being questioned and the Comando Militar para a Independência de Cabinda (CMLC), later renamed FLEC-Renovada, was formed with Antonio Bento Bembe as its leader. For many years the two FLECs operated in separate politico-military zones, with FLEC-FAC operating in the northern and central areas and FLEC-R in the south. In 2006, FLEC-R signed the peace agreement with Angola to the exclusion of other armed and civilian groups. In 2010, FLEC-FAC suffered another significant splintering with the emergence of a group led by former VP of FLEC Alexandre Tati and General Estanislau Boma. The dissident group wanted to keep Nzita Tiago as an honorary figurehead but essentially dethroned him. From their perspective, one was FLEC interior and the other was FLEC exterior, given that Nzita Tiago had remained in exile in Paris for many years.

Several attempts were made in the 1990s to find a compromise to the conflict. However, a solution to the problem involving force became the default strategy. The government estimated that it would take the army three months in 2002 to crush the armed groups. After UNITA was defeated, most of the army units moved north to Cabinda, in what became a brutal crackdown. In October 2002, the FAA began the final assault on Cabinda with Operação Vassoura (Operation Broom) aimed at destroying FLEC-FAC. A report, "Terror in Cabinda", was published by a human rights commission detailing atrocities committed in Cabinda, mainly by the FAA. Building on the success it had against UNITA, Luanda sent a massive military contingent to sweep away any remaining insurgents and fully neutralise their activities. It failed to achieve this even with the tremendous asymmetry experienced by FLEC, which was severely depleted but not eliminated. Having realised it could not impose a final military solution, the government pursued a divide-and-rule strategy by signing peace with one FLEC faction in 2006. Once the accord was signed, the situation deteriorated significantly.

The Memorando de Entendimento para a Paz e Reconciliação da Provincia de Cabinda (Memorandum of Understanding for Peace and Reconciliation in the Province of Cabinda) was signed on 1 July 2006 by the government and the Forum Cabindês para o Dialogo (FCD), a civil society group led by Bento Bembe and his FLEC faction. The agreement, however, failed to calm the situation in the enclave. Its ultimate success was the division of the armed and unarmed resistance in Cabinda. FLEC elites, civil society leaders, and priests who had aligned to negotiate with one voice in 2004 were now divided. This was part of the government's strategy. The key government positions awarded to Bembe's commanders and politicians were subsequently withdrawn or had remained ineffective through lack of integration. While Bembe was appointed Human Rights Minister and three of his deputies nominated for Deputy Minister positions of agriculture, oil and interior, all four were later demoted. His main commander, General Zulu, who retained the position as the Deputy Chief of Staff for Social Issues in the FAA, later retired. There was clear and open disillusionment and renewed calls for renegotiation. Efforts to unite the Cabindan factions began gaining ground in 2015, although the government continued to deny it had a conflict.

The average Cabindan was faced with living in a highly militarised environment tightly controlled by the armed forces and the intelligence services, creating an underlying sense of fear and control. In July 2006 the only independent human rights organisation, Mpalabanda, was banned by court order for allegedly inciting violence and carrying out political activities. Cabindans claimed that since the signing of the 2006 peace agreement, the situation deteriorated significantly—with the FAA staging cross-border raids to attack Cabindan refugees and FLEC forces. The infiltration of the security services into public life intensified, and they actively disbanded civil society groups. Once the most respected institution in Cabinda, the Catholic Church became instrumentalised and was actively dividing communities. Dismantling the unity of the church and neutralising the capacity of the resistant priests to conduct community work and human rights activism resulted in the expulsion of several highly respected priests.

Critical aspects of the 2006 agreement remained unimplemented. The "special status" provision awarded to the enclave was intangible and illusory. It was meant to open the possibility of autonomy but was left sufficiently vague to allow for non-implementation. The Governor was thought to have continuously diverted the 10% of oil revenues that were to be injected into local development projects.[92] Monthly, depending on currency fluctuations, this could have amounted to $7 million. The enclave had a small population of 600,000, and these monthly revenues would suffice to create jobs and deliver basic services. Yet poverty deepened and food insecurity increased, as rural communities were unable to work the fields impeded by the military. It was also unclear if the integration of the FLEC fighters from the 2006 agreement was fully implemented and concluded. A group of FLEC combatants were in a quartering area in Yabi for over seven years without being formally demobilised or integrated into the armed forces. Many perished over the years, as did other FLEC fighters who were subsequently captured.

A political and social clampdown began growing incrementally from 2010 when the government started detaining civilians and activists accused of having connections to the remaining armed FLEC factions. The strangulation of rural life worsened with "civilians in the Maiombe forests being restricted from farming and fishing and only allowed two kilos of foodstuff each, with the purpose of cutting off access to food for the guerrillas".[93] The enclave was being fenced off from the Congos to completely circumvent FLEC's movements and allow the military commanders to extract and exploit their commercial interests in timber and other resources.[94] Despite these attempts to isolate the FLEC, the armed groups continued to recruit and were estimated to have over 1000 fighters.[95] Having changed their tactics, the FLEC reorganised their military commands to operate in smaller autonomous groups instructed to act throughout the territory, making them harder to detect and neutralise. In 2011 there was a rapprochement between

Tati's group and the government, but these talks ended in disagreement and the FAA reacted with another major offensive. In March 2011, the FAA began an offensive to pursue key commanders in their rear bases in the Congo and the DRC to capture and execute them. Increasingly the FAA and military intelligence colluded with Congolese forces to identify FLEC members in return for money. The Congolese army did not always cooperate with the Angolans, as the FLEC commanders were also able to pay them off for security. Key commanders like Nhemba "Pirilampo" (chief of staff of FLEC after Estanislau Boma defected) and Lubota "Sabata" (FLEC FAC operational commander of Northern region) were killed through these rendition operations.

In June 2016, the long-time leader and founder of one of the FLEC factions, Nzita Tiago, passed away in Paris aged 88. His leadership of FLEC-FAC over decades was both a unifying and divisive force. Efforts by influential Cabindans immediately began to try to unite the FLEC groups and mediate a smooth succession process. Emmanuel Nzita, his son, took over the leadership of the movement. In 2016 several brigades of the army, the border police, the Rapid Response Police (PIR), the naval commandos and construction brigades were deployed in the enclave. The presence of the intelligence services was everywhere, and their infiltration capacity was widespread. There was general anger and frustration as the expectations for peace—the most minimal being development and demilitarisation—failed to transpire. FLEC intensified its attacks in 2017, causing the government to continue deploying diverse units in the province. The deployments were shrouded in secrecy and dreaded by soldiers and junior officers who understood the risk of death when being sent to Cabinda. FLEC increasingly began to issue war communiques of the number of FAA soldiers killed, the number of police detained, and the numerous confrontations in the enclave. Videos circulated of their military formations, parading their prisoners of war.

The activists of the older generation—retired priest Raul Tati, father Jorge Congo, lawyer Francisco Luemba, and others—who never gave up demanding justice and freedom for Cabinda changed strategies in 2017–18 and decided that they would work from within the system to change it. Tati joined the UNITA ticket and was elected into parliament for the province of Cabinda. Father Congo was nominated

Secretary for Education in Cabinda, and advocate Luemba was appointed to the Superior Council of the Judiciary in January 2017. This had the unintended effect of allowing a younger generation of activists to become more vocal and fearlessly take to the streets. Many have been jailed and awaiting trial since 2018. One group, in particular, became very vocal. The Movimento Independentista de Cabinda (the Independence Movement of Cabinda, MIC) rallied support from the youth. In February 2019, over 40 protesters were detained after marching for self-determination and celebrating the 134th anniversary of the Treaty of Simulambuco. They remained in police custody for three months. Several other protests were called by the movement, demanding that Angola hold a referendum to determine the future status of Cabinda.

When UN Secretary-General Antonio Guterres called for a global ceasefire in March 2020 as the Covid-19 pandemic raged, FLEC became one of 16 armed groups that heeded the call during April. Guterres mentioned the countries whose groups responded positively to the cessation of hostilities—including Libya, Sudan, Syria, Yemen and others—and, by mentioning Angola, placed the Cabindan conflict in a small but significant limelight that brought renewed energy to the Cabindans. By June, the FAA had resumed hostilities in the enclave. For the first time in 14 years, the government also conceded that guerrilla operations were active in the enclave.

## *Lundas: The Curse of Diamonds*

The Lundas provinces, like Cabinda, remained unappeased with a constant stream of violent deaths and human rights violations. Like Cabinda, overriding resource extraction interests led to serious underdevelopment and visible instruments of coercion in the northeasternmost part of Angola that bordered the DRC. Located in a highly forested area in Chokwe territory, the Lunda provinces remained a historically complicated area where the government had to deploy the army, the national police and private security companies to provide security for the diamond concessions. The Lunda Sul and Lunda Norte provinces, which held the largest diamond fields in Angola, were the most isolated and least developed of the country.

They were also one of the regions where the FAA, like Cabinda, were deployed to deal with social issues.[96] While exploration was organised in a centrally controlled industrial complex in the Lunda Sul province, the province of Lunda Norte was chaotically left to the control of the private diamond companies mining in the remote fields of the Cuango river. The region suffered from decades of political neglect and social marginalisation, coupled with generalised poverty, which fuelled popular resentment against the government. Human rights activists and local populations referred to it as the government's killing fields. [97] Over the last decade, torture, extrajudicial killings, and other human rights abuses regarding livelihoods and the appropriation of lands have been recorded.[98] In the Xa-Mutemba municipality in December 2009, the FAA buried 45 illegal miners alive. The atrocity was exposed by both the Angolan paper *Semanário Angolense* and the *Wall Street Journal*,[99] yet no investigation was launched (Marques 2011). Between April and June 2015, over 21 civilians were killed, and 174 disappeared after a 'collection round' by the police to deport foreigners.[100] The mass deportation of *garimpeiros* (informal miners) has generated tensions between Kinshasa and Luanda over the last ten years. Angolan security forces, led by the FAA, expelled over 400,000 illegal immigrants, primarily Congolese. Included in many of these rounds were local populations.

Communities were forced to live on the border of the diamond concessions and were subjected to constant expropriation of land, the destruction of harvests, and severe limitations on their freedom of movement (Marques 2011). Communities urged the government to divert the Cuango river so that the extraction of alluvial diamonds could occur elsewhere. Yet there was little if no redress for these state-sponsored actions. "The dense bush allowed the government to kill at will ... Here we were not considered citizens; we were treated as animals".[101] Community leaders in the area confirmed that the more disorganisation there was, the more the government and their international partners could extract.

As Angola took over the Kimberley Process (KP) in 2016, nine senior generals were facing investigation for alleged crimes against humanity, following charges against them by an Angolan human rights activist with the Attorney General's Office in Luanda. The generals were accused of being behind the orchestration of 100 killings and 500 cases of torture in their capacity as co-owners of private security companies. One fundamental failing of the KP process remained its continued definition of 'blood diamonds' that removed any culpability of states. The KP Certification Scheme had in the last few years also proven to be corruptible, with extensive schemes available to alter the certificate of origin of the diamonds.[102]

As one of Africa's top diamond producers, Angola's diamond industry included joint ventures with Brazilian, Russian, Israeli and Belgian companies.[103] It exported mainly to Dubai, Israel, Switzerland and EU countries. The ruling elites' interests in diamonds were secured under several companies: the national diamond company Endiama,[104] Iaxonh (formerly TAIS),[105] the Sociedade Mineira do Cuango,[106] Sodiam,[107] Ascorp,[108] Sociedade Mineira de Luminas, and Sociedade Mineira do Lapi,[109] among others. Like oil, revenues from diamonds were a main source of patronage. Each of the joint ventures involved key generals and the dos Santos entourage, who carved out large fortunes. De Beers estimated that 90% of the prospective area in Angola remained unexplored,[110] pointing to the extended presence of these diamond companies and their corresponding private security companies.

Diamond exports generated $1.2 billion in 2014, with an additional $73.7 million in taxes.[111] In 2019 the country sold over 9 million carats of rough diamonds resulting in $1.3 billion in revenue. However, the Lundas saw little return on this, exacerbating their sense of alienation. Despite the presence of the Catoca mine, the fourth largest kimberlite mine in the world, on the outskirts of Lunda Sul capital Saurimo, neither schools, nor hospitals, nor employment-generating activities were developed. It was estimated that over 80% of Angola's diamond production came from Catoca, which was jointly owned by Endiama (32.8%), Alrosa (32.8%), Odebretch (16.4%), and the Chinese company LLI Holding (18%). The only income-generating activity left for the communities in this area was the *garimpo* (wildcat mining). "The Lundas didn't know what it was to have industry or formal employment. ... *Garimpo* was the only survival tool we had".[112] Yet it was a very dangerous activity. The population entered into informal agreements to help mine the diamonds but were not afforded any protection. In many cases, private security companies, the national police and other diamond miners changed the terms of agreement with the communities and *garimpeiros* invariably got killed. The collaboration among all the armed elements (police, private firms and the army) resulted in a more vicious clampdown on illegal miners and engendered widespread *garimpo* protection rackets.

Mobilisation of any form in the area carried significant risk, although there was a stance of defiance and peaceful resistance. The Lundas' political interests were nationally represented by the Partido de Renovação Social (PRS), founded in 1991 to campaign for a federal system. Yet other social movements emerged to represent the demands of the population. In 2007 a manifesto was prepared by the Protectorado da Lunda Tchokwe organisation calling for administrative and financial autonomy of the region. The author of the manifesto, Jota Filipe "Malakito", was detained and spent two years in jail for his separatist stance. Another organisation emerged in 2013, after a leadership dispute with Malakaito, called the Movimento do Protectorado Lunda Tchokwe (the Lunda-Chokwe Protectorate Movement, MPLT) led by José Mateus Zecamutchima. The ultimate goal of MPLT was to achieve independence for the Lunda-Chokwe kingdom that comprised Lunda Norte, Lunda Sul, Moxico and parts of the Kuando Kubango provinces. This was the Machiamba kingdom that had been disputed between the Portuguese and the Belgians in 1891–4. They claimed that the Lunda-Chokwe had a protectorate agreement with Portugal between 1885 and 1894. The independence claim was based on the fact that the Portuguese had not ruled this territory until the 1920s, with local administration structures emerging only in the 1950s. The Protectorate Movement took a very visible role in exposing atrocities and demanding greater justice in the Lundas. Support for the movement grew over the years yet its pacifist stance led to calls for a more forceful campaign.

In March 2019 a group of traditional chiefs (Sobas) travelled to the Lulo mine to ask if youths could work there too. They were met with police violence. One Soba was killed and over 70 people were detained. In November of the same year, a group of men armed with machetes attacked the Luzia jail near Saurimo (the capital of Lunda Sul province) to free an independence leader who had been calling for armed resistance. Self-styled as the leader of a separatist movement called the Revolutionary Front for the Integration and Sociological Independence of Lunda-Chokwe, commander Trovoada's call for action was dismissed by authorities as a lone-wolf attempt by an army deserter to seek justice for his region. The attack on the jail resulted in the deaths of five attackers and the detention of 18 others.[113] While the probability of an armed insurrection gaining any traction in this heavily fortified region was remote, this was evidence of the mounting frustration and anger directed by the population against Luanda.

The situation escalated in early 2021 when, on 30 January, authorities opened fire on a group of protesters in Cafunfu, Lunda Norte, killing 28 and wounding several more. Several security forces intervened, including the FAA, the PIR and the police. Versions of events differed, with authorities claiming self defence against a group of 300 armed MPLT members that attacked a police station. Others placed the number of protesters at around 93 unarmed civilians.[114] MPLT claims it had written to local authorities to inform them that they would be staging a protest marking the 127th anniversary of the protectorate treaty with Portugal. Across Angola, influential bishops condemned the response, deeming the incident a "massacre", denouncing the use of extreme violence and demanding justice. The church, civil society and the opposition rapidly called for an investigation. Calls began to emerge for dialogue between communities and the government so that they could resolve the "issue of structural separation and exclusion in Angola with urgency".[115] Days after the massacre, reports surfaced that the bodies of those killed were stolen from the morgues and thrown into the Cuango river to hide evidence.[116] On 9 February, the MPLT leader, Zecamutchima, was detained by the investigative police unit (SIC) and taken to Luanda. He was held without access to his lawyers or family members, much like Kalupeteca (the leader of the sect involved in the 2015 religious massacre explored in the previous chapter) and many others who dared rail against the status quo. Zecamutchima was accused of the crime of rebellion and awaited trial.

Events in the Lunda Norte province and the reactions of security forces became João Lourenço's first attributable massacre. This securitised response to a political issue signalled his incapacity or unwillingness to reform the system, and the fear that small protests would catalyse social disobedience and "convulsion" throughout the country. These events also brought about a renewed sense of urgency towards the holding of local elections and the possibility of sharing power with the opposition to appease political instability.[117] Local elections had never been held in Angola despite being promised for decades. The requirements of rigging and influencing the outcome of local elections in line with previous electoral experiences would require a larger and costly securitised footprint on the ground, the gerrymandering of municipal boundaries, and an update of the electoral roll. An exercise meant to devolve power and potentially disarm socio-economic tensions had so far been perceived as far too risky and unpredictable.

This chapter has highlighted some of the traits and pathologies surrounding the FAA and their post-war role. Emerging from decades of war, the national army morphed from an instrument of political dominance to a fragmented tool for the enrichment of its chiefs on one side and the last remaining symbol of national unity on the other. The pathologies that characterised its quotidian and future challenges were a result of political miscalculations on behalf of the Presidency. The FAA remained a key vehicle for regional stability, offering the option for military intervention if Angola's national security was threatened. The opportunity to use the army for peacekeeping missions in 2014–15 provided an alternative use for the FAA's military enterprise and helped to alleviate pressure on the state budget. However, issues surrounding its mandate, initial costs, mission leadership, troop composition, and political concerns kept the FAA from assisting in multilateral peace missions. Instead, the FAA continued to focus on its domestic role. The actions of the FAA in the Lundas and Cabinda placed it on a war footing with the civilian population as it aided in military as well as political strategies to repress and impoverish these communities. Increasingly, the identities of the Cabindans and Chokwe were solidifying against Luanda because of these actions, a process that required more consensual approaches than the ones used against UNITA in the 1990s. The FAA would continue to remain a conduit for popular control in 2020.

5

# CHANGING THE GUARD

## JOÃO LOURENÇO'S PRESIDENCY

In September 2017, Angolans elected a new President. After 39 years, dos Santos decided to step down and hand over power to his Defence Minister, João Lourenço, when his tenure had lost its lustre and was entangled in decadence and decay. Calls for dos Santos to retire from politics were widespread and numerous but he stayed on even after the 2012 elections revealed the fragilities of the MPLA's political standing with the people. Decades of theft had entrenched inequality, and no amount of rhetoric of grandeur and failed promises could erase this legacy. Faced with dwindling domestic support, left exposed by corruption scandals, and with an economic recession caused by the oil crisis in 2014, his decision to retire was laden with self-interest. Dos Santos decided to leave power before the country had to face the consequences of decades of malfeasance and exclusionary political and economic policies. Before departing, he and his group of SCP generals and technocrats drafted a bill restricting the future President from changing the security chiefs, which would ensure that the SCP would retain ultimate control. Dos Santos had also left the main levers of the economy—oil, diamonds, construction and the sovereign wealth fund (SWF)—in the hands of his children and his closest advisors. Weeks into his Presidency, Lourenço reversed these decrees and reshuffled the leadership of the different branches of the security apparatus. He removed Isabel dos Santos from the oil company Sonangol and her brother José Filomeno from the SWF, sidelined their siblings' economic interests, and began targeting officials with corruption charges. With the stroke of a pen, he annulled contracts worth $20 billion that his predecessor had awarded to his daughter Isabel.[1] To shield himself from the political aftershocks of these actions, Lourenço further increased the securitisation of non-military sectors of the state by placing generals and other officers in civilian roles across the executive and judiciary.

This marked the beginning of a new era and brought an abrupt end to the captured economy of the dos Santos clan but continued a similar strategy of securitisation, political hegemony and government disengagement with its people. The new President distanced himself from the previous administration in several important ways. Lourenço chose to reform rather than witness the country's unravelling under the weight of political decline, economic mismanagement, and unaddressed poverty. He inherited severe pathologies but began tackling the most urgent issues, including the economic recession and breaking the pattern of systemic and institutionalised corruption. Despite this, in the short political life of Lourenço's presidency, he rapidly passed the enchantment phase to experience the phase of realism. His promised economic miracle had not materialised, and his government continued to replicate the ineptitude of the past. Satisfying public expectations of change required more than merely reducing the influence, wealth and patronage network of his predecessor. To survive the massive aftershocks of the recession, Lourenço should have taken steps to ease the social tension which posed the greatest risk to his government. However, development programmes remained purely rhetorical and directed towards electoral campaigning and political gains. The most vulnerable should have been protected from the effects of austerity measures, and social services had to be bolstered, staffed and funded. The youth needed jobs and sustainable livelihood strategies. Above all, the state and the ruling elites should have found avenues to dialogue with the Angolan citizenry to prevent the multiple crises from developing into instability. Instead, Lourenço opted for a hybridised response and chose to reform enough to survive these crises but not enough to ultimately threaten the political hegemony and stranglehold of the MPLA elites on the state and the economy. If the four decades of dos Santos rule were defined by war, peace and corruption, Lourenço's rule can be defined by factionalism, poverty, and inequality.

Two years into the changing of the guard, Angola was hit with two existential threats. The Covid-19 pandemic and the vertiginous drop in oil prices in April 2020 meant that Angola was facing twin crises of unprecedented dimensions. All the fault lines became enhanced, pushing the level of resilience, adaptability, and survival of the Angolan people to extremes. This chapter outlines the changes enacted by Lourenço as he took the helm of the Presidency and the challenges he faced while navigating these difficult political and economic fault lines.

## The 2017 Presidential Transition

The biggest debate in private circles among the elites and analysts working on Angola was guessing the form the presidential succession would take and who would eventually replace dos Santos. As one of Africa's longest-standing leaders, dos Santos' replacement was expected to fit within two possible options: a figure of proxy-power akin to what Vladimir Putin achieved in Russia with Dmitry Medvedev, controlling the Presidency from afar and ensuring political continuity; or a dynastic option with one of the children taking the helm. This debate slowly began to grow after the 2012 elections, yet dos Santos would only confirm his intention to retire from politics in December 2016. His successor came as a surprise to many who had speculated that the former Sonangol chairman and vice-president Manuel Vicente, indicted for corruption in Portugal, might be selected as a proxy. Vicente lacked any constituency of his own, had no political pull within the party, lacked military credentials, and was linked to the dos Santos clan through business interests. He would have served dos Santos well. Others were convinced that one of the dos Santos children, installed in key economic positions since 2011, would be put in place. The 2010 constitution had already been devised to secure and concentrate power in the Presidency and the party as a necessary tool for a future successor.[2] Whoever took over needed to retain sufficient power to govern after years of growing decay and social dissatisfaction, but the successor would also depend on the party to define his policies, even if the structures for MPLA collective leadership had, over time, lost all power.

Instead, dos Santos opted to elect a former political commissar and general as his successor. Lourenço became the first President of Angola with a military background. The reasoning for such a move was unclear, especially given the difficult history between the two men. Lourenço had been side-lined by dos Santos after publicly commenting in 2001 on what that President had stated—that he wanted to retire from active politics—in a party meeting when Lourenço was MPLA Secretary General. His imposed political hibernation lasted from 2003 until 2014, during which he served as first Vice-President of the national assembly, a relatively powerless position. Lourenço was rehabilitated in 2014 when dos Santos nominated him Defence Minister. The succession altered several important relationships and standings among elites and MPLA factions. Dos Santos had prioritised the elites from Luanda and had placed many people of mixed race in positions of power. Lourenço began dismantling this by empowering the elites from Malange and bringing back the prominence of the Black leaders of the MPLA. While dos Santos had placed generals of smaller ethnic groups (for example the Kuanhama) in sensitive positions of the security forces but had also allowed some southern commanders (in particular the Ovimbundu) to lead several units, Lourenço placed Bakongo commanders in key positions of the security apparatus. In many ways, Lourenço began to dismantle the system of personal rule that dos Santos had built, replacing "his relatives, friends, lieutenants, clients and followers ... (threatening) the political peace" (Jackson and Rosberg 1982).

The opacity of the Angolan state and security apparatus, upheld by rapid economic growth, led to the perception of a sustainable and stable political order. However, Lourenço inherited several pathologies that he had to contain, address or entrench. Inequality was one of the most damaging legacies of the dos Santos regime. The extreme distortion in the distribution of resources and national wealth, a legacy of the war and post-war reconstruction, would be the hardest trend to address. An inadvertent hierarchy of citizenship emerged from those who were entitled citizens to those who were marginalised. The cleavages were most visible within the gap between the super-rich elites and the poor, although they had many nuances. In 20 years of peace, Angola's prosperity had impoverished the majority of its population. Inequality peaked in 2008 with its oil boom. The Gini coefficient, measuring economic wealth and income distribution, went from 0.43 in 2008 to 0.51 in 2019.[3] Over half of the population (51%) was multi-dimensionally poor, meaning that the poor were exposed to numerous deprivations in their daily lives such as lack of education, poor health, disempowerment, and inadequate living conditions.

A second legacy linked to this was the way the government superficially developed its economy based on extractive priorities rather than diversifying to develop employment-generating sectors. The country lost an opportunity to invest in job-creating industries during the oil windfall (2004–13) where state coffers were filling up with double-digit growth. Instead, elites looted, and any foundations for pro-poor development were set aside. Corruption, the third legacy, kept the political elites united, stemming away any potential factionalism within the MPLA, and delegitimised state institutions, weakened the economy and destroyed relations between the state and society. It became so entrenched that it began defining the way citizens interacted and engaged with public institutions and each other. The last legacy was the instrumentalisation of democratic procedure and principles. A veneer of democracy, upheld by the procedural practices of elections and parliamentary debates, hid a difficult reality of authoritarianism. The country had never had free, fair and transparent polls despite numerous international observation missions legitimising the results. Senior MPLA leaders privately acknowledge the fraudulent practices they engaged in when tampering with results and what this meant for their legitimacy in governing. They also understood how the opposition had gained ground and was stronger, potentially capable of winning in future polls. Underpinning and driving these legacies was the structure and practice of securitisation. To address these fault lines the political order had to be desecuritised.

To govern this system, Lourenço needed to restructure power. His first step was to control the security apparatus. His second step was to define a strategy to stop the recession and ensure growth. To do this he had to make political choices in defining who within the MPLA was necessary and therefore protected, and who could be chosen to face criminal prosecution. The political battleground fundamentally shifted to within the MPLA. "Fear (was) displaced from society to the MPLA elites",[4] as corruption charges were laid against the dos Santos entourage. Lourenço's economic strategy could not have been disconnected from any political front, given the embryonic link between politics and enrichment in Angola. In this way, he fused his second and third steps—political purging and economic sanitisation—to secure his tenure. The anti-corruption battle served both purposes well.

Meanwhile, the ruling party had underestimated the levels of disengagement and disenchantment felt by the population during the dos Santos presidency. The political decay surrounding years of unapologetic looting of state funds, repression and economic mismanagement weakened Lourenço from the onset. The way he came to power also brought his credibility into question. The MPLA campaigned on the promises of job-creation, tackling corruption, decentralising power, diversifying the economy and improving essential services like health and education, revealing an accurate diagnosis of the country which would echo with the electorate. But it also ran the risk, like previous MPLA campaigns, of being merely slogans that were left unimplemented and disregarded after the polls. Given this background, the 2017 elections were marred by controversy and allegations of mass fraud.[5]

Evidence of electoral misconduct was presented to the courts in September 2017 by the opposition but the executive-controlled judiciary dismissed these cases. The four main opposition parties— UNITA, CASA-CE, FNLA and PRS—united in their bid to have the results overturned. Their main contention had been that no tabulation process occurred at the provincial level and therefore numbers at the national level could not possibly have been based on real results. They also claimed that ballot boxes had disappeared, that new ballot boxes were delivered to polling stations, that electoral sheets were switched and that ghost polling stations had been in operation.[6] Across the continent, the Kenyan Supreme Court dismissed the results of their elections, held a month earlier, that had awarded the incumbent President Uhuru Kenyatta victory, despite the stamp of approval of international observation missions. In Angola, similar strategies to those argued for and upheld by the

Kenyan court, of irregularities and illegalities in the way votes were transmitted from polling stations to the central tallying centre, were at the heart of the electoral fraud that gave Lourenço his victory. The figures initially released by the electoral commission, the CNE, did not add up, literally. Officially, provisional results were only shared 24 hours after polls had closed but without the participation of opposition representatives in the tabulation process. The CNE's first provisional results totalled 100.37%, while the second came to 99.99%. Of the 12,000 polling stations across the country, it was impossible to determine how the results were arrived at, given that the provincial tabulation process did not occur and was therefore not the basis of the final tabulation of national results. The President of the CNE, Julia Ferreira, admitted in a press briefing that results were arrived at by other considerations and not just the result sheets. According to the official figures announced by the CNE, the MPLA was awarded 61%, UNITA increased its vote share to 26%, the CASA-CE party gained 9%, while the PRS's vote share decreased, with 1.3%, as did the FNLA's, with 0.9%, and the National Patriotic Alliance (APN) achieved 0.51%. The opposition's parallel tabulation—based on copies of the original result sheets—internally revealed that the MPLA's margin of victory was closer to 54% and UNITA's was closer to 35%. Had the MPLA achieved just over 50% it would have lost its two-thirds majority in parliament, which would have given the opposition greater strength. For the MPLA, a loss in vote share would have threatened the interests of the elites and potentially brought instability into the presidential palace. While the MPLA had retained a majority, with 150 out of 220 seats in parliament, the opposition and the urban population were acutely aware of the fragility of the ruling party and the possibility of defeating them in the next polls in 2022.

Immediately after the election, dos Santos boarded a TAP Air Portugal plane, refusing to use the national airline TAAG or any protocol service, indicating that tensions were already mounting between him and his successor. The elder statesman also signalled that he no longer trusted the state to protect him or ensure his safety. Dos Santos moved to Barcelona, a city he knew well after decades of medical treatment there. He would be free from prosecution until 2022. His life transitioned rather painfully from one of absolute power and the reverence of his entourage and supporters to one of a muted yet sieged existence. Rumours circulated among the Luanda elites that he was visited by his closest advisors and allies requesting he release documents and information discrediting Lourenço. Dos Santos had so far witnessed targeted, but unavoidable, attacks on his children, who, except for Zenu and a few younger siblings, no longer lived in Angola. A fall from grace of this nature was one of his alleged fears. Angolan intellectuals had repeatedly commented on how the 2009 corruption trial of former Zambian President Frederick Chiluba, brought by his own party, was his greatest fear. A dos Santos trial will likely never occur, given the political backlash it would cause within elite circles, but his children's trial and its legacy were damaging enough. The year of Chiluba's trial (he was later acquitted) coincided with a deep introspection made within the corridors, affairs and accounts of government by the Presidency. A trusted dos Santos advisor retells how, in 2009, he was called to the Presidency and assigned the mission of undertaking a comprehensive study of the extent of corruption among the elites. "We brought in 100 British auditors, as the President did not want Portuguese or South African auditors, to help with our study. In the end we handed in our report to the President who never shared it with anyone and after 2012 corruption escalated. It is still unclear why this happened when at the time he was so concerned."[7] The dos Santos family fortune was valued at almost $10 billion.

*Changing the Guard*

Behind closed doors, within MPLA meetings, assurances were provided of continuity and "amnesty" for previous governing mishaps and maladministration of public money. Lourenço would have struggled otherwise to have secured the nomination had he been openly targeting the dos Santos faction, which held tremendous influence. However, once he was elected, Lourenço began to build his power base and take the necessary steps to counteract any backlash his policies would release. To achieve this, he changed the security and military chiefs in contravention of one of dos Santos' last decrees determining the permanence of the generals he appointed. In July 2017, in his last months as President, dos Santos passed a decree that would prevent his successor from nominating different security chiefs for eight years (until 2025). This one act was the biggest admission of where power truly lay in Angola: the SCP.

Lourenço's drive to change the security apparatus and strengthen his grip on the SCP was both to ensure that his power base was built outside the meanders of MPLA political wrangling and to safeguard his personal security. Given the fragmentation within the MPLA, the support his predecessor still retained within the party, its chairmanship (until 2018), and the need to sacrifice political heavyweights in the corruption drive, Lourenço had to ensure his own survival. Within the first year, rumours circulated in Luanda that he had suffered two attempts on his life from elements within the security apparatus that managed to enter the presidential compound using the cover of night. Details were sketchy, but generals within the FAA commented that the changeover and schedules of his personal guard altered after these alleged incidents. Unlike the dos Santos era, when coups and threats to the Presidency were either fabricated or enhanced to ensure power grabs by competing security agencies, these alleged attempts were kept secret. The President's brother, General Serqueira, who already held a leading position within the SCP under General Kopelipa, was promoted to deputy chief of the SCP and head of the Presidential Guard. Lourenço began placing close colleagues and friends from his days as an MPLA political commissar in leading roles. Although he made changes in the leadership of the FAA, the Presidential Guard, the intelligence services, police and Ministries of Defence and Interior, he retained its structure and potentially even expanded the role and duplication of intelligence branches within the Presidency.[8]

The first to go were Generals Kopelipa of the SCP and José Maria of Military Intelligence (SISM). Many were replaced by former political commissars of the FAPLA and placed in leading positions of the security apparatus. The most important of these former commissars was Pedro Sebastião, who substituted General Kopelipa as head of the SCP. When Sebastião took over, he proceeded to replace the police and the PIR leadership and began transferring FAA soldiers to the police (who were better paid). In September 2019, an estimated 15,000 soldiers were heading into the police force. Sebastião's appointment was not without controversy. The general was accused of illicit enrichment when he was governor of Zaire province by profiting from the LNG-Angola project in partnership with Escom.[9] Lourenço's appointment of former commissars was justified on loyalty but they held few military credentials. These officers did not command troops in battle nor were they instrumental in strategy, operations and tactics. This represented a significant problem for an army that endured 27 years of war and whose mythology of national pride provided it with an important level of social stature. In this way, he catalysed "the era of the political commissars and the ending of the era of generals".[10] This had two effects: it helped Lourenço place trusted colleagues in roles that would defend his interests and secure his administration but weakened the command structures of these organs because of politicisation. The role of commissars in the military was to supervise political education and ideological indoctrination, as well as to ensure the civilian control of the army. During the civil war and in following the Cuban, Russian and Chinese doctrines, political commissars were a crucial part of command and control of the military. Both UNITA and the MPLA used them as political/ideological counterweights to military commanders. From military fronts and regions to regiments through to the platoon level, commissars continued to operate in the FAA during peacetime but under the title of officers responsible for patriotic education. Others were placed in key roles, such as General Domingos Manuel Junior as Director of the Military Institute (the military academy), among others. The militarisation of the justice system also occurred in tandem with the appointments of Brigadier Manuel Miguel da Costa Aragão as Chief Justice of the Constitutional Court and General Helder Pitta Grós as the country's attorney general.

The President also appointed military chiefs that alone held no political constituency and therefore owed their power to him. The Bakongo generals had no strong political organisation within the MPLA or in the opposition, given the ineptitude of the FNLA party. Key Bakongo security chiefs included General Fernando Miala for intelligence, Pedro Sebastiao of the SCP, and General Marques Mbanza as military inspector. He strategically placed in a leading role General Miala as head of the SINSE intelligence service, whose mandate was redirected towards recovering stolen assets and investigating corruption. Under Miala the SINSE was also strengthened and funded to allow for increased surveillance and training capacity. SINSE was thought to have begun acting as a tool for political punishment, much like the SISM military intelligence office was under General José Maria. Miala was given an opportunity to begin settling scores with former comrades that aided in his indictment and very public trial. The court case brought against General José Maria was interpreted as a revenge trial. He was charged with misappropriating military documents (documents and maps relating to the Cuito Cuanavale war in the 1980s) and insubordination. His defence team claimed that none of the documents were classified and therefore were not a threat to national security. José Maria was sentenced to three years in prison in late 2019.

Five months into his presidency, Lourenço replaced the respected FAA Chief of Staff, General Nunda, with General António Egídio de Sousa Santos "Disciplina", who previously headed the Department of Patriotic Education and had built his military career as a political commissar. This was part of another major shake-up with the retirement of over 100 generals and the replacement of many others. Under Disciplina's tenure, there was general discontentment and demoralisation within the FAA. He was accused of having politicised the army and removed the former UNITA officers that had given the FAA a national character. Disciplina's previous role as head of Patriotic Education of the FAA would inform his approach as its chief general. He primarily acted as the main auditor and enforcer of partisan alignment of the FAA, a role he was expected to continue playing as the new CEMG. Following Nunda's dismissal, Army Chief Lucio Amaral and Generals Apollo and Wambu (all Ovimbundu), as well as Generals Vietnam and Hilario (both Kuanhama), were all either removed or retired. Under Disciplina's command the condition of the FAA as a national army deteriorated. He actively politicised the command of the armed forces and began turning it into an instrument of partisan power.

The partisan deployment of the FAA also set a dangerous precedent. During the VII Extraordinary Congress of the MPLA that deposed dos Santos as Chairman in 2018, the FAA was used alongside the USP, UGP and the police to ensure the safety of party leaders. The USP, allegedly wearing civilian clothes, were the first security cordon around the President while the UGP was stationed on the surrounding streets with the support of the national police and the FAA.[11] Disciplina justified the

FAA's deployment as a preventative measure to avoid incidents that could disrupt and threaten public order during the congress. The move was unconstitutional but fell in line with Disciplina's flagrant disregard of the law when, in 2010, he became the only active-duty general to hold a party membership (as part of the MPLA's central committee).[12] His party position was later suspended in 2011. Lourenço also placed General João Antonio Santana "Lungo", Kopelipa's deputy and head of the SCP intelligence bureau, in Disciplina's position as head of FAA patriotic education. The intelligence office he had headed—the Oficina Secreta da Presidencia—was a mix of operational intelligence, propaganda and patriotic education. Lungo was known as a key political commissar who controlled the media, censored information and spied on social networks under dos Santos.

Having safeguarded control over the security apparatus and redesigned the command structures to ensure loyalty to him personally, much like dos Santos, Lourenço then turned to secure control of the party. His ability to reform was constrained during the first year because of the duality of power of the state Presidency and the party chairmanship under the control of dos Santos. He was unable to fully define the course of action within the party and the economy until he took over as Chairman of the MPLA in September 2018. His predecessor had hoped that by retaining control of the party, he could counteract any reform processes that would put at risk the interests of his family and entourage.

Once in control of the MPLA, Lourenço began shifting power from the dos Santos elites to his own. During the VI Extraordinary Congress, the politburo of the MPLA suffered a massive overhaul. Many historic figures and strong supporters of dos Santos were released from the party's top decision-making organ, including its former vice-president Roberto de Almeida, key generals Antonio dos Santos França Ndalu, Francisco Magalhães Paiva N'Vunda, Higino Carneiro, Kundy Paihama (former Defence Minister), Antonio Paulo Kassoma (former Secretary-General), and long-term Secretary-General Juliao Mateus Paulo "Dino Matrosse", among others. Out of 52 only 27 retained their seats in the Politburo, with the remaining positions filled by different members of the executive, and close allies to Lourenço. In June 2019, during the VII Extraordinary Congress, the President further consolidated his influence by expanding the central committee by 134 new members (now composed of 497 members). With this, he diluted the support still harnessed by dos Santos and brought in a younger generation. In his time as Chairman of the MPLA and President of the country, power had become vertically aligned even with the ruling party becoming more fragmented and internally divided. Powerful members were scrambling to find their place in this new political dispensation. For the first time since 1977, members of the MPLA and civil society began witnessing a new era of political reckoning that injected a sense of fear and persecution into the nomenclature. Fear became displaced. It relocated from the population to the ruling elites that were either dispensable or were too exposed to be salvaged. However, Lourenço understood that this would win him credibility but also expose him to threats from within.

Fears of political reprisal led Lourenço to securitise further. The levels of paranoia and mistrust led to a replication of intelligence services and reporting channels. "Miala reported to the President in the morning, Zé Grande (head of the SIE) reported in the afternoon, Sebastião had to report his own and different findings, as did the Presidential Guard".[13] This hinted at an expansion of the intelligence services. Several measures were adopted to extend surveillance. In May 2020, Luanda's equivalent of a CCTV system came online with 244 cameras placed across the capital. The Centre for Electronic and Public Security (CESP) was inaugurated by the Minister of Interior, Eugenio Laborinho, as an operational support structure to help reinforce public safety. The project was financed by South Korean Eximbank and was meant to apply the technological approach and surveillance strategy used by China. Laborinho established a partnership with the China National Electronics Import and Export Corporation in setting up a coordinating entity called the Integrated Centre for Public Security (CISP).[14] An independent and critical news outlet joked that even the dustbins in Luanda would be watched given the increase in surveillance.[15]

## Fighting Corruption

Paradoxically, while corruption was a strategy to retain control over power and ensure loyalty, it also undermined political stability in

Angola. Different forms of corruption were allowed to spread over decades, including the misuse of public funds, differing layers of extortion for services and security, and rent-seeking efforts to control opportunities for enrichment. These practices became entrenched because of a lack of checks and balances, a pervasive culture of impunity, wide patronage networks and opaque tendering processes in high-risk sectors like oil and mining. Although this system was concentrated in its most brazen form within the political elites of the ruling party, it was also widespread and included law enforcement, public officials, the judiciary, land administration officers, and provincial governments. "The MPLA had a very strong economic machine that was deeply linked to the state. All expenses were covered by the state and all the necessary capital for businesses came from the state".[16] One company in particular was mentioned as an example of this incestuous dynamic. Created in 1992, the management company GEFI (Sociedade de Gestão e Participações Financeiras) transferred state assets to the private realm of MPLA-owned businesses, representing over 60 companies in banking, the hospitality industry, construction, real estate and other sectors.[17] The main objective of GEFI was gratification and the assured enrichment of elites.[18]

Determining the amount of money lost to corruption between 2002 and 2014 was impossible. In an interview with the *Wall Street Journal*, Lourenço estimated that $24 billion had been stolen over the years.[19] The Governor of the Central Bank (BNA) estimated that at least $30 billion dollars were being held abroad.[20] However, the amount lost over two decades to corruption could have been as high as $80 billion.[21] Billions of dollars circulated through numerous ministries and state entities and companies over that period. Tenders were awarded to elite-owned businesses. State funds were used for investments abroad and for the monopoly of industries domestically. Contracts worth over $14 billion were awarded between 2006 and 2016 by dos Santos to companies owned by family members.[22] Many more billions would have been diverted directly or indirectly to party, security and local elites. The opposition claims that billions more were left unaccounted for, pointing out that the strategic reserve of the state alone had accumulated over $93 billion between 2011 and 2014.[23]

In December 2018, Lourenço created a multisector commission composed of SINSE, SIC, the Attorney General's office (PGR), Sonangol and others to determine all the private investments that were made with public funds. Within three months, the commission had reportedly detected deals totalling over $4.7 billion. The President began his crusade with the objective of recovering tens of billions that had been squandered during the post-war years (2002–17). The drive served three main objectives. It was as much about aligning political support and subverting allies of the previous president as about allowing for a relatively cost-free strategy to internationally renew the country's image. The strategy also aimed to bring back enough money to bridge the budget deficit. "Lourenço believed that the repatriation of stolen money would cover the $6 billion budget deficit but that was impossible because government running costs and salaries alone were worth billions. The money wouldn't resolve it. … This was a rentier economy and corruption was the key motor that made it work".[24]

While Lourenço had campaigned on an anti-corruption ticket with the acquiescence of the party, the agreed strategy was towards future corruption rather than retroactive retribution. Before the 2017 elections, a manifesto was drawn up within the party that determined a *tabula rasa* for corruption committed before September 2017 and a commitment to stop any practices thereafter.[25] Prosecutions and asset recovery were never part of that agreement within the MPLA. Once elected, Lourenço faced a crisis of credibility because of the widespread accusations of result tampering. He rapidly understood that if he attacked the symbols of the previous administration's stranglehold on the economy, his popularity rose. It also became clear that, had the new President remained a hostage of the previous regime, he would have been a weaker and more fragile leader. While several officials believed they would be covered by the 2015 amnesty passed by dos Santos, the crimes of which they were accused exceeded the terms of the amnesty.[26] The Attorney General's office clarified in 2018 that embezzlement and other financial crimes that were punishable by 12 to 16 years of jail time were not covered by the amnesty.

Leading the fight against corruption was the Attorney General, General Grós. A specialised corruption bureau was created within his office. However, the attorney general, like other top positions of the state, was politically appointed by the President, which reinforced an existing dynamic that weakened his mandate and held him captive to presidential whims. The judiciary remained constrained by political interference and subservient to "superior orders" from the Presidency.[27] Until 26 December 2018, individuals were given a grace period to voluntarily return stolen assets over $100,000. If they presented themselves to the authorities, they would not face prosecution. This strategy failed to produce results, leading the government to explore more robust measures. In 2018 the government passed the Law for the Coercive Repatriation of Assets after the Law of Voluntary Repatriation was ineffective. The government and the Central Bank came under considerable criticism for not divulging the values so far recuperated. Although the Service Desk for Asset Recovery of the Attorney General's office claimed that almost $4 billion were recovered, no other entity made any pronouncements or allowed for parliamentary oversight.[28] The entire process was shrouded in secrecy, which boded badly for the fundamental need for transparency and accountability that underpinned any anti-corruption drive.

Magistrates, lawyers and the entire judicial system were ill-prepared for the speed with which the corruption cases were being brought to investigation and individuals indicted. Over 5,000 cases had yet to be investigated, with 637 cases investigated in 2018 and several hundred in 2019.[29] Cases ranged from comparatively small amounts stolen to hundreds of millions of dollars. General Higino Carneiro, the former governor of Luanda, was facing corruption charges over the misuse of $115 million while he was Minister of Public Works in 2007. Dos Santos' former spokesperson, Manuel Rabelais, was accused of having stolen $90 million from the Central Bank. Norberto Garcia, a former spokesperson for the MPLA and former director of the Technical Unit for Private Investment, was charged with fraud, money laundering and document falsification regarding the setup of a fake state project worth $50 billion. The former Minister of Industry Joaquim Duarte David was also investigated for having secured a loan from Sonangol worth $731 million to build his cement business in 2003.[30] The first to be convicted was the former Transport Minister Augusto Tomas, sentenced to 14 years in prison (later reduced to eight years) for having diverted funds from the National Council of Transports.

In a move that gained Lourenço respect across the political aisle, Zenu dos Santos and his partner Jean-Claude Bastos de Morais were arrested and accused of theft, embezzlement and money laundering in connection with diverting funds from the Angolan Sovereign Wealth Fund (SWF). They were detained from September 2018 until March 2019. Zenu was additionally charged with having transferred $500 million from the Central Bank to the UK.[31] Bastos de Morais was released in March 2019 after the charges were controversially dropped and his bank accounts were unfrozen. He was thought to have aided government efforts in recovering stolen funds, which, until late 2019, amounted to $2.3 billion in financial assets and $1 billion in physical assets from the SWF. In August 2020, Zenu was sentenced to five years in prison. Former Governor of the Central Bank Valter Filipe received eight years.

Isabel dos Santos was the next member of the dos Santos clan to be targeted. Her downfall was not a surprise. As Africa's first female billionaire, she had accumulated an indecent amount of money from business dealings involving the state. She disputed allegations that any of her businesses profited from her father's connections and denied using public money. Isabel was initially investigated over a $38 million transfer from Sonangol after her dismissal as chairwoman of the national oil company. Once the Luanda Leaks exposé broke out in January 2020, revealing a wide web of corruption, international and local efforts intensified against her. The investigation into Isabel's business dealings, headed by the International Consortium of Investigative Journalists (ICIJ), examined in detail how the first daughter amassed a personal fortune with the aid of Western consultancy firms, accountants and lawyers over two decades. Assets were seized 'preventatively' in response to investigations conducted in Portugal and Angola. As part of this seizure was her stake in the Portuguese telecommunications company NOS, worth $442 million, adding to the $2 billion worth of previously confiscated assets.[32] The Portuguese Securities and Market Commission requested that the energy company GALP, where she held shares, provide clarifications on their internal procedures, a measure that it should have taken years before. Portugal, to a large degree, was complicit in many of the actions that allowed the dos Santos elite to accumulate and store their wealth in the country. By either choosing not to ask where the money was coming from or by giving privileged access to their interests, Portugal benefited significantly from the transfer of wealth.

The state claimed that Isabel owed it $4.9 billion for several business deals that involved state companies, her husband Sindika Dokolo and their Portuguese asset manager Mário Leite da Silva. Her Angolan bank accounts were frozen, as were her interests in BIC and BFA banks, telecom company Unitel, Finstar, Cimangola, ZAP, Continente Angola and Sodiba.[33] By freezing her majority stake in BIC, Isabel was unable to keep crediting Sodiam (a public diamond company) for money loaned and used to finance the purchase of the jewellery company DeGrisogono.[34] Isabel and Dokolo acquired the Swiss company in 2012 for the amount of $200 million, in what was a status purchase. Sodiam invested $147 million for this deal, with money taken from the BIC bank (majority-owned by Isabel).[35] She denied any wrongdoing and denounced judicial actions against her as a political "witch hunt". Immediately she and her husband began working on countering the public relations disaster ahead of them. They began issuing statements on how two decades of investment had provided jobs for 20,000 people. They also began counteracting with lawsuits. Together they had interests in over 400 companies and subsidiaries worldwide.

The recovery of assets faced numerous difficulties. Several of the most corrupt officials invested in listed companies abroad, many of which were in Portugal and Brazil, creating a barrier to their recovery given the imperative of the stability of these companies and the economies of their countries. The repatriation of capital would also severely affect the balance sheets of banks in numerous jurisdictions, which could possibly require legal reinforcement internationally.

For the first time in almost two decades the concentration of wealth fell outside the group with political power. The wealthiest Angolans—mostly linked to the dos Santos Presidency in the form of family and government members—no longer retained political power. These included Kopelipa, Isabel dos Santos, General Leopoldino Fragoso de Nascimento "Dino", Manuel Vicente and others. This created a serious problem within the MPLA, given the design of the political economy of the country. Lourenço had to pragmatically adjust his strategy to allow for political targeting of some elites while protecting others. A former advisor to President dos Santos admitted that "if the anti-corruption drive were real Lourenço wouldn't have a government".[36] Within the MPLA an elite was spared because they were necessary, while others were rehabilitated and protected.[37] When former MPLA spokesperson Norberto Garcia was absolved in April 2020 of any wrongdoing in connection to the fake $50 billion project known as the "Burla Thailandesa", he was rehabilitated and installed as the head of the department of psychological action and information of the SCP.[38] Former vice-president Manuel Vicente was being shielded from Portuguese justice and was thought to still be advising Lourenço on Sonangol reform and the economy.[39] Vicente was charged with bribing a Portuguese prosecutor €763,000 to drop charges of money laundering brought against him in 2011 relating to a €4 million property purchased in Portugal. Lourenço lambasted Portugal publicly in 2018 and demanded that the case be tried in Angola instead. He chose to strain diplomatic relations with Angola's closest trading partner rather than hand over Vicente to face trial in Lisbon. In 2018, Portugal agreed to transfer the case to Angola. Back channels claimed that key generals and allies to the former president, dos Santos, began returning some money and properties and, in that way, remained outside the legal "sweeps".[40]

For the first two years of Lourenço's administration, the business trio (Vicente, Dino and Kopelipa) were relatively unscathed by the anti-corruption drive. In mid-2019, Vicente and Kopelipa began returning their interests in the Banco Economico (which was created after the collapse of the BESA bank) held through their company Lektron SA. The Attorney General's office was investigating how the trio benefited from a $125 million loan from Sonangol to buy a 30.98% stake in the bank.[41] General Dino also held 19.9% of the shares in the bank and equally benefited from a $53.2 million loan from Sonangol. In January 2020, the provincial court of Luanda confiscated some of Dino's assets that were bought with public funds. He had retained positions through the holding company Cochan S.A. in numerous companies including Grupo Kero (supermarkets), Pumangola, Biocom, Medianova and others. In October 2020, Kopelipa and Dino surrendered 837 houses, 271 buildings, yacht clubs and shipyards, and numerous factories associated with the universe of China International Fund (CIF) companies to the state. Billions in reconstruction money that Kopelipa controlled in the SCP had been siphoned off via CIF. The infamous Sam Pa, their partner in

CIF, was jailed in 2015 in China's own anti-graft clampdown. This, however, was just the tip of the iceberg.

The business trio would still have to answer for their role in the collapse of BESA, the Angola subsidiary of Portugal's Banco Espirito Santo (BES), which played a central role in its downfall in 2014. The collapse of BES in Portugal wreaked havoc on the country's financial system and brought generations of family wealth to an end. The threesome, together with other leading MPLA elites, had contributed to the high levels of toxic debt that had been contracted through several of their companies. When the bank collapsed, it had over $5.7 billion in toxic debt. In late 2020 no individual or top executive had yet been jailed for their role in bringing down a financial institution that would greatly impact the economy of Portugal and erase the life savings of hundreds of thousands.

Relationships with large conglomerates revealed the insidious layers of patronage and corruption. One case exposed these clearly. Brazilian construction conglomerate Odebrecht, the largest private employer in Angola, became the focus of a scandalous corruption deal exposing how private interests were infiltrated into the political system. A New York court fined the company $2.6 billion in 2017 after Odebrecht acknowledged it had paid almost $1 billion to politicians, lawmakers, regulators and other middlemen over the course of several years in its dealings with Angola, Mozambique and ten Latin American countries. Part of their construction money was diverted to pay commissions to politicians. An Angolan minister, whose name was omitted during testimony to Brazilian prosecutors, was revealed to have been paid $20 million by Odebrecht.[42] As investigations continued in Angola and elsewhere, the incestuous links between international companies and corrupt public officials would be increasingly exposed. Many within Angola would, however, question the veracity of Lourenço's clampdown. "Those found guilty are tried, convicted and then when they finish their short prison sentences come out to their lush bank accounts".[43] Dos Santos' ex-wife, and former head of the National Agency for Private Investment (ANIP) Maria Luisa Abrantes, echoed this scepticism in a Facebook post. She, like many other elite members, placed this drive as a matter of theatrics and instrumentalised purges. All buildings and assets affiliated to CIF that were handed over by

Kopelipa and Dino, she argued, belonged to the state, and CIF was merely contracted to build them; she further argued that all other companies had been stripped of all capital prior to the handover.[44] Many in Angola agreed that the corruption drive was a stunt with few real consequences for the elites. The attorney general was also accused of tackling corruption in biased ways. Some suggested his links to former dos Santos allies, such as his marriage to General Kopelipa's cousin, may have added personal pressure on him.[45]

In some cases, corruption was occurring during Lourenço's presidency unconstrained by efforts to clean up political access. One case disconcertingly touched upon MPLA royalty. Founding president Agostinho Neto's son-in-law Carlos São Vicente, married to Irene Neto, had over $900 million frozen by Swiss authorities in early September 2020 as part of a money-laundering investigation. This became the largest personal asset freeze in Swiss history.[46] São Vicente had been involved in the government's monopoly to insure the oil industry. As former CEO of the AAA insurance company, he was accused of transferring almost $1 billion between 2012 and 2019 from the company into personal accounts. The story reported a similar pattern of a kleptocratic elite using political office to create webs of shell companies to defraud the state of millions by transferring funds into foreign banks. The amount stolen, one corruption activist highlighted, was similar to the combined annual budget of ten of Angola's provinces that governed 12 million people.[47]

The President was both criticised and congratulated for correcting mistakes as they happened under his watch. Two deals particularly embarrassed his Presidency. In April 2019 the Angolan company Telstar outbid 26 more qualified local and international companies (like MTN) for the fourth telecommunications licence, worth $120 million. Lourenço annulled the tender that had been awarded to a company created in 2018 whose majority shareholder was the Minister for Telecommunications and Technology, General Manuel João Carneiro, and re-opened the bidding process.[48] The second deal reversed was over the $3.6 billion "Ministries Neighbourhood" project in Luanda, which saw the state selling land to itself worth $340 million via a company held by GEFI. The President cancelled the deal after it was exposed by anti-corruption watchdog Maka Angola.[49] Other deals involved his closest advisors. Air Connection Express, a private con-sortium operating domestic flights, benefited from a sovereign guaran-tee for the acquisition of six aircraft purchased in Canada. Key partners included General Serqueira, the President's brother, who owned the SJL aviation company, Frederico Cardoso from the Civil Cabinet of the Presidency, who owned the company Air26, and the head of the SCP General Pedro Sebastião and his company, Mazewa. The deal occurred in early 2018 and by May that same year Lourenço had reversed it.

Lourenço would, however, continue protecting some officials. The most blatant disregard for the law occurred when the President chose to shield his chief of the Civil Cabinet, Edeltrudes Costa, accused of transferring at least $17 million of public funds into his personal account in Banco Angolano Investimento (BAI) when he served dos Santos' Presidency. Costa had already been criticised for the advisory services he provided to Sodiam, the country's sole diamond trading company, for which he was paid $25,000 monthly.[50] There was total silence from the Presidency as Costa remained in his position. Many other deals involving generals, advisors and Lourenço's friends would continuously emerge as stark reminders that the system could not be changed.

### Deepening Recession and Depths of Poverty

When Lourenço took the helm, Angola was deep into an economic recession. The country had been badly affected by the 2014 oil crisis, with the drop in oil prices leading to a loss of billions of dollars a year in revenue. Within seven years, Angola's GDP had fallen from $120 billion in 2013 to $89 billion in 2016, and further decreased to $51.3 billion in 2020. Oil accounted for 80% of government revenue, with a large portion of the remaining 20% coming from foreign loans. In 2019, Angola's oil production stood at 1.4 million barrels per day (bpd), down from 1.9 million bpd at the height of its oil boom in 2008. The country's production was expected to decrease further given the lack of investment and prospect of new projects and wells, a situation that the top five oil companies had already been drawing attention to.[51] The Finance Ministry estimated that production would decrease as much as 36% by 2023.

Protecting the oil industry naturally became a priority for the new government. A month into his Presidency, Lourenço met with the top oil companies (Chevron, BP, Total, Exxon, Eni and Statoil) and created a task force to help define the future of the industry. As a result of their work, the government began introducing legal reforms in 2018 and further restructuring Sonangol. Several of these reforms included the creation of a national concessionaire, the National Agency for Petroleum, Gas and Biofuels (ANPG); a simplification of the control mechanism for oil-related tenders and procurement; the establishment of a new fiscal regime for marginal fields development; and a law regulating national gas exploration, among others. ANPG began managing bids for new oil concessions and production-sharing arrangements, a responsibility previously held by Sonangol.[52] These reforms were greatly welcomed by the industry and injected a sense of reliability into a partnership that had become somewhat strained under the previous administration. In October, ANPG launched the public tender of ten blocks, with an additional 40 blocks due for auctioning by 2025.[53] Plans also included the construction of four refineries, aimed at decreasing the exorbitant costs of fuel imports. Government imports of oil derivatives cost between $150 and $170 million a month, the result of a monopoly held by key dos Santos allies.[54] The projected refineries were an important step but they are only profitable if they can produce between 200,000 and 400,000 bpd. In 2019, Angola's domestic market consumed 100,000 bpd, which required Angola to export in the region and directly compete with South Africa, Nigeria and Côte d'Ivoire. All of these plans were also contingent on the ability of the government to inject accountability and transparency into a sector that had been greatly appropriated for illicit gains.

This restructuring also aimed to sanitise the country's international image, hoping to gain access to new sources of capital and investment. Efforts towards macroeconomic stability were pushed forward with reforms intended to cut costs and consolidate public finances. These reforms were enacted in coordination with the International Monetary Fund (IMF) after Angola applied to receive a total loan of $3.7 billion from the fund. The 36-month Extended Arrangement under the Extended Fund Facility began in December 2018 and was aimed at helping Angola buffer itself against volatile oil prices, stymied growth and its current account deficit.

A year into the programme, the government had managed to implement several measures and meet the programme's benchmarks through increased exchange rate flexibility, structural reforms (privatisation and governance reforms to diversify the economy), fiscal consolidation (non-oil revenue mobilisation and increased taxes), prudent debt policies and appropriate monetary policies (reducing inflation).[55] However, it faced several internal and external risks. Some of the external factors revolved around lower oil prices, the impact of waning global growth, tighter market access restrictions, etc. Internally, Angola had to deal with its declining oil production, the need to cut spending on an overinflated security apparatus and the social impact of its reforms on deepening levels of poverty. This, coupled with the inability of the government to respond to the socio-economic needs of the most vulnerable due to lack of capacity, infrastructure and disengagement with the population, had already become a threat to stability before the crises of 2020.

Diversification of the economy and the privatisation of parastatals were key to economic revival. Over 195 state-owned enterprises (SOEs) were earmarked for privatisation, including the national airline TAAG, the diamond company Endiama, several banks, and Angola Telecom. This aimed to raise money, attract private investment, and drive efficiency gains.[56] While the new privatisation law imposed restrictions on who could be involved in purchase bids, the entire process was handled by the same political elites that benefited from opaque dealings and preferential treatment. Many of these assets were deeply indebted, had big workforces and inefficient management structures and operated in a country that retained many layers of political bureaucracy. Selling off SOEs was, therefore, going to be racked with difficulties in 2019, a prospect that increased exponentially in 2020. The government attempted to accelerate the sell-off of loss-making parastatals during the pandemic, hoping to bring in much-needed cash. However, of the 195 companies planned for privatisation by 2022, only 14 had been sold by the end of 2020.[57]

Generating non-oil revenues was a major part of the IMF's intervention. To achieve this, several taxes were introduced and several subsidies eliminated. The immediate impact of these measures was greater hardship for the working population. The Angolan middle class had, for the first time, started to feel the impact of the recession in a way that limited their purchasing power. Subsidies were a huge part of their benefits (housing, transport etc.). The slashing of these and other expenditure control measures led to an increase in water and electricity costs, and inflated food prices. In late 2019, the government introduced a 14% VAT tax aimed at generating more revenue for the state in order to balance its accounts. However, since 2014 the average Angolan had lost an estimated 43% of their purchasing power which, coupled with rising inflation and increased taxes, created an unsustainable austerity effect on populations that had no financial recourse.[58] A few days after the tax was introduced, the Minister of Finance, Archer Mangueira, resigned after facing heavy criticism for failing to explain how it was going to be implemented and for mismanaging this move in the context of latent social convulsion. The poor were once again the most sacrificed. The minimum wage, roughly $50 (25 million Kz) a month, was insufficient to cover the most basic living costs of the average Angolan. In 2017, a bag of chicken cost 3,000 Kz ($6) and in 2019 that rose to 9,000 Kz ($18). Before the 14% VAT tax was introduced, a box of fish cost 15,000 Kz ($32) and afterwards it cost 25,000 Kz ($54). "The mistake made by the government was to bring the poor into the discussion".[59] Economists argued that too many reforms (fiscal, monetary, exchange) were being implemented at the same time which had an impact across Angolan society and was plunging the population into deeper levels of poverty without support mechanisms like subsidies and programmes to combat unemployment.[60] Austerity was even felt within the intelligence services and the military. "In 2018 we had over 2,500 suicides, even in the military barracks, because people became desperate."[61] Poverty that had been relatively cordoned off from downtown Luanda to uphold a façade of modernity became increasingly visible. The misery and desolation of the urban populations were widespread and commented on by elites, security agents, civil society, intellectuals and the opposition. For once, it became difficult to deny the manifest effects of distorted growth.

*Social Tensions and Austerity*

The perceived and real unfairness of a political and economic system that had kept the majority of its citizens in poverty while allowing others privileged access to capital, opportunities and resources had created a situation of generalised public anger. In 2019, latent social tension was felt throughout the capital Luanda. Citizens were acutely aware of the long-term inability of the government to ameliorate their suffering and were rapidly reaching breaking point with regard to their livelihood strategies. The risk of a social convulsion was very real but was being tempered by the support Lourenço's anti-corruption drive had gained. Despite this, people's patience was continuously being tested with constant extravagant displays of wealth by the elites,[62] commonly referred to as "*marimbondos*". *Marimbondos* are wasp-like insects whose sting is extremely painful. They are considered a pest in Angola and this became the popular term used to show disdain for the elites. As much-needed economic reforms were implemented and the levels of austerity rose, so too did the frustration against the *marimbondos* and the government.

Transforming the country's socio-economic fabric and the political system that created structural impediments to diversified pro-poor development was a difficult task. Lourenço may have had some intention to alleviate the public suffering and reform the system but his capacity was constrained by the system itself and the people still operating it. The dimension of the problem evaded quick fixes. Angola continued to rank 149th out of 188 countries in the UN Human Development Index (HDI). In early 2020, the National Statistics Institute (INE) revealed how over 12 million Angolans survived on 500 Kz a day (equivalent to $0.09), with the majority living in rural areas, particularly the provinces of Cunene, Huila, Kuando Kubango and Namibe.[63] This number is expected to rise exponentially after the catastrophic effects of the Covid pandemic. Within a year, the number of poor in Angola had risen by over a million (to a total of 13.19 million people) in 2020, continuing on an upward spiral with future projections reaching 17 million in poverty by 2030.[64]

Fears of social convulsion over harsh economic conditions during the 2015 recession had led dos Santos to invest over €1.3 billion in measures to ensure the import and affordability of basic foodstuffs (*cesta basica*) including rice, corn and wheat flour, palm oil, beans and sugar (Roque 2020). Efforts were focused on ensuring that the general population could still access these products through regulatory measures on the import market and distribution networks. Advisors claim that dos Santos invested this amount of money to ensure that the country would remain stable until the 2017 elections and the presidential succession.[65] While Lourenço's government planned, with World Bank assistance, to begin operating a cash-transfer programme to mitigate the effects of austerity on the poorest, no relief materialised for the first two years. Youth unemployment stood at 53%, with youth making up two-thirds of the Angolan population. To address this, the government defined an Action Plan for the Promotion of Employment (PAPE), to fulfil an MPLA election promise. PAPE was meant to generate jobs for 250,000 youths until 2021 by launching a micro-credit programme and distributing professional kits, and conducting extensive skills training in Luanda, Zaire, Kwanza-Norte and Bie. It would cost the government $50 million. In mid-2020, the government approved an Integrated Plan for the Acceleration of Agriculture and Fishing (Plano Integrado de Acceleração da Agricultura e Pesca Familiar, or PIAAPE), which was the first time a programme had been launched to deal with agriculture. In a country where 70% of the rural areas are mainly dedicated to subsistence farming, this seemed like a serious oversight. While hailed as a good move, the programme faced the difficulties of not having a system for accessible micro-credits, lacking stable land tenure procedures, and depending on ministries that lacked human resources and were deeply corrupt. PIAAPE, like PAPE and other programmes, revealed noble intentions, but the system itself was broken and reforming it would be politically costly.

In order to fulfil another election promise, the government had hoped to lift over 3 million people out of extreme poverty by 2022, but it faced insurmountable difficulties. The elites had completely hijacked the economy's structure, and untangling that mess of patronage, nepotism, and favouritism would entail serious political reform, not just a corruption clean-up. Access to loans, job markets, and business opportunities would be conditioned by this. In addition to the systemic partisanship through MPLA specialist committees, lack of skills training to counter the need for foreign technical know-how, and a reduced employment market that was primarily urban-focused, would also condition any steps in the right direction. Job creation also required both private and public investment, which, given the pre-coronavirus economic setting, and the post-coronavirus global outlook, would make this even harder to achieve.

Parts of the country had reached such levels of vulnerability that any development had to be preempted by sustained emergency aid to stabilise them first. From 2015 to 2020, Angola, like much of southern Africa, had been facing a massive drought and populations were struggling to farm. Extreme climatic conditions had plunged entire communities into distressing levels of hunger and malnutrition. In the south, years of consecutive drought and inadequate land policies coupled with land grabs and the diversion of water sources placed millions at risk of starvation.[66] In 2019, UNICEF alerted that at least 2.3 million people were at high risk of malnutrition. Civil society and the church had been highlighting this risk in the provinces of Namibe, Cunene, Huila, Kuando Kubango and parts of Moxico for the last decade.[67]

As the IMF reforms were being implemented, the government tried to mitigate some of the risks of the austerity measures with surgical interventions in the provinces. It launched an Integrated Programme for Municipal Intervention (PIIM) to provide key development infrastructure, 4,000 schools and 200 health centres across the 164 municipalities in all 18 provinces. The programme would cost $2 billion and would run from November 2019 to August 2020. By May 2020, the government had allocated 20 billion Kz to these projects (an estimated $33.9 million). The PIIM also aimed to provide the necessary conditions to allow municipalities to curb urban migration by supporting agricultural production and reintegrating ex-combatants. The PIIM was an apparent step towards administrative decentralisation. It presupposed that municipal authorities could absorb the funds, allocate them correctly after conducting a needs assessment and manage priorities and resources (human, financial and physical) in accountable and transparent ways. Under dos Santos, a similar programme had existed as an institutional predecessor to PIIM. The Integrated Municipal Programme for Rural Development and to Combat Poverty (PMIDRCP), managed by close collaborator Rosa Pacavira, had achieved few tangible results. Launched in 2010, the PMIDRCP aimed to reach 15 million Angolans. Its purpose was to lower poverty indices, improve people's lives, implement infrastructure and provide access to public services. The programme, however, failed to translate into the general improvement of rural populations' lives and livelihoods and became a vehicle for decentralised patronage instead. The opposition claimed that the PIIM was an election strategy of the MPLA to win support ahead of the local elections. The MPLA had avoided conducting municipal elections since the end of the war. The MPLA had promised to schedule local polls but continuously postponed them over the last decade. Delays were justified on bureaucratic, financial and legal grounds. MPLA proposals in parliament, defining the legal instruments for the holding of local elections, aimed to regulate and control the local levels while the opposition aimed to create distance between the central government and the municipalities. For decades UNITA had lobbied for a constitutional review aimed at empowering local governments with financial autonomy and the direct election of governors. Municipal elections would undoubtedly benefit the opposition that had maintained its support base in the provinces and the rural areas.[68] Given the heightened social tension arising from the economic crisis, the ruling party was fearful of defeats in more than eight of the 18 provinces where the opposition rallied significant constituent support. In 2019–20, the majority of Angolans (75%) considered that the government was doing a poor job on unemployment, improving living standards of the poor, and other economic issues.[69] This negative reaction to the economic situation bodes ill for the MLPA's chances of electoral victory in 2022.

*Political Opening and Reconciliation*

For decades, political reform in Angola has been whitewashed with practices of illiberal democracy and the puppeteering of parliament and the "free press". Laws that were passed only centralised power further, creating an institutional framework that denied citizens any participation. It also narrowed the space for the opposition and civil society. While Lourenço did not come in as a reformer of the political system but of the economy, several symbolic gestures earned him the respect of the opposition. He was credited with allowing for the political opening that the opposition, civil society and the population more broadly had hoped for since the end of the war. The country had in the first two years of his tenure become freer and less repressive. He established a dialogue with civil society and the youth. His meeting with key objectors like Luaty Beirão (who came to epitomise the youths' struggle against dos Santos) and other NGOs and civil society leaders marked a sharp turn away from dos Santos' securitised handling of activists. Lourenço presented key writers, activists and prominent members of society with national awards honouring them for their commitment to the country and their work. The majority of those selected were vocal critics of the MPLA and the dos Santos regime. In November 2019, the President handed out 70 awards, divided among three categories of commendations (the Order of Independence, the Order of Bravery and Social Merit, and the Order of Civic Merit) to individuals and institutions for "their outstanding contributions as patriots and Angolans who bravely fought against colonialism, for independence, and the construction of the Angolan state". Among those awarded was anti-corruption activist Rafael Marques de Morais, known for exposing the highest levels of corruption in government and one of the elite's most severe critics.

In another symbolically important move, Lourenço chose to launch an initiative to help communities heal from decades of war. Reconciliation had in the past remained an elusive and amnestied process. Since the first peace agreement in 1991, amnesties for crimes committed during the conflict were continuously renewed with the subsequent accords in 1994 and 2002. This served to appease the military and the political leadership of both the MPLA and UNITA but did nothing for the millions of civilians who suffered at the hands of both armies. The nature of the war left deep and enduring scars in Angolan society. Atrocities were committed on all sides against each other and from within. Historical revisionism and victors' justice had denied millions an important portion of their history by failing to recognise legitimate grievances and their ability to contest versions of events. Recent debate among the military elites, and subsequent publications, around the Cuito Cuanavale war had reactivated competing accounts of key battlegrounds. It also initiated a process of fact-finding for younger generations. In August 2019, the Commission to Memorialise the Victims of the Conflict was launched by Justice and Human Rights Minister Francisco Queiroz. The commission was composed of all political parties represented in parliament, the church, civil society, and the Ministries of Justice, Interior, and Youth. It aimed to create forums for national and provincial discussions about the past. It was meant to allow for the burial of victims and end with the construction of a memorial. This commission became an important step but was insufficient in addressing the need for justice, truth-telling, reparations, and correcting historical injustice. For Angolans to heal, so much more needed to be done, particularly as inequality was not only a socio-economic phenomenon but also political, historical, and partisan.

In another unexpected move, the government allowed for the burial of UNITA's founder and wartime leader Jonas Savimbi in June 2019. After 17 years, Savimbi was given a dignified and very public burial by his family and supporters in his village in Lopitanga in the province of Bie. UNITA's leadership had requested that the DNA of the remains be analysed and verified by different laboratories, with experts sent from South Africa and Portugal. The funeral was attended by 20 of Savimbi's children, and tens of thousands of party members and historical friends (politicians and military officers from Portugal and South Africa). The burial of key leaders killed in combat remained an important issue for UNITA, which began preparing ceremonies for their senior leaders killed during the 1992 Halloween Massacre in Luanda. The closure provided by these political gestures was significant, especially for UNITA, because the 1992 massacre in Luanda and the killing of Jonas Savimbi were two of the most traumatic events in the history of the movement, crystallised in the memories of the leadership and millions of supporters.

In March 2021, just 18 months before elections, Lourenço announced a constitutional review process aimed at enhancing the power of parliament, eliminating impediments to the holding of municipal elections and guaranteeing the Central Bank's independence.[70] The announcement came weeks after the Cafunfu massacre in Lunda Norte and amid a rising wave of police aggression, latent social tensions and economic despair. The opposition initially welcomed the announcement but soon began contesting the proposed changes. This constitutional review was, in their opinion, clearly aimed at eliminating political adversaries. Two articles, in particular, were aimed at invalidating the running of the opposition's strongest leaders, UNITA's new

President, Adalberto da Costa Júnior, and PRA-JA's Abel Chivukuvuku, on the basis that presidential candidates who had renounced their parliamentary seat in the past were disqualified (Chivukuvuku), as were those who had held dual nationality in the decade preceding their candidacy (da Costa Júnior).[71] The MPLA was playing a very dangerous game by legally blocking UNITA from running. It seemed like a last desperate attempt. Ruling elites and intelligence services had already begun an ugly political campaign of defamation, including an alleged attempt by SINSE to force testimony accusing UNITA's leader of sexual crimes against minors.[72] SINSE and the Presidency's intelligence service GAPI were also thought to be the instigators of a campaign that portrayed UNITA's leader as racially and linguistically non-Bantu.[73] More strategic was the suggestion that if UNITA or the opposition proceeded to revise the proposed amendment, it would delay the process resulting in national polls being pushed to 2024 rather than 2022. The strategy was, as expected, brilliant and Machiavellian. Da Costa Júnior was *mestiço*, urban, young, eloquent and popular with the youth. For the MPLA, he was a real threat because he was not easily portrayed as the leader of a "tribalist and backward African party". As explained throughout this book, political threats were always translated into security threats which in the context of a wounded and financially constrained MPLA, struggling to taper over the deepening levels of poverty and social frustration, meant that the last year of Lourenço's mandate had the potential of seeing a surge in securitisation strategies, utterances and actions. The signs of that perception of danger being escalated were clear.

In a surprising move, President Lourenço dismissed the head of the SCP, General Pedro Sebastião, on 31 May 2021 and replaced him with hardliner General Francisco Pereira Furtado. The move came after an officer of the SCP was caught carrying millions in foreign currency, a scandal that became known as "Operation Crab", which instituted a broad investigation into the financial dealings of FAA officers. General Furtado's reputation for heavy-handedness led some within the FAA to question if his nomination was a strategy to deflect from deep internal MPLA fissures capable of threatening Lourenço, rather than a corruption purge.[74] Trained in Cuba and Russia in his FAPLA days, and commanding several military regions during the war, Furtado was also involved in the commission overseeing the 2002 Luena accords and the 2006 Cabinda agreement. From 2006 to 2010, he served as Chief of General Staff of the FAA and was deeply unpopular. In 2011 Furtado had $40 million confiscated from a bank account in Cape Verde, where he was born, which SISM claimed were from FAA budgets and the operational funds of the army.[75] He was viewed as a corrupt general who came to substitute another corrupt general.

Swept away in this clean-up were seven other SCP senior leaders, and, more importantly, the head of military intelligence (SISM). General Apolinario was replaced by General João Pereira Massano. It was clear not only that Lourenço was unable to change the securitisation infrastructure, but also that his administration was knee-deep in corruption. His popularity plummeted daily, as socio-economic hardship increased among the masses. Many within the services[76] claimed that the tensions felt were similar to those during the 1992 electoral debacle, when uncertainty and fear of political destitution and of being overrun by rapidly shifting events had led the Presidency to securitise further and unite after a premeditated massacre of the opposition. Lourenço could opt for a different route, but his options for existential survival were rapidly decreasing.

While João Lourenço had inherited a difficult situation, a country plunged into a state of chaos due to decades of corruption, securitisation, socially disengaged governance, poverty and inequality, he made several mistakes during his initial years. He chose to reform the economic system while maintaining many of the people who had been the architects and enforcers of the old system. He allowed practices that had torpedoed sustainable and transparent development to continue. He also benefited politically from previous mistakes to entrench his grip on power. Lourenço securitised further and initiated an era of greater surveillance and the politicisation of the security forces, further delaying the much-needed process of defence transformation. The President's attempts at reform were in many ways conditioned by the exoskeleton of securitisation and the shadow government with which he governed that both protected him and kept him from being able to bring about genuine change. Securitisation under Lourenço was undoubtedly a continuation policy from the dos Santos era—a protection against external and popular threats—but was also a tool used to entrench power against MPLA factionalism. Despite the intention to reform, Lourenço was left managing decline rather than resetting Angola's economic and political path. Contestation was rising under Lourenço's tenure, making the securitisation policy an assured avenue for the survival of his administration. However, all of these constraining and debilitating dynamics would pale compared to the twin accelerants of the Covid-19 pandemic and the drop in oil prices. What would transpire would be a Presidency limping along a difficult road without an end in sight. As elections approached in 2022, Lourenço would be facing an emboldened opposition and a combative public that had reached the limits of the suffering it was prepared to endure.

6

# THE TIME OF MONSTERS

## ANGOLA'S RESPONSE TO COVID-19

Around the world, metaphors of war were uttered by presidents and their ministers in tackling the Covid-19 pandemic. Political polarities, policy hesitations, sprawling lockdowns, and emergency measures were enacted by political actors, who securitised their responses to a health crisis. The world had changed overnight, but the effects of this securitisation had yet to be fully grasped. As "the old world (wa)s dying, and the new world struggle(d) to be born: now (wa)s the time of monsters",[1] the world faced an uncertain future. Across the constellation of actions, motivations and securitising actors, the response to Covid-19 brought about a sense of legitimacy to securitisation. It defined an objective existential threat, determined a morally legitimate referent object, and defined an appropriate security response (Floyd 2011).

Nevertheless, the costs of securitisation were rapidly felt through the economic disaster it unleashed in most countries, and the difficult trade-off of other values such as liberty and community empowerment. Governments globally used emergency procedures to curb freedoms while some enacted unrelated authoritarian measures. In pre-existing securitised countries and polities, this moment was exacerbated by the existing fragilities brought about by the enduring effects of a policy that bred inequality and fragmented national communities.

While security discourses were about alternative futures and counterfactuals (Buzan et al. 1998: 32), securitisation in Angola was also a legacy of the past and the projection of fear and instability. However, Covid-19 positioned Angola squarely in its present. At once, the country was faced with the inadequacies of a system meant to keep people and livelihoods safe and serve the actors it was morally induced to protect. Covid-19 immediately placed importance on the population as they became the referent object for the first time. The system had not been built to protect the state or the population but the Presidency. The inconsistencies in mission, objective, and strategies would expose the fragilities of this policy and the dangers of maintaining the status quo. Covid-19 threatened to unleash a level of disorder the Angolan securitised state was unprepared for, especially among already vulnerable populations. The present was unrefined, raw and brutal. It was one of "abandonment, fear and misery".[2] Covid-19 would bring death to areas where death was commonplace. The difference this time was the widespread anger, hunger and despair fuelling a rise in contestation and dissent. Deprivation, a collapsed healthcare system, popular disillusion, an expanding humanitarian crisis, and empty state coffers were rapidly becoming real threats to national security.

As the old world was dying and the new world of Covid-19 emerged, Angola stood at a crossroads. It could potentially unravel, or it could use the moment to desecuritise. A "business as usual" approach would no longer suitably address a situation beyond the immediate control of the Presidency. Securitisation had deepened too many fault lines. It impacted the functioning of the state. It appropriated the process of defining a national identity. It politicised fear and instrumentalised poverty. It also entrenched exclusionary dynamics because it created autonomous realms between sovereign power and the people themselves. As a result, the value of desecuritising these states became even more urgent. If securitisation occurred in a field of struggles (Balzaq 2011), desecuritisation would occur within a context of unpredictable, unstable and contested fields of social mobilisation. Enemies would need to be deconstructed, power renegotiated, and existential threats replaced by recognised resistance.

*Death of the Old World? Covid-19 and the Oil Collapse*

Angola's securitised state was prepared to counter different types of enemies. Rebels attempting to launch a guerrilla war would be met with counterinsurgency strategies and the might of a depleted but vast army. Criminals were subdued and killed on the street by the amassed and militarised police force. Real or imagined plans for popular protests that could lead to social insurrection were diffused by the intelligence services and special security units. Where money and the promise of influence and patronage were ineffective, force, intimidation and brutality were applied. A seemingly invincible system was unable to defeat an invisible enemy, embedded throughout society, levelling its victims across the socio-economic divide, camouflaged and undetectable, with a great capacity for destructive longevity. The coronavirus would reach Angola, imported from abroad, in late March 2020. The securitised state responded, as did many countries globally, with a securitised response. War rhetoric, emergency powers, the curbing of liberties, the deployment of the military and police, and increased surveillance characterised both democratic and autocratic countries' responses. The Covid-19 pandemic became an existential threat that propelled governments to centralise powers and justify drastic measures by shifting politics away from the normal to the emergency. This was perhaps the single most defining moment, globally, of securitisation of an entire generation. It was unprecedented in its dimension but also the menacing tone shifted a health issue into a threat against the state, society and the nation's cohesion.

Initially, citizens across the globe accepted the securitised measures and radical confinement. They were moved by the patriotic calls of their leaders to mobilise for "war". But ideology, misinformation and political manoeuvrings from competing actors began to wither away the unified stance initially achieved. Protests erupted because of the repressive "big government" measures, and everywhere deconfinement occurred outside the control of the state. Many were unable to comply with government directives because of the extreme threat of hunger, state inaction and incompetence. Others reacted against the curbing of civil liberties. The unmeasured desire for normalisation led societies to defy reason, scientific evidence and solidarity. Mass securitisation unleashed a backlash that, while ill-informed and certainly dangerous given the dimensions of the pandemic, created an opportunity to rethink securitisation. Like the responses to Ebola and HIV/AIDS, the militarisation of a public health emergency once again removed the problem from structural factors (Elbe 2006; McInnes and Rushton 2013). Development, poverty, and underfunding in services were sidelined by the employment of securitised responses and the security forces sent to enforce them. Leadership, messaging and national cohesion were, together with protective gear, medication, hospital space and staff, the most dramatic levelling deficit across the globe.

President Lourenço declared a state of emergency on 26 March 2020 in an attempt to impose a general quarantine to stop the spread of the coronavirus. Masked ministers determined security and economic measures meant to infuse some order. Borders were shut, public gatherings forbidden, schools closed, masks made mandatory and the population placed in lockdown. Two months later the state of emergency was scaled down to a state of calamity, easing some restrictions. By June, Angola had only registered four deaths and 69 infections although testing was scant and had mostly been targeted at individuals coming from abroad. The FAA were deployed in Luanda, patrolling the capital and enforcing the state of emergency. The military and the police also began enforcing a curfew in the provinces. The military's logistics and personnel provided a more effective and easily coordinated effort during the initial lockdown. Military flights distributed aid and supplies to the provinces. FAA personnel bolstered the police patrols in critical areas of the country. However, the government came under widespread criticism by civil society for the heavy-handed approach of the security forces and their lack of "solutions for the people that had no food".[3] Many in the *musseques* and elsewhere chose to defy the restrictions preferring to die of the disease than to die of starvation as they continued to circulate through the cities searching for some form of income. By June, the police had arrested over 15,000 people for breaching restrictions and seized 10,000 vehicles and 20,000 motorbikes.[4] The militarised approach to a public health emergency only further revealed the government's lack of political and social policies in its arsenal.

The President placed his top security chief General Pedro Sebastião of the SCP at the head of the intersectoral commission, replacing health minister Silvia Lutucuta who had initially managed the effort. Sebastião and State Minister for Social Issues Carolina Cerqueira jointly coordinated the government's response. The FAA's logistics and coordination were chosen over ineffective and overly bureaucratised ministries. It meant to decrease the possibility of corruption of civilian administrators handling the crisis without a counterbalance. The police and health officials monitored movement between provinces through the health cordons that had been imposed countrywide. Their ineffectiveness allowed the virus to spread from Luanda to 14 of the 18 provinces in seven months. The nursing and police teams monitoring the health cordons lacked biosafety material, were unable to check all passengers for fever at all times and were unable to track vehicles effectively.[5] Mistakes were made across the board due to incapacity and systemic failures. Two weeks into the state of emergency, the President staged a major government shake-up by replacing 17 ministers and 24 secretaries of state (equivalent to deputy ministers) reducing executive portfolios from 28 to 21. This led to the creation of five "super-ministries" that merged several executive portfolios.[6] The government justified this move as a need to cut spending. The reshuffle was interpreted as Lourenço's need to politically align allies rather than seek qualified individuals to help define a crisis response and a recovery plan (Roque 2020).

Lourenço's Presidency was facing a challenge that it was not remotely prepared to tackle. Decades of underfunding, understaffing, corruption, maladministration, and neglect had left the healthcare service in a state of turmoil. Gutted by corruption and austerity, the system would easily be overwhelmed. Containment and prevention had to be prioritised because the healthcare system could not adequately respond. Preventable and treatable diseases like malaria, diarrhoea and pneumonia remained major causes of death among small children. Hospitals lacked appropriate facilities, medical supplies were insufficient, and healthcare workers remained underpaid or lacked training. The country had roughly two doctors per 10,000 inhabitants and a total of 110 intensive care beds in the public healthcare system. While Luanda was in a difficult situation, the provinces were worse off. In 2011 over 40% of doctors were stationed in Luanda (which represented 24% of the population) to the detriment of rural areas. The healthcare system had become decentralised in peacetime with a greater focus on developing municipal centres, yet little was done to address the inadequacies and limitations of the system. In Huambo, with over 2.5 million inhabitants, hospitals only had three ventilators. Doctors shied away from treating Covid-19 patients, lacking personal protective equipment (PPE). In some provincial hospitals, the lack of PPE led to absurd situations. In the main hospital in Moxico, ten masks were distributed weekly to protect more than 30 doctors.[7] Information was restricted and doctors who revealed numbers of patients, death rates and difficulties within the health system were punished.[8]

The danger of the spread of the virus being underestimated and underreported was real given past experiences and the lack of general testing. A game of illusions and deniability was always part of the system. In 2015–16 a yellow fever outbreak was greatly mismanaged by authorities. On a single day—14 March 2016—a doctor inside the paediatric ward of the Samba Hospital in Luanda reported the deaths of 27 children due to the outbreak.[9] The opposition accused the government of deflating the numbers of deaths claiming that in November 2015 alone, four cemeteries in Luanda had registered 8,339 deaths.[10] Seven months later, the Angolan health ministry reported that over the course of six months it had 2,954 confirmed cases and only 328 deaths. The public health response was severely criticised by civil society and the opposition, who drew attention to the lack of investment in the healthcare system. In 2016 the Health Ministry operated with a budget of $136 million. By 2020 this number had marginally risen to 9 billion Kz (equivalent to $154 million). Health spending was allocated to public health services, to the detriment of maternity care, ambulance services and medical centres. With the state unable to provide solutions, strategies mushroomed across the health sector that put many at risk. Hospitals and their staff became part of the corruption networks, demanding that patients and family members pay them extra for services while sending them to purchase medication. Ways to profit from the tragedy of a broken public health system emerged with schemes such as purchasing blood bags for over 30,000 Kz (equivalent to $51) with blood donors being called upon regularly to save lives and make money.[11] Existing systemic problems would inevitably inform any response to the coronavirus emergency.

Treatable diseases like malaria continue to kill large numbers in Angola. From January to May 2020, Angola registered over 2 million cases and 2,548 deaths from malaria (up from 460 cases in the same timeframe a year earlier). The National Doctors Syndicate (SINMEA) came out in June, criticising the inaction and underfunding of initiatives to help address preventable diseases in Angola. By July, 5,767 people had died of malaria (32 daily), a number far superior to that of Covid-19. Seven months after the initial lockdown, Angola was faring badly in comparison to its neighbours. Poorer countries were managing to tackle their coronavirus outbreaks in a way that eclipsed Angola's efforts. While South Africa had been devastated by its first wave, ranking fifth in the world registering 650,000 cases by mid-2020, its recovery rate was 89%, a rate only surpassed by the DRC (94%), Zambia (93%), and Madagascar (91%). With 3,569 cases and 139 deaths by mid-September, Angola's recovery rate in contrast stood at 37% while its death rate of 4% was far higher than the continental average of 2.4%. The African Centres for Disease Control and Prevention (CDC) was unable to explain the mortality discrepancies in countries like Angola, Chad, Liberia, Nigeria, Egypt and Libya, with few common denominators across those states.[12] Moreover, each Covid-19 patient cost the Angolan state 16 million Kz (€23,500), making this response far costlier than any action ever taken to address fatal diseases in the country. Despite this, civil society began calling for the government to revise its biosecurity measures and the medication being given to patients.[13]

It would take months for authorities in Angola to consider community transmission of the coronavirus even as death rates in hospitals rose and were attributed to existing diseases. Testing was insufficient, which partly accounted for the low number of positive cases. Inaccurate tests repeatedly gave negative results when all symptoms pointed to the coronavirus, even among members of the military who had greater access to testing.[14] The government had purchased five laboratories from the Chinese company BGI, worth $6 million, to increase its testing capacity, and labs were expected to be placed in the border provinces of Lunda Norte and Uige and the most populous cities of Huambo and Luanda.[15] Until the arrival of these laboratories, transmission would continue rapidly, especially in Luanda. A former health minister anonymously stated to a Portuguese paper that "without tests the population could be falling victim to a dangerous manipulation of data."[16] The health minister predicted that Luanda could have 45,000 cases by September 2020, a potentially serious underestimate given the extreme overcrowding of the urban and peri-urban areas, the lack of sanitation and services, and the millions of day-wage labourers who were not able to socially distance. By October, several government members were infected, including the Presidents of the Constitutional and Supreme Courts, the Ministers of Justice, Interior and Commerce, and the head of the Civil Cabinet of the Presidency; the Governor of Uige and the Deputy Attorney General would not survive. Much-needed doctors would also begin to die, averaging one a month. In March 2021, a year into the pandemic, Angola had only registered 21,500 total infections and 522 deaths, numbers that reflect poor testing capacities and disengagement from the responsibility to monitor infection rates and address healthcare fragilities across the country.

The government's pandemic response strategy was developed with foreign assistance in mind.[17] It followed previous humanitarian responses, delegating care and funding to external partners. The European Union committed $12 million, while the US provided over $3.5 million for testing supplies and assistance to vulnerable populations and training programmes for contact tracing. Qatar, Portugal and others donated personal protective equipment (PPE). The World Bank made $15 million available for urgent health sector response and made further funds accessible for the long-term strengthening of the healthcare system and activities for socio-economic development. UNICEF responded by helping the government with cash transfers, infection prevention, nutrition care, education support and community engagement. The government invited 240 Cuban doctors into Angola in April to help address the shortage of medical staff. The doctors would be placed in all the 164 municipalities. The cost of such a measure was financially unsustainable, given that it had cost $71.3 million at the signing of the contract without any clarity on what it would cost for the team to remain in Angola.[18] By early June, the government was reported as having invested 1 billion kwanzas in a military campaign hospital of 600 beds. The hospital would be equipped with 31 ventilators and run by General Alberto de Almeida,

Chief Director for Health in the FAA. Four months in, the hospital had treated only 705 patients.[19]

Globally, the pandemic has wreaked chaos in the economies of the most developed countries. Millions have been made permanently unemployed, with industries unable to recover and entire sectors failing to adapt to the social distancing required to contain the spread of the virus. In countries like Angola, the effects are even more consequential. Populations that scraped a living of minimal standards in the urban centres would become food insecure, no longer able to pay for basic health and education services. The small middle class would be plunged into uncertainty with unemployment, mass lay-offs and the inability to pay rents and keep the standard of living they worked hard for. Moreover, the rural areas would become zones of emergency with few safety nets able to secure basic needs. The government tried to adopt several measures to ease the social and economic effects. Two existing policies—the PIIM and the PAPE mentioned in Chapter 5— were expected to be accelerated to address unemployment. The Finance Ministry announced it would mobilise $1.5 billion from the sovereign wealth fund, while the Ministry for Economy and Planning would continue to promote the Credit Support Programme (PAC).[20] Measures for economic relief were abysmally inadequate even with programmes such as "Kwenda" meant as a temporary social protection measure. The "Kwenda" programme aimed to benefit 1.6 million vulnerable families in a four-phased approach, spending a total $420 million. Of that amount, $320 million were funds loaned from the World Bank, with the remainder supported by the national treasury.[21] Under the programme each household, with an average of five family members, would receive 8,500 Kz ($13) a month. Civil society rapidly pointed out that if any of these families needed to get tested, they would have to spend months without eating, given that individual tests cost between 6,000 Kz and 75,000 Kz.[22]

Every household across the country has been affected by the recession, which was compounded by the severity of the economic effects of the pandemic. The government struggled to respond to the humanitarian crisis that was beginning to unfold. In the first six months of 2020, Luanda registered an 183% increase in Severe Acute Malnutrition (SAM) cases due to Covid-19 restrictions.[23] SAM refers to the most visible and extreme form of malnutrition, being a major cause of death in children under the age of five and requiring urgent life-saving treatments. Children suffering from SAM were also the most vulnerable to Covid-19. News outlets began reporting on how 46 children were dying a day of starvation, two every hour, with over 76,000 having been treated for malnutrition in hospitals across the country during the first half of 2020.[24] The government was unable to stabilise the prices of the *cesta básica*, the basic staples of the population. Prices suffered a 400% increase during the first three years of Lourenço's administration.[25] Economists began alerting that the effects of a prolonged recession and the austerity caused by Covid-19 would have a catastrophic impact on Angolan society. Suicide levels began increasing rapidly due to the public's abject despair, with 739 registered in the first six months of 2020—an average of four a day.[26] Over 467,000 Angolans had lost their jobs (in the formal market) and an additional 1.3 million had joined the informal market to seek sustenance.[27] Before the pandemic, Angola registered 12 million living in poverty, corresponding to 41% of the population.[28] That number rose exponentially in mid-2020 to 22 million (35% living in extreme poverty and 34% in moderate poverty) with few immediate solutions to reverse the upward trend.[29]

A month after declaring the state of emergency, the price of oil fell vertiginously. The April 2020 global oil crash caused the government to lose 40% of its revenues (equivalent to 9.6 billion dollars). Exports from oil had already fallen from $34.7 billion the year before to $16.7 billion.[30] By June 2020, it had become clear that Angola would be facing many more years of recession, with oil expected to average at levels way below what the budget supported. Covid-19 achieved what 27 years of war were unable to—an oil drilling shutdown. The five biggest oil companies operating in Angola—Total, Chevron, ExxonMobil, Eni and BP—stopped all drilling activities and focused their operations on existing wells. Angola had expected, through these partners, to bring into operation an additional ten platforms, but these plans were shelved.[31] OPEC's decision to decrease exports was also affected by prospects for recovery, which reduced Angola's share by 10%, down to 1.18 million bpd. In May 2020, the country was exporting oil at an average price of $15.41, an unthinkable prospect for a country wholly dependent on oil revenues. The Angolan economy contracted by 5.1% in 2020, the biggest drop in four decades. As a result, Angola's 2020 budget (worth €27 billion) was slashed by 40%. The expenditure available had to be enough for the government to fund its securitised system, repay its debt, and continue with its development programmes to alleviate the pressure of the ongoing recession.[32] Half of this money would go into repaying the country's debt. Before the pandemic, public debt, largely external, stood at 90% of GDP. By the end of 2020, Angola's debt to GDP ratio reached a crippling 129%.[33] Budget priorities, however, failed to prioritise the social sector adequately. In the revised budget, defence benefited from an increase of $73 million compared to health which increased by only $31 million. The government set aside 4 billion kwanza (over $6 million) to acquire medical equipment while allocating 17 billion kwanza (over $26 million) to the budget of the intelligence services SINSE. Removed from the budget were a dental clinic and presidential library worth $7 million after the opposition criticised the amount allocated to these superfluous projects, which was double the funds allocated for the refurbishment of 17 hospitals.[34] It was not just the lack of money that created hardship; it was the incongruity between how it was applied and the needs it was meant to meet.

Several decisions confirmed the impression that the Presidency was unable to adjust its policies to reflect the real threats it faced. In May, the government spent $180 million on defence, in a context of extreme military overspending, to pay for technical and military projects re-equipping the armed forces.[35] That same month, the government announced that construction of the new international airport in Luanda would proceed, with spending capped at $1.4 billion. This highly controversial project, initially budgeted at $300 million, had over time cost $9 billion.[36] The government also invested $185 million in expanding Catumbela airport, 650km south of Luanda, intending to turn it into the second international airport. Lourenço would again step falsely into another ill-conceived purchase of aeroplanes for TAAG in March 2020 as airlines across the world were filing for bankruptcy and securing government bailouts after international travel was globally halted. The purchase was made with a $118 million bank loan from ABSA. All these measures revealed deep dissonance with the situation

Angola was experiencing. The opportunity to make significant changes to spending and begin injecting money into sectors benefiting the population was, yet again, lost. Grand infrastructure projects that would have little impact on job creation or poverty reduction continued to be prioritised. Emergency aid to feed the most vulnerable, address the healthcare crisis, and stabilise food prices were discarded measures. Continuity seemed inevitable in 2020 at a time when the country needed bold and reforming leadership.

When the Covid-19 pandemic hit Angola, it seemed it could plunge the country into instability as an accelerant to the looming and interconnected socio-economic crises. The perfect storm of a deepening recession with unprecedented levels of poverty in peacetime was colliding with the disillusion felt across society with the "business as usual" approach of the Lourenço Presidency and his doubling-down on securitisation. A collapsed healthcare system, bankrupt state coffers, and food shortages would result in an unacceptable loss of life and expose the government's vulnerability to threats from the masses. Weekly, the image of the President and the MPLA deteriorated as protests continued in small but recurrent forms. Hundreds of youth would take to the streets across Angola on 26 September 2020, marking the third anniversary of Lourenço's presidency. They demanded freedom, justice, jobs and education. "Our intention is effectively (to achieve) democracy. We want to build a citizens' republic and not the militants' republic".[37]

The government's fear was palpable, especially when the opposition raised their voices. Youths from UNITA, PRS, and Bloco Democrático joined a protest on 24 October. Immediately the intelligence services started their misinformation attack by launching a cancellation notice using UNITA's letterhead announcing the party's decision to withdraw from the protest. It did not work. The organisers negotiated social distancing rules with the police, as well as the trajectory and time of the protest. The day before, the government had announced the country was in a State of Calamity, forbidding any gathering of more than five people. Constitutionally only a state of siege, emergency or war could stop protests. People took to the streets. Their march for citizenship, demanding services and local elections, was, as expected, met with brutality. The Presidential Guard, PIR and other police units were deployed against them. But they fought back this time. Within a few hours, over 500 demonstrators were held in different police stations; several had been killed. Over a hundred were charged and facing trial, including four journalists. The risks of civil unrest were real. Across social media, Lourenço's actions were severely criticised. A veteran UNITA general would deconstruct the new President as an "apprentice dictator ... hiding in the palace and giving orders for gunmen to beat and shoot their children and brothers".[38] The events in Cafunfo in January 2021 further exemplified Lourenço's continuation of a securitisation policy that brought about more repression but also greater resistance from the population. The country was heading in a direction of increased securitisation with cosmetic reforms validating a continued direction of a country desperately seeking a governance model that would reflect popular needs rather than elite fears.

As oil recovered in late 2020, the time of monsters may have been attenuated temporarily. The government was able to once again export at $60 per barrel in February 2021. With the rise in the oil price, the country drafted its 2021 budget using an average price of $36 per barrel giving the government an estimated financial cushion worth $3.6 billion.[39] However, the breathing room afforded by these billions was tempered by the reality that Angola was heading into an election year and possibly the most difficult elections that the country has faced since 1992. That money would likely be used to feed the propaganda machine, buy votes, double down on technological strategies to impose fraudulent results, and make palliative investments to improve governance records, rather than repay its foreign debt, invest in poverty reduction programmes, and mass healthcare interventions like vaccinations. The year 2022 will most likely be characterised by a general downward trend in oil production capacity resulting from structural decline and a permanent change to the country's economy. Angola was expected to produce 400,000 barrels less in four years if no new oil was found. Economists were increasingly aware that the peak of 1.8 million bpd of 2015 would never be met again. In 2021 the country was only producing 1.2 million bpd. Oil dependency, caused by a lack of diversification and competitiveness, is on a finite timeline. The country desperately needs to rethink its economic model and speed up its non-oil economy for future growth, focusing especially on the areas of renewables and agriculture. The Covid-19 pandemic and the oil crash are accelerants to a crisis that was already unfolding. Angola is living its time of monsters, with an old world that has died and a new world teetering dangerously towards greater securitisation, authoritarianism and contestation fuelled by popular dissatisfaction and a disarticulated society seeking to speak above the noise of a state of emergency.

# CONCLUSION

This book set out to explain how securitisation embedded itself in the entrails of power, profit, plunder and survival of the MPLA and the all-powerful Angolan Presidency for three decades. It has introduced a new framework for the historical interpretation of Angola, placing securitisation as a mechanism for stabilising the complementary policies of political hegemony, economic appropriation and social engineering. As an infrastructure and system of operations, securitisation became a vital instrument to maintain political order, preserve arcane power structures and allow for the personalisation of political and economic interests to operate above the neutered authority of the state and society. The purpose was always to shield the Presidency and the ruling elites from losing power, from accountability, philosophical defeat and the ignominy of mismanagement and inefficiency. The shadow government and its securitised policies hid behind a façade of public norms, constitutionalism, bureaucratic organisation and legitimising international partners. It functioned through a range of routine practices undertaken by securocrats, bureaucrats and politicians who became "professional managers of unease" (Bigo 2002: 65); networked into a larger economic and administrative system of reward and a security system that interpreted and enhanced threats in order to meaningfully justify the need to centralise power and operate in the shadows.

*Governing in the Shadows* has analysed how securitisation occurred and why it was deemed necessary. As a strategy, it was underpinned by defining moments of crisis and political threats which brought about reform to the system, aligned it with other complementary political and economic actions and increased opacity. Defining moments included the 1977 internal "coup", the 1986 economic collapse, the 1992 elections and the 1997 Government of National Unity, the 2002 humanitarian crisis, the 2011 "Angolan Spring" protests, the debilitating 2014 oil crisis, the 2017 presidential succession and the Covid-19 pandemic of 2020.[1] For different reasons, each of these moments represented important shifts in the ruling party and the Presidency's capacity to govern. The securitised responses that accompanied the shadowing and centralisation of power at each of these junctures followed the logic of differentiation and interpretation of danger. Somehow governing was always about existential survival. Securitisation practices and infrastructures came to provide the best defence against any form of defeat, in the process deeply embedding security in how politics and the economy functioned in Angola. Whenever the MPLA's political project was threatened, securitisation increased. Differences in political thinking and identity came to be viewed as indicators of danger, social dysfunction and anomie, fed by decades of entrenched animosity between political rivals in wartime but also the fear of losing power and privilege in peacetime.

The war mentality that underpinned securitisation functioned with a simple logic. The enemy (instability, reform and loss of power) had to be contained (through intimidation, surveillance and co-optation), and society had to be mobilised and deployed in a total war scenario (MPLA structures, assimilation and control). This simple logic was founded in a state of permanent crisis that never existed. Angola stabilised after the war despite a devastating humanitarian crisis. UNITA demobilised, and the FAA remained loyal to the President even as several pathologies threatened their operations, command and cohesion. Development partners and private sector investors flocked to the country as its resource-based economy grew. Elections were held, but political contestation was largely peaceful. Human rights and anti-corruption activists, together with civil society and journalists, exposed the government's failings, but the population was no longer interested in providing any front for the government in their quest for reform. Paradoxically, the threats Angola faced in 2020 were enhanced by securitisation and the unintended consequences of a false sense of political security among the ruling class. The threat-centred management approach to government obfuscated the many other approaches available to the Presidency, and, more importantly, its reductionist way of thinking and of seeing Angola blinded it from the systemic crises that were developing. The economic crisis, the illegitimacy and emasculation of the state and the social crisis of inequality intensified each other, potentially resulting in the very instability that the securitised state had worked so hard to avoid.

As has been detailed in this book, the MPLA and the political elites supporting the Presidency were well served by the securitisation of the state. The various security forces and infrastructures provided an alternative to a fully functioning executive at national, provincial and local levels. They became the link between how the state was represented for most Angolans due to its coordination of governance, as well as the fact that service delivery and other state interventions that could have provided a better and more benevolent link to the state were inefficient or largely absent. While subverting the more political and philosophical tools normally used to build an inclusive and transformative post-war recovery programme, the MPLA fell back on a strategy of patronage and securitisation. The Presidency understood the state and the party as a site for extracting value, power and the legitimacy needed to govern it. Both were severely weakened by depleting these institutions of decision-making capabilities and allowing patronage and corruption to inhabit their structures and operations. Weak state institutions also allowed the Presidency and the MPLA elites to exacerbate collective action in society (Acemoglu, Robinson and Verdier 2004). The infiltration and co-optation of traditional authorities, the church, civil society, and the media further aggravated this lack of recourse for civilians in need of redress for a state that had failed them. The intrusive way in which any form of dissent or activism demanding services, transparency and development was squashed allowed the MPLA to control the direction and narrative of the post-war years. A façade of democracy, development and stability hid a very different reality for most Angolans who remained poor, disenfranchised and marginalised.

In Angola, securitisation is part of everyday politics, departing from the realm of the extraordinary. It is not so much a failure of "normal" politics as a form of post-war politics. It is neither urgent nor transformative but rather part of the status quo. Security invoked a rationale that had become part of the institutional, behavioural and historical DNA of the ruling party and the elites that ran it. The shadow government and the securitisation architecture that supported it sought to fill a patriarchal role as the nation's protector that would evoke "feelings of allegiance, safety, submission" and fear (Burke 2002: 20–1). The Presidency and the SCP cabinet that ran operations crafted a sophisticated link between the elites and security forces, which became tied to a system that regenerated and reinforced loyalties, patronage, and aligned their purposes. The Presidency simultaneously persuaded (or imposed) the need for securitisation at the micro-level of elite fears and the macro-level of popular uncertainties about the future. By legitimising themselves as the solution to dangers that existed within, these shadows gained the political acceptance of the party and its supporters but widened the disconnect with those who were not persuaded by its vision or policies.

In 45 years, very little has changed in how power is structured in Angola. It was founded on a strong Presidency, the overwhelming might of the security apparatus, the MPLA's historical "right" to rule, on a captured economy, and the acquiescence of international allies and financiers. Throughout the plethora of transitions that the country experienced—from one-party rule to multiparty democracy, from a centralised socialist economy to predatory capitalism, from war to peace, from an oil bonanza to permanent recession, the transition to a Second Republic and two internal MPLA presidential successions—the mechanics of power remain characterised by opacity and exclusion and underpinned by threats. The securitised state did not emerge in a vacuum, nor was it imported or a carefully enacted strategy of control and authority. It emerged from the backdrop of war, ahead of difficult political and economic transitions and was consolidated in the context of a hegemonic peacetime political order. As the movement that "won" independence, the MPLA embodied the role of guardian, promising unity and identity. The form of political monism that fused the state, party and government into one tangled entity allowed the MPLA and the Presidency to view any alternative political thought or calls for change as a threat to their survival. Even internal dissidence became a question of security because of the way it threatened to expose the

CONCLUSION

failures "and the consequences of these for the multitude of interests and forces that the new order should be uniting" (Buur, Jensen and Stepputat 2007: 13). Overwhelmingly, securitisation occurred because of political threats, not just military ones. Considerations about security naturally permeated most of the government's policy during almost three decades of civil war.

In wartime, the militarisation of political power seemed an acceptable strategy for the party and society, given the context of an ideological and identitarian war of competing states and societies. National security was an issue of political survival of the nation and the people on each side of the war. The massification of war machines on both sides engulfed all political and social spaces; they legitimised the righteousness of causes and were reinforced by proxy support. Although power had gradually migrated from the party and the state to the Presidency, a process that began under Agostinho Neto in the late 1970s and increased in the 1980s as the war intensified during dos Santos' first decade in power, the utilitarian purpose of shadowing was never more evident than after 1991. The 1991 peace process promised to bring to Angola a reformed political and economic system, dismantling the one-party state and releasing the grip of Cuban and Russian strategy. Elections meant that the MPLA had to be rebuilt as a massified party, fusing corporatism and patronage into political strategies of differentiation with the opposition. Until then, politics was always closely tied to national security imperatives and military and political leaders' survivalist needs. The economy had been geared to serving the war machine, a policy that changed in form and focus over the years but was consistently underpinned by the need to maintain a large security apparatus and a narrow pool of powerful loyalists. As UNITA edged closer to securing power in Luanda through the political process, the restructured securitisation machine weaponised politics and elections. Paradoxically, if UNITA had won the elections or secured a military victory, the mechanisms of securitised governance would have been replicated. In Angola, everything was political but supporting the political were considerations about security and survival. The degrees of separation between the MPLA and UNITA were great in many respects but not in others. The political machines of both were powered by strategies built on contrasting programmes but secured by their intelligence and securitised units. Mistrust among leaders on both sides fed mutual paranoia and the fear of governance by their opponents. The last decade of war revealed this and a large part of the MPLA's post-war securitisation was informed by these dynamics.

Throughout the 1990s, as political calculations informed military and diplomatic attempts to undermine peace efforts, the securitisation policy began to change in form, reflecting the change in the international environment and how internal politics had been reorganised. The Government of National Unity's (1997–2008) feeble capacity to override decisions from the Presidency revealed where the real power lay. The shadow government in Futungo became a remarkable operation that managed perceptions, interests, and contradictory mandates, and conciliated diverse objectives. It guaranteed the asymmetry of power necessary for all other strategies of economic and political dominance to succeed. The aim was to ensure that the asymmetries never overtly defined political configurations, institutional arrangements or economic interests so that UN-brokered reforms and peacebuilding efforts could simultaneously operate with strategies to entrench MPLA hegemony. It was a highly successful strategy that isolated, weakened and eventually defeated an insurgency that had denied the MPLA the full benefits of sovereignty and legitimacy for 30 years.

The military victory that brought peace to the country in 2002 signalled a definitive shift in the MPLA's capacity to govern Angola for the first time. With UNITA, which had been the biggest existential threat to the ruling elites, severely wounded and weakened, the Presidency proceeded to strengthen its shadow powers in order to streamline decision-making and ensure the careful control of events. Civil society, traditional authorities, the media, NGOs and other voices were given the space to operate in circumscribed ways with the unconcealed oversight of the MPLA. The policy attempted to encapsulate all the peoples and regions of Angola and bring them into the MPLA's ecosystem while fortifying the system around the Presidency and ensuring political longevity. The "psychological shackles of fatalism and fear" that characterised the civil war were used with surgical precision at times of partisan fear (Hodges 2004: 206). In peacetime, the MPLA and the Presidency were fundamentally unable to detach themselves from practices that determined that control, power, surveillance and violence were necessary for survival and to ensure the safety of their political project. From 2002 onwards, securitisation had become a clear strategy to protect the President and the MPLA's interests and buffer them from any dissent, demands for popular inclusion or reform. Parallel security forces and an extensive intelligence community allowed President dos Santos to build a counter-power to manage threats. He shadowed the state with two super-structures within the Presidency, created parallel institutions and ensured that hierarchy and control were vertically aligned. The intelligence services took on a broader surveillance role, spying on the elites and opposition and infiltrating society. Competing interests allowed some generals leading the services to capture and direct these institutions personally. The array of forces within the security ecosystem became a form of social advancement and power.

Paradoxically the process of securitisation meant a weakening of the militarised ethos of the past. While the FAA were deployed when necessary to tackle other internal threats, they, by design, became a weakened pillar of the state. With the end of the war, the armed forces had to be controlled by allowing the enrichment of many of its commanders, shadowed by the Presidential Units and guarded by military intelligence. The resulting pathologies weakened the only institution that had retained a spirit of national unity and was regionally, racially and ethnically representative of Angola. The image and standing of the FAA was somewhat spared despite the corruption, mismanagement, disrepair of equipment and partisan encroachment. That would change under the presidency of João Lourenço.

The end of the dos Santos era brought some adjustments but retained the securitisation strategy. President Lourenço took over at a difficult time. He rapidly understood that saving the party's image and saving the economy had to become his priorities if he was to survive in a country experiencing a deep recession and widespread disillusion. Cleaning up corruption kept the elites loyal and bought him much-needed popular support. It also created international credibility with donors to help rescue the failing economy. However, in order to protect himself and his reform agenda, the new President fell back on the same old securitisation strategy. The strength of the securitised state, the SCP that managed it and the Presidency that designed it was dependent on the solidity of the political and financial apparatus and structures that gave it legal, national and instrumental projection. The weakening of the MPLA, through Lourenço's purges and the subsequent realignment of power, undermined the foundations of that political apparatus. This was compounded by a lack of funds so that there was little possibility of politically containing further dissent and dissolution. The trifecta of securitisation, patronage and political corporatism was off-balance, leaving securitisation as an important stabilising strategy. Lourenço chose to redouble his focus on securitisation to safeguard his rule, given the instability of personalised governance and the institutional damage caused by the dos Santos era. He maintained the existing structures and entrenched their power by strengthening the intelligence services and the police, "purifying" the FAA and making it an instrument of partisan power, and empowering former political commissars as trusted lieutenants in key positions of his administration. Lourenço took the reins of reform but failed to understand that the securitisation policy had become the cornerstone of the country's inequality, citizens' disenfranchisement, and government's failings. It was the biggest impediment to genuine reform.

At no point were the fragilities of the securitised state more apparent than in 2020 when Angola, like the rest of the world, faced an invisible enemy tearing apart healthcare systems, economies and societies. The Covid-19 pandemic laid bare the competing realities of Angola and the incapacity of the Presidency and government to fundamentally shift their modus operandi to protect what should have been the real priority: the people. Despite this, in Angola, Covid-19 never posed a threat to the Presidency and the security bureaucracy that upheld it. Instead the pandemic presented another dimension to the forces that exposed government inaction, malfeasance and disengagement with society. What rapidly rose to threaten the ruling party's grip on the country was a social and economic disaster that was unfolding due to years of recession, lack of economic diversification and falling investor confidence. The economic miracle of the 'Angola rising' years had failed and no amount of securitisation could counter the possibility of social unrest.

This book takes the concept of securitisation beyond the linguistic act of positioning specific actors or issues as threatening. Securitisation

# CONCLUSION

is described as a process and infrastructure that creates a web of centralised control of information, people, and politics in support of a
hegemonic leader and their elite using multiple forces and agencies to
ensure stability for wider economic and political policies. In this
regard, securitisation is not just the moment of intervention but very
much tied to a historical process and institutional context. The way in
which securitisation is described here takes the act of securitisation
further by discussing the rationale behind the intentionality of legitimising threats in peacetime. It reveals a sustained effort of imprinting
authority and partisan influence in areas of governance that are not
always tied to national security imperatives. As a strategy geared
towards the possibility of real or perceived ubiquity, it was effective in
managing contestation. The security prism was in this way "the result
of the creation of a continuum of threats and general unease in which
many different actors exchange(d) their fears and beliefs in the process
of making a risky and dangerous society" (Bigo 2002: 63). However,
while Angolan society was neither dangerous nor risky, it was undoubtedly divided and stratified, but also capable of diffusing the many forms
of violence and aggression that permeated its everyday interactions.
Different episodes of how securitisation collided with the political and
social projects that operated outside the confines of the government's
corporatist strategy have been described throughout the book. The
examples of the Cassule and Kamulingue assassinations, the 15+2 book
club, and the Mount Sumi massacre became the most known and stood
out because of the counter-narratives and counter-propaganda efforts
of activists. Described in the different chapters are the systemic reach
and structured interventions of the different agencies of the securitised
system in assisting in containing dissent (SINSE and SISM), deterring
youth protests (militias and PIR), neutralising the rise in community
mobilisation in the peripheries (FAA, private security and intelligence)
and suppressing opposition politics in all areas. They reveal the broad
reach of the intelligence services and their chaotic coordination with
different security forces, and the use of MPLA political cells. Despite
this, securitisation was not meant to govern people against their will.
It was meant to guard the nation and the state in suggestive and coercive ways so that actions that contradicted its political order remained
contained. These nuanced contradictions, competing values and the

complementary strategies that placed securitisation during a modernising post-war reconstruction programme expose the complexities of analysing Angola.

## Legacies of Securitisation

The legacies of securitisation can be found in Angola's damaged institutional capacity, in its conduct of politics, and in economic distortions and relations between the governed and the government. It has also left enduring after-effects in less palpable areas. Securitisation had inadvertently entrenched poverty, inequality and contested identities in two ways. As a policy of default survival, it removed the urgency of instituting policies that could legitimise a political project beyond the patronage and clientelism of party massification. These policies were discretionary and partisan. They were also directed towards political outcomes rather than developmental ones. Securitisation also justified the use of surveillance and intimidation as a tactic against social and political concerns that could have been diffused through socio-economic distributive policies and forums for civilian participation. Issues like inequality, poverty, identity and political contestation were securitised when internal threat perceptions pushed them to the top of presidential priorities. Just like elections, the securitisation of issues invalidated other viable avenues to mitigate against the more dangerous alternatives of contestation. Decades of securitisation impacted the very nature of political communities and the way they articulated different issues. In this way, post-war nation and state-building became enmeshed in the language, context and continuity of security because of the prism of constant threats to competing visions. The preservation of preferred identities meant the denialism of others and the conflation of partisan survival with the preservation of sovereignty (McDonald 2008).

Securitisation impacted the nation's identity by placing history within the system of meaning used to legitimise it. Historical revisionism and propaganda, implicit in the legitimisation of securitisation, impacted the nation's identity by claiming portions of that history and using it as threats against the present. The memory of massacres and the war were references used to rapidly achieve compliance and exact a re-ordering effect on power relations. When the war ended, the MPLA was allowed to impose its political identity as the driving force of *Angolanidade*. It proceeded to inadvertently define the nation by what it wanted it to be rather than comprising the different realities that encompassed it. This sense of *Angolanidade* failed to bring harmony to the competing visions in which the wide diversity of Angola's realities and identities coexisted. What the government misunderstood for 50 years was that the nation was not the party and that society's security was based on the retention of identity and sustainable livelihoods. Protecting the MPLA's vision for a new Angola, through assimilation and securitisation, would unleash multiple forms of contestation across the country. The many 'Angolas', the parallel realities, the refracted experiences of reconstruction and reconciliation, were all symbolic of the disharmonious engagement with history, the present and the future. Existential threats came from tangible threats to lives and livelihoods but also spoke to the intangibility of sustaining the idea of a contested Angolan nation. It had been this very idea that fuelled a highly destructive war and yet peace removed the need for any further interventions.

No agreement was ever reached by the ruling party, the opposition and the population on what it meant to be Angolan. By putting aside the imperatives of genuine reconciliation and political dialogue, securitisation became the alternative, distorted route to nation-building. Societal security was destroyed by assimilation and the political push into modernity and development that negated competing identities and made invisible the different socio-economic realities of the peripheries and the urban poor. In the same way that "a state that loses its sovereignty does not survive; a society that loses its identity fears it will no longer be able to live with itself" (Waever 1995: 67). Peace brought the emergence of a post-nationalism that was interpreted as fealty to the MPLA. Political hegemony and securitisation implied the assertion of the MPLA's identity over all others, with the ruling party consecrating its leaders, history and military victories as the only history of Angola. This denied many Angolans a place in their own history and a sense of belonging to their nation. It aimed to redeem the past and save the people from being tempted to create a social space marked by alternative political visions. Securitisation entrenched this further through the levelling effect of the "with us or against us" paradigm that became the overriding unification logic during peacetime. This paradigm "suppressed alternatives and negated differences".[2] This alienation was not just felt by UNITA supporters or members of other opposition groups, but across the different regions of Angola where marginalisation became transformed into a political issue of identity. The quest for belonging created subaltern resistance against a reductionist historical hegemony that "produced a messianic present" (Blanes 2016). This messianic present was securitised and disjointed.

Securitisation was also based on the need to manage fear. Fear of "the other" was a strategy the MPLA used during the war as a unifying factor but also aimed at dominance (Messiant 2001). Although the subject of that fear was UNITA, the mentality of imposed silence and the weight of political dominance over dissent became embedded within the MPLA. The secrecy and paranoia of the security services were a version of this effect, although it permeated society. Levels of disorder were created to instil fear in the population so that political emergencies required state interventions, where the securitised "state offered itself as the solution" (Faria 2013: 251). What impeded large public demonstrations of dissatisfaction was the "culture of fear" referred to in many interviews over the years, which was used as a way to intimidate the population and remind them who was there to protect them.

Meanwhile, during peacetime, the elites and the Presidency were afraid of a social awakening, of the day justice was demanded at the political and socio-economic level so that decades of marginalisation, inequality, moral bankruptcy and corruption could be reversed. The private press and the voices of dissent portrayed this as the MPLA "fearing the people and fearing itself. It feared that they, the people, would take to the streets and form an irresistible force".[3] Securitisation created a barrier to this threat and allowed the elites to continue defending their self-interests. As a result, citizenship remained contested because of these asymmetries of power. It re-ordered social relations because of the way it managed fear. Entire categories of people became embodiments of threats at different times when they became dissenting voices that attempted to counter the securitisation of politics and social interactions. As a result, securitisation buffered the rulers from the population but also separated them amongst themselves. Those who were for the MPLA were for stability and peace, whilst those who insisted on demanding reforms and asserting rights were the enemies of peace. Securitisation had, as expected, created enemies from categories of people that were framed as threatening (Beale 2020).

Access to citizenship oscillated between degrees of inclusion in the new post-war society and marginalisation. Those degrees were determined by need and utility. During elections, civilians were useful and their citizenship role was highlighted. They were "seen" and their needs were spoken to. They were co-opted and courted by the political parties. Elections also became securitising exercises. The message conveyed in the run-up to national polls was that a vote for the MPLA was a vote for peace. The alternative could bring serious instability to the country. As a rhetorical strategy, it was divisive and dangerous. It attempted to connect with the population through fear while implicitly portraying political competition and contestation as a national security threat. The language of security increased with every electoral cycle, culminating in 2017 with planes airdropping leaflets into the *musseques* in Luanda, warning the population to stay home and not protest the results.[4]

Securitisation allowed the government to implement another strategy that would maintain a high degree of submission: poverty. The daily battle for survival kept the population focused on other matters that deflected them from asserting their rights and demanding better governance. Deprivation became the way the MPLA structured the public sphere, in particular in situations where it had sufficient resources to manage poverty selectively (Faria 2013). The government presented access to basic goods, services and other citizenship rights as gifts by the state (Messiant 2001). Socio-economic inclusion, mostly aligned with political inclusion, was discretionary and exercised through access to economic opportunities, favours and access to the state. This allowed the government to retain social control by managing the different degrees of acceptance and difference, as well as creating alterity and organising access (Martins 2016). The gateway to the economy passed through the MPLA, but more specifically through the Presidency, as the way to achieve social mobility and accumulate wealth. Clientelism and patronage allowed the government to embed control at all levels, from the traditional authorities at the local level, to civil society at the national level. The threat of economic hardship was also implicit to the elites who risked having their privileges revoked if they behaved badly. Securitisation factored into this strategy as key elements of the security forces became the gatekeepers to the most important means of elite patronage—reconstruction money, revenue from diamonds, and the off-shoot services and tenders related to the oil industry. Generals guarded this portfolio within the SCP, and many others also benefited from it. The richest provinces in terms of mineral wealth in Angola (Cabinda and the two Lundas) were kept underdeveloped, repressed, and secured by military, paramilitary and private security forces. They represented the extreme version of this securitisation and its effect on poverty and exclusion. "By maintaining the majority in poverty, the state had the opportunity to politicise, to control, and to limit its people".[5] Poverty, like securitisation, contained the aspirations of a generation and demands for reform. It also carved spaces of social rebellion.

The threats that the system tried to contain were, in fact, created by it. Intensifying levels of surveillance, enlarged patronage pools, the management of marginality, and society's containment were insufficient to allow small threats to challenge the system. This revealed the fragility of the system itself. Communities that had been conditioned to think of survival in terms of security and order began to think instead of their liberties and rights. Their welfare no longer depended on the security provided by the state but on protection from it. Society became mobilised once more, abandoning the mentality that had led to its retreat. Even if society had not begun to assert itself in the form of protests and voting for change, the system's stability is finite. Growing economic hardship, the almost permanent state of recession and the exposure of government failings heightened a sense of insecurity for all. The coercive strategies of the past could not manage this insecurity. It required a level of empowerment and reform that placed citizens in a position to participate in rebuilding after the pillage of peace.

At the time of the publication of *Governing in the Shadows*, Angola is heading into a year of elections. The August 2022 polls could represent a turning point for the country, given the trajectory of political decay of the MPLA and the opposition's assertiveness. However, the elections are likely to follow the discourse of securitisation, the infiltration of opposition parties and the intimidation of leaders and voters, with the physical presence of security forces to "ensure stability". The shadow government and the SCP are expected to show little restraint in perpetuating a policy that has invalidated the democratic exercise, exacerbated domestic tensions and coordinated actions to disarticulate the opposition.[6] The process will likely be directed at renewing João Lourenço's mandate, not out of conviction or fairness to the electoral process but out of an existing dynamic of fraudulent practices and last minute co-optation and vote-buying. Observers anticipate a sense of continuity within the political order, both of MPLA hegemony and presidential absolutism. The difference this time is that the MPLA and the Presidency are in a heightened sense of insecurity and threat and could set the country on a dangerous path, given the many fault lines described in this book. The Covid-19 pandemic has been an accelerant of change in many countries, bringing societal disaggregation to the political foreground and highlighting governmental inadequacies, contradictory policies and the recurrent preference for short-term political gain. Angola has not escaped this. While the continuation of the status quo and a policy of muddling through seems the most likely election outcome, the resilience of the shadow government and the securitised state has certainly begun to wither.

Within the next decade, the country could either reform and desecuritise or enter an era of greater authoritarianism. One path is dependent on the forces of liberalisation and democratisation, the other on overt repression and overt securitisation dependent on force rather than patronage and surveillance. With a budget shattered by decreasing oil revenues and galloping public debt, the government's options are either to invest in areas that would make society less rebellious or rearm and reinforce the security apparatus to quash the possibility of a social insurrection. The options are between a warrior people and a besieged president, or effective change. One implies greater violence, the other political sacrifice. Both require fundamental shifts in public policy and the role of society.

While securitisation entails portraying issues as catastrophic threats, any process of desecuritising requires framing these same issues as manageable and amenable to public policy interventions (Sears 2020).[7] Desecuritisation highlights the type of politics that would no longer normalise "exceptional politics of speed and enemy exclusion" (Aradau 2004) but instead foreground accountability and social empowerment. The unmaking of securitisation implies deconstructing the apparatus that edifies the strategy and the political structure that defined it as necessary. Democratisation and the reform of social, political and power relations would be necessary to take reform out of the purview of security so that it is not conceived as a focus of instability. By reaching out to civil society and the opposition, the government could potentially suspend the need to hold onto the "logic of vulnerabilities" (Buzan et al. 1998) that until now has characterised its levels of fear and its cosmology of constant political threats.

Reforming the system will be difficult. The legacy of Angola's authoritarian past casts long shadows over its democratic future (Svolik 2012). But political reform cannot be avoided forever. It has to be conducted in parallel with the major socio-economic transformation that the country desperately needs. Two dynamic issues could decisively push Angola out of its continued policy of securitisation: political decentralisation because of the demand for local elections and economic diversification because of the oil crisis. Either one of these could naturally unlock the centralised control of politics and the economy. They represent the push-pull forces that the shadow government has worked so hard to curtail. One of the hardest aspects of recovering the functioning state and creating credible institutions will be untangling the intricate webs of elite collusion over financial and political power. Many of these elites have deep links to the security network, which makes the dismantling of this stranglehold so dangerous. Reforming the army, police, intelligence services, the Presidential Guards and all supporting institutions would mean relegating them to a secondary role, led and directed by elected civilian officials. With a sustainable economic programme to supplement the loss of income from demobilisation, a gradual process of desecuritisation could occur without the risk of instability. Merely reforming their structures would be insufficient: they would need to transform their entire orientation, purpose, mission and behaviour.

Desecuritising also implies allowing civilians a greater role in the economy. The fundamentals of a modern economy—resilient supply chains, productivity, fair wages, and robust infrastructure—must align with concrete programmes to address the multiple causes of poverty as well as intersectional issues such as gender and the environment. This requires a fairer distribution of resources and opportunities. Above all, growth needs to be decentralised. The Covid-19 crisis and its long-term socio-economic effects cannot be tackled with the same mentality as a wartime economy. Angola desperately failed at that during the war so replicating it in peacetime could result in complete economic collapse. This means that the massive upscaling of oil production and other resource-generating areas—which is an impossibility given the oil crisis—has to be rethought. Production must occur in a socially just and distributive way so that there can be food security, employment and buying power across society. Covid-19 also presents the government with an opportunity to desecuritise society so it can join forces in a moment of crisis, and help repair the distortion of state-society relations. A self-motivated and empowered population would be more effective than a population contained by surveillance, policed and intimidated. Co-operation needs to be resurrected so that an element of trust in the authorities can restore a sense of inclusive citizenship. A shared vision of the future "and a strategy built on social consensus" (Moura Roque 2000) is still the only viable route. Democracy cannot arise from the comfort of elites but must be built "from below" by the sustained mobilisation of the poor, changing the country's political economy and negotiating a way out of authoritarian rule (Wood 2000).

Failing this, Angola faces the risk of becoming a militarised, deeply securitised and increasingly unstable country. This alternative is a harsher response built on the security apparatus without the more appeasing dynamics of political patronage and clientelism to manage competing interests. The Presidency's problem of authoritarian control (Svolik 2012), which led it to enhance and share power with securocrats, will become a recurring issue only resolved by greater repression. The possibility of a more militarised and unstable situation would make the military politically indispensable, further weakening civilian institutions and reversing the few electoral gains of civil and political liberties. This reality would shut down all avenues for social and political contestation, postponing elections and repressing both the opposition and civil society.

A post-pandemic Angola will have to face the reality that, for now, securitisation seems to have become the Presidency's and the MPLA's defining praxeological fate. It would be unlikely that both are prepared to reform themselves out of power. But the way forward is not set in stone. President Lourenço and several reform-minded MPLA technocrats could still take the bold move to desecuritise. This would require great courage and conviction but would also allow the ruling party to truthfully gauge its political support and capitalise on the power behind conciliatory measures. Angolans across the political aisles expect more from their hard-won peace. Bringing the government out of the shadows to share power and privilege with society remains the only way to deliver much-needed security to all Angolans.

# NOTES

## INTRODUCTION

1. Conversation with a military intelligence officer, Luanda, November 2015.
2. Author interview with the President of UNITA, September 2012, Luanda.
3. De Giorgi, Alessandro, 2006, *Re-thinking the Political Economy of Punishment: Perspectives on Post-Fordism and Penal Politics*, Aldershot: Ashgate, referenced in Hallsworth and Lea 2011: 142.
4. "Ethiopia: New Spate of Abusive Surveillance." Human Rights Watch, 28 October 2020, www.hrw.org/news/2017/12/06/ethiopia-new-spate-abusive-surveillance. Accessed April 2021.
5. Palmer, Jason, host. "Like hell out of a bat: SARS-CoV-2's origin." *The Economist*, 10 February 2021.
6. "Out of Sight, Not Out of Reach." Freedom House.
7. "Report: No Refuge: South Sudan's Targeting of Refugee HRDs Outside the Country." Front Line Defenders, 18 March 2021.
8. "South Sudan: Rampant Abusive Surveillance by NSS Instils Climate of Fear." Amnesty International.
9. Mandaza, Ibbo, "The Making of a Securocrat State in Zim." *The Zimbabwe Independent*, 14 April 2016.

## 1. THE COMPONENT PARTS

1. The popular power units were part of the securitisation of society whereby civilians became part of militia-like forces, acting as auxiliary forces for civil defence. They played different roles throughout the decades. The latest reincarnation of the ODC is explained in Chapter 3.
2. "A Convicção messiânica de Nito Alves", *Angonoticias*, 27 May 2005. www.angonoticias.com/full_headlines.php?id=5485. Accessed 1 May 2021.

3. "The orphans of Angola's secret massacre seek the truth", BBC News, 5 September 2020. https://www.bbc.com/news/world-africa-5402 5264. Accessed 29 April 2021.

4. Valles, Edgar. "27 De Maio: Reconciliação e Perdão Em Angola?" *Público*, 27 May 2020.

5. Author interview with opposition leader, Luanda, September 2008.

6. The MPLA claimed to have more than 4 million members: "Vitória Do MPLA Foi Preparada a Rigor?" Voice of America, 25 September 2008.

7. Neto 2008, referenced in Faria 2013: 171.

8. Correspondence with an Angolan journalist, October 2020.

9. Author interview with a senior officer in the Ministry of the Interior, Luanda, September 2019.

10. Vidal, Nuno, "The Angolan Regime and the Move to Multiparty Politics", in Chabal and Vidal 2007.

11. Messiant, Christine, 1992, "Social and Political Background to the Democratization and Peace Process in Angola", paper for Seminar on Democratization in Angola, Leiden, the Netherlands, quoted in Hodges 2001: 54.

12. Author interview with UNITA member of the GURN, August 2008, Luanda.

13. Vital Moreira, a Lusophone constitutionalist and member of the European Parliament, in "Presidencialismo Superlativo—Espaço Público", *Público*, 9 February 2010.

14. Crawford, Adam, "'Contractual Governance' of Deviant Behaviour", *Journal of Law and Society*, Vol. 30, No. 4, 2003, pp. 479–505.

15. "Long-term Socio-economic Impacts of COVID-19 in African Contexts: UNDP in Africa." UNDP.

16. Study conducted by the Permanent Commission of the Council of Ministers, 2010, in Ernesto, Alexandre, "A economia informal de Angola: Caracterização do Trabalhador informal", Open Society Report, 2018.

17. Da Costa Júnior's bid revealed deep divisions within UNITA around regionalist and racial prejudices (he was mixed race) although he was supported by the core of UNITA's senior leaders.

18. Aliança Patriótica (PADDA-AP), Partido de Aliança Livre de Maioria Angolana (PALMA), Partido Nacional de Salvação de Angola (PNSA), Partido Pacífico Angolano (PPA), PDP-ANA, and the intellectuals-based party Bloco Democratico (BD).

19. A letter, allegedly from the former President of the Supreme Court, Rui Ferreira, instructing the constitutional court to sink the bid, was circulated on social media as evidence of this interference.

20. "Excessos Policiais Embaraçam Lourenço", *Africa Monitor*, No.1258, July 2020.
21. Author interviews with officers from military intelligence revealed that in the province of Kuando Kubango alone there were 6,000 SINSE operatives, which (if multiplied by 18) would make 108,000 operatives in total. SINSE is one of three intelligence agencies. Some of these numbers could have been "ghost operatives" reflecting the need of some commanders to steal money. Nevertheless, the numbers could have been higher if they included other intelligence services.
22. "Authorities collect firearms and explosives", Angola News Agency, 11 April 2007.
23. Civilian Firearms Holdings, 2017, Small Arms Survey.
24. Author interview with a military intelligence officer, Luanda, October 2019.
25. In 2002, the government passed a bill banning NGOs from conducting any political or partisan activities or approaching politically sensitive issues (peace in Cabinda, human rights, etc.).
26. The Acção Para o Desenvolvimento Rural e Ambiente (ADRA), created in 1990, was one of the first NGOs to work on sustainable rural development projects and the empowerment of the poor. Mãos Livres, founded in 2000, was a human rights organisation whose members were mainly lawyers offering free legal assistance. The Associacao Justicia, Paz e Democracia (AJPD), established in 2000, was another organisation that worked on human rights.
27. "Sobas Guardam Urnas e Material Eleitoral Em Casa." Em Defesa Da Democracia, Contra a Corrupção, Maka Angola, 21 August 2017.
28. "Kwanza-Norte: ONG Causa Solidária e Nosso Soba trabalham na provincial", Angop, 13 July 2005.
29. Throughout this book, the Angolan national currency, the kwanza (Kz), is used in conjunction with the dollar, euro and British pound to follow how different government documents, news pieces and reports reported the amounts at the time. Currency fluctuations of the kwanza make this a slightly more complicated issue to tackle, hence referring to other currencies.
30. This pattern continued into 2019 with the director of TPA, Joana Toma, and an anchor of TV Zimbo, Djamila dos Santos, being nominated onto the central committee of the MPLA. "A Relação entre o jornalismo e o poder em Angola", Deutsche Welle, 20 June 2019.
31. "Unfinished Democracy: Media and Political Freedoms in Angola", Human Rights Watch report, July 2004.
32. Author interview with FALA ex-combatant, Luanda, September 2012.

33. Author interview with former GURN Deputy Minister, Luanda, September 2008.
34. Generoso de Almeida, Claudia. "Angola—The President and the 'New Alliance' with the Catholic Church." Presidential Power, 18 December 2019.
35. Global Group. "Igreja de Coligação Cristã de Angola Propõe-Se a Reunir 1200 Seitas Numa Só." DN, 12 May 2015.
36. Author interview with Ovimbundu member of the MPLA, Luanda, September 2012.

## 2. A STRATEGY OF SECURITISED HEGEMONY: OUTMANOEUVRING THE ENEMY

1. UN sanctions on UNITA were defined by UNSC Resolutions 864 (1993), 1127 (1997, 1173 (1998), and 1295 (2000).
2. UNAVEM I was established in 1989, following UNSC Resolution 435 and the Brazzaville Protocol of December 1988, which linked the withdrawal of Cuban and South African troops from Angola to the subsequent independence of Namibia in 1990.
3. "UNAVEM II", 1996, *The Blue Helmets: A Review of United Nations Peacekeeping*, New York: UN, Department of Public Information, p. 238.
4. Numbers provided by General Kamorteiro, Deputy Chief of Staff of the FAA (most senior UNITA official in the military), in an author interview, November 2019, Luanda.
5. Human Rights Watch, 1994.
6. Author interviews with diplomats, Lisbon, Pretoria and Washington, 2011–16.
7. Partido Democratic Angola (PDA), Frente Nacional de Libertação de Angola (FNLA), Partido Social Democrata Angolano (PSDA), Partido Democratico para o Progresso-Aliança Nacional (PDP-ANA), Convenção Nacional Democrática de Angola (CNDA).
8. These numbers were revealed in a book written by a UNITA member of the CCPM who had access to the electronic and official printouts. See Moura Roque 1994: 74.
9. Two news pieces came out in the state-controlled *Jornal de Angola* reporting that UNITA had accepted the election results and that a second round of elections would move ahead: "Savimbi diz que aceita Resultados como Estão" and "Vamos ter Segunda Volta", 17 October 1992.
10. Author interviews with UNITA leaders, Lisbon and Luanda, 1998–2017.
11. Author virtual conversation with a former Angop state news journalist, July 2020.
12. Author interviews with journalists and politicians, Luanda, 2004–19.

13. Author interview with former UNITA Chief of Staff, Luanda, October 2019.
14. Author interviews with witnesses, Luanda and Lisbon, 1998–2019.
15. "Angola: Assault on the Right to Life", Amnesty International report, August 1993, p. 5.
16. Personal recollection of UNITA former CCPM member, 1990s.
17. "Ending the Angolan Conflict: Our Time Has Come to be Heard", National Society for Human Rights (NSHR), 29 March 2000.
18. "Angola: Assault on the Right to Life", Amnesty International report, August 1993, p. 7.
19. "Angola: Internal Security Forces and Organization", Library of US Congress Country Studies, 1989.
20. UN Security Council, S/25840, 25 May 1993.
21. Numbers provided by Save the Children, referenced in "Angola the Spoils of War", Africa Report, Vol. 39, Number 1, the African-American Institute, January/February 1994, p. 14.
22. "Angola the spoils of war", Africa Report, January/February 1994, p. 16.
23. EO was also thought to have trained the Reconnaissance Regiment and the Special Tactical Intervention Units of the government. With their help and training, in July 1994 the FAA captured Cafunfu from UNITA in what was deemed one of their most successful operations. Detailed news piece from the *Mail & Guardian* newspaper based in South Africa, September 1994, quoted in "Angola: Arms Trade and the Violations of the Laws of War since the 1992 Elections", Human Rights Watch, November 1994, p. 20.
24. "Angola Unravels", Human Rights Watch, September 1999, p. 103.
25. "Angola: Arms Trade and Violations of War since the 1992 Elections", Human Rights Watch, November 1994, p. 7.
26. Human Rights Watch, 1999, p. 99.
27. Attempts to cover up details and deflect judicial accountability in France years later led the Presidency to employ widespread diplomatic measures including the nomination of Falcone to UNESCO as Angola's representative to provide diplomatic immunity, and withholding economic opportunities from Paris.
28. Africa Report, 1994.
29. Human Rights Watch, 1996.
30. Angola Peace Monitor, 1997.
31. "Report of the Secretary-General of the United Nations Mission in Angola", United Nations, 17 June 1998.
32. "War drums sounding", *Africa Confidential*, Vol. 39, No. 16, 7 August 1998. www.africa-confidential.com/article-preview/id/4500/War_drums_sounding. Accessed May 2021.

33. Ibid.
34. Médecins Sans Frontières (MSF) Press Release, "Angola: a population sacrificed by war and abandoned in peace", October 2002.
35. Ibid.
36. "A Crude Awakening", Global Witness, December 1999.
37. Testimony of a close advisor who spoke with Savimbi weeks before he was killed. Lisbon, 2008.
38. Numbers cited by the Government of Angola and the UN Common Country Assessment 2002, *Angola: The Post-war Challenges*, authors unknown.
39. MSF, 2000.
40. Author interview with a senior church member, Luena, May 2004.
41. "Angola: Year-ender 2002—Political Challenges for the Future", Office for the Coordination of Humanitarian Affairs (OCHA), UN, 22 January 2003.
42. MSF, 2002.
43. UNICEF Angola country profile, 2008.
44. "Angola's government doesn't seem to care about humanitarian crisis", Afrol news, 13 August 2002.
45. Author interviews with IDPs and ex-combatants, Huambo and Moxico, April 2004.
46. Author interview with an IDP from Huila, April 2004, Huambo.
47. Witnessed firsthand by the author in the city of Huambo, mid-2004.
48. Author interview with a Soba, May 2004, Huambo.
49. Kaun, Alexandra, "When the Displaced Return: Challenges to 'Reintegration' in Angola", research paper 152, Office of Refugee and Asylum USCIS, January 2008.
50. See UN OCHA Humanitarian Coordination Update, December 2002.
51. "Dealing with Savimbi's Ghost: The Security and Humanitarian Challenges in Angola", International Crisis Group Report 58, 26 February 2003.
52. Author interview with a FALA demobilised colonel, Huambo, May 2004.
53. Author interview, IOM, April 2004, Luanda.
54. Author interview with a member of the organisation assisting the DDR process, Luanda, April 2004.
55. Human Rights Watch, 2003.
56. Author interview with a demobilised soldier, Moxico, April 2004.
57. Author interview with an FAA general, Luanda, May 2004.
58. See Relatorio Social de Angola, 2014, Universidade Catolica de Angola.
59. Author interview with an FAA general, Luanda, April 2004.
60. Chatham House, 2005.

61. Author interview with a former advisor to CEMG, Lisbon, February 2020.

62. See IRIN, "Angola: Savimbi's ghost still haunts UNITA".

63. "Economic Growth in Angola to 2017: The Main Challenges", Angola Brief, CMI, December 2012, Vol. 2, No. 4.

64. White, David, "Infrastructure: Benguela railway transformed by loans from Beijing", Financial Times, 17 July 2012.

65. Pushak, Nataliya, and Foster, Vivien, "Angola's infrastructure: a continental perspective", in Africa Infrastructure Country Diagnostic Reports, World Bank 2011.

66. "Angola's Corrupt Building Boom: 'Like Opening a Window and Throwing out Money'", New York Times, 24 June 2017.

67. Marques de Morais, Rafael, "The New Imperialism: China in Angola", World Affairs Journal, March/April 2011, p. 71.

68. "The Queensway Syndicate and the African Trade", Economist, 13 August 2011.

69. "Angola: where did all the money go? Part 2 the parallel economy", Africa Report, 22 October 2019.

70. "Top 10 largest companies", African Business Review, 12 June 2013.

71. Ovadia, Jesse Salah, "The Reinvention of Elite Accumulation in the Angolan Oil Sector: Emergent Capitalism in a Rentier Economy", Caderno de Estudos Africanos, no. 25, 2013, pp. 33–63. Accessed May 2021.

72. Paiva, José Francisco (ed.), 2011, A Política Externa de Angola no Novo Contexto Internacional, Lisbon, p. 137.

73. Angola Country Report, Economist Intelligence Unit, January 2015.

74. Portugal supplies 14.7% of imports, followed by China with 12.6%, Singapore with 11.4%, the U.S. with 8.8% and the UAE with 5.1%. "China is leading importer of goods from Angola in 3rd quarter of 2014", Macauhub, 6 January 2014.

75. Author interview with Portugal-Angola Forum, Luanda, March 2015.

76. Seabra, Pedro and Gorjão, Paulo, "Intertwined Paths: Portugal And Rising Angola", Occasional Paper 89, South African Institute of International Affairs, August 2011.

77. "Angola ends partnership with Portugal", Deutsche Welle, 17 October 2013.

78. "Rui Machete pediu desculpa a Angola", Diario de Noticias, 4 October 2013.

79. "Luanda shouts back at Lisbon", Africa Confidential, Vol. 54, no. 23, 15 November 2013.

80. Author interviews with civil society members and church leaders, Luanda September 2012.

81. Redvers, Louise, "Living in the world's most expensive city", BBC News,

2 February 2012. https://www.bbc.com/news/business-16815605. Accessed May 2021.

82. Kollewe, Julia, "London, Birmingham and Aberdeen now cost more to live in", *The Guardian*, 25 June 2018. https://www.theguardian.com/ business/2018/jun/26/london-birmingham-and-aberdeen-now-cost-more-to-live-in. Accessed May 2021.

83. Neto, Alexandre, "Aparato de Guerra usado nas demolições em Cacuaco", Maka Angola, 5 February 2013.

3. THE SHADOW GOVERNMENT: GUARDING THE GUARDIANS

1. Included key ministers, Secretary-General of the Party, the Vice-President, opposition leaders and some representatives from civil society.

2. The committee and its secretariat (President, Vice-President and Secretary) were dominated by MPLA functionaries. Only four of the 26 committee members were drawn from the opposition. International Transparency's Angola 'Government Defence Anti-Corruption Index— 2013", Transparency International UK, 2013.

3. The law also defined the consultative organs of the SCP which included a technical council, a council of personnel, and support structures for the Minister, his advisors and consultants. In addition, special offices were deputised to support the President, in particular on issues of health, security studies, psychological action and information, telecommunications, and presidential transport.

4. "Neutering UNITA", *Africa Confidential* Vol. 43: 20, 11 October 2002. https://www.africa-confidential.com/article-preview/id/867/ Neutering_UNITA. Accessed May 2021.

5. Author interviews and correspondence with Angolan elites, February and March 2015.

6. Author interviews with different political and military figures in Luanda, January 2015.

7. Author interview with a former FAPLA navy commander, Luanda, January 2015.

8. Author interview with a former FAPLA general, Luanda January 2015.

9. Author interview with a former dos Santos advisor, Luanda, October 2019.

10. Author interview with a leading Cabinda activist, Cabinda, November 2015.

11. Art. 11.2 of the 2013 state budget.

12. Marques de Morais, Rafael, "Orçamento para o presidente, as Forças Armadas e os Espiões", Maka Angola, 21 January 2013.

13. Author interview with a military intelligence officer, Luanda, January 2015.
14. Author interviews with different military sources, Luanda, January 2015.
15. Author interview with different FAA military sources, Luanda, January 2015.
16. Author interview with an intelligence officer, Johannesburg and Luanda, December 2014.
17. Author interviews with different military sources, Luanda, January 2015.
18. Author interview with an FAA sergeant, Luanda, January 2015.
19. Ibid.
20. "Orçamento para o presidente, as Forças Armadas e os Espiões", Maka Angola, 21 January 2013.
21. "Efectivos da USP denunciam condições precárias, injustiças, nepotismo e corrupção", Angonoticias, 24 November 2019.
22. Author interview with an SHP officer, Luanda, January 2015.
23. Ibid.
24. "Se Voltarem, Vamos Matar-vos", Human Rights Watch report, 21 May 2012.
25. "Crise na unidade de operações 'Chacal' da presidência da república", Folha 8, 30 March 2014.
26. Author interview with a DPCS captain, Luanda, January 2015.
27. Ibid.
28. "Chineses controlam unidade Presidencial fantasma", Maka Angola, 24 September 2012.
29. "Fuqing crime and punishment", Africa-Asia Confidential, Vol. 15, No. 12, 2 October 2012.
30. "Chineses Outorgam Diplomas de Mérito a Soldados da Presidência", Maka Angola, 6 February 2015.
31. "Fuqing crime and punishment", op. cit.
32. "Presidential Guard Presidential Guards at the service of Private Business", Maka Angola, 25 September 2012.
33. "Fuqing crime and punishment", op. cit.
34. Author interview with a captain of DPCS, Luanda, January 2015.
35. Author interview with a military officer, Luanda, January 2015.
36. Author correspondence with a military intelligence officer, February 2015.
37. Africa Monitor, AM917, 24 February 2015.
38. Capalandanda, António, "Guarda presidencial Angolana reforça segurança", Voice of America, 20 May 2015.
39. Author interview with a senior dos Santos advisor, Luanda, October 2019.
40. Author virtual conversation with an Angolan journalist, October 2020.

41. Decreto-Lei number 3/75 of 29 November 1975, *Diario da Republica* I Serie no. 17, 29 November 1975.
42. Law 7/78.
43. Law 46/81.
44. Author virtual conversation with an Angolan journalist, October 2020.
45. Author correspondence with an Angolan investigative journalist, October 2020.
46. National Security Law 8/94 was passed on 6 May 1994.
47. Law 8/94 on National Security.
48. Law 12/02.
49. Presidential Decree 1/10.
50. Author interviews with intelligence officers, Luanda, January 2015.
51. Author interview with a SINSE collaborator, Luanda, January 2015.
52. See Maka Angola, "Kamulingue, Cassule, CIA, SINSE e mandantes dos assassinatos", 17 November 2014.
53. Author interview with a political analyst, Luanda, January 2015; also reported by *Novo Jornal*, 11 March 2011.
54. "SINSE encomenda aparelhos de intercepção de mensagens na internet", Club-K, 6 July 2011.
55. Angola 2014 Report, BertelsmannStiftung Transformation Index, BTI.
56. Ibid.
57. "Inteligência Externa com Novo Centro de Formação", Club-K, 12 March 2013.
58. Author interview with a captain of military intelligence, Luanda, January 2015.
59. Ibid.
60. Author interview with a human rights activist, Luanda, January 2015.
61. Martins speech in January 2013 at the opening of the Methodological Seminar on the Integrated Planning System of SINSE, Luanda.
62. Author interview with an intelligence officer, Luanda, January 2015.
63. Author correspondence with military intelligence, February 2015.
64. Author interview with a captain of military intelligence, Luanda, January 2015.
65. Ibid.
66. Author interview with a military intelligence officer, Luanda, January 2015.
67. "The Angosat-1 communications satellite", Russian Space Web. http://www.russianspaceweb.com/angosat.html. Accessed May 2021.
68. Author interviews with opposition leaders, Luanda, 2008–19.
69. Marques de Morais, Rafael, "O poder e a sucessão de José Eduardo dos Santos", Maka Angola, 31 January 2012.

70. Author interview with a military intelligence officer, Luanda, January 2015.
71. "Oliveira Sango, DG do Serviço de Inteligência externa", Club-K, 5 July 2011.
72. Author interviews with political analysts, Luanda, January 2015.
73. Author interview with a former FAPLA general, Luanda, January 2015.
74. "Presidente Angolano inaugura academia com cursos de serviço de informação", *Correio da Manhã*, 20 May 2019.
75. Author interviews with several UNITA leaders, Luanda, 2012–19. See also "Adolosi Mango Alicerces, ex-SG da UNITA—In Memoriam", Club-K, 10 September 2014.
76. "'Puseram-me no Buraco', Detenção Militar, Tortura e Processo Injusto em Cabinda" / "'They Put Me in the Hole', Military Detention, Torture, and Lack of Due Process in Cabinda", Human Rights Watch report, June 2009.
77. Author interview with a captain of military intelligence, Luanda, January 2015.
78. Author interview with an FAA colonel, Luanda, September 2012.
79. Author interview with a captain of military intelligence, Luanda, January 2015.
80. Author interview with an SISM officer, Luanda, January 2015.
81. "General Ze Marias Partisan Plot to Destabilize the Army", Maka Angola, 2 July 2014.
82. Author interviews with a captain of military intelligence, Luanda, January 2015.
83. Ibid.
84. "Alemães montam Sistema de Escuta em Angola", Club-K, 23 April 2013.
85. "Regime ensaia sistema para banir sites criticos", Club-K, 27 July 2015.
86. "Angola: government seeks to impose an internet clampdown", Economist Intelligence Unit, 14 April 2011.
87. Quaresma Dos Santos, D. for Maka Angola, part of the Guardian Africa Network, "Angola passes laws to crack down on press and social media", *The Guardian*, 19 August 2016. https://www.theguardian.com/world/2016/aug/19/angola-passes-laws-to-crack-down-on-press-and-social-media. Accessed May 2021.
88. Author interviews with Angolan analysts and opposition leaders, Luanda, August 2008. See also Roque 2008.
89. "General Rogerio Saraiva, o presidente da 'outra CNE'", Club-K, 25 August 2012.
90. "Vitória do MPLA foi preparada a Rigor", Voice of America, 25 September 2008.

91. Author interviews with civil society members in Luanda and church leaders in Huambo, August 2008.

92. Author interview with a former Secretary-General of the MPLA, Luanda, September 2008.

93. Author interview with a UNITA provincial leader, Huambo, September 2008.

94. "Documentos de fraude de 2008 embaraça MPLA", Club-K, 1 July 2012.

95. SAPA, "Angola vote body accused of irregularities", 13 July 2012. https://www.iol.co.za/news/africa/angola-vote-body-accused-of-irregularities-1341213. Accessed May 2021.

96. "Livro Branco sobre as Eleições de 2008", Instituto de Desenvolvimento e Democracia, 2009.

97. Author interview with a CNE member from the opposition, Luanda, August 2012.

98. Author interview with a journalist, Lisbon, June 2019.

99. Marques de Morais, Rafael, "Angola: the stolen elections", Maka Angola, 25 August 2017.

100. See Amnesty International's Annual Report 2014/15.

101. Decree 41/96.

102. Decree 20/93.

103. Author interview with a former Ministry of the Interior official, Luanda, January 2015.

104. Marques de Morais, Rafael, "Angola's killing fields: a report on extrajudicial; executions in Luanda 2016–2017".

105. Author interviews, Luanda, September 2012.

106. Author interview with a human rights activist, Luanda, January 2015.

107. Author interview with a former FAPLA general, Luanda, January 2015.

108. Author interview with a FALA ex-combatant, Luanda, September 2012.

109. Redvers, Louise, "Brutal crackdown fuels Angola rage", *Mail & Guardian* (Johannesburg), 29 November 2013.

110. Marques de Morais, Rafael, "O Assassinato de Ganga e a impunidade da UGP", Maka Angola, 26 November 2013.

111. BTI, Angola 2014, p. 10.

112. Amnesty International, Punishing Dissent: Freedom of Association, Assembly and Expression in Angola, 13 November 2014.

113. Marques de Morais, Rafael. "Kamulingue, Cassule, CIA, SINSE e os mandantes dos assassinatos", Maka Angola, 17 November 2014.

114. Author interview with a member of the accused legal team, Luanda, January 2015.

115. Marques de Morais, Rafael, op. cit.

116. "Cassule foi morto à pancada; Kamulingue com tiro na cabeça", Club-K, 14 November 2013.
117. "Como Cassule e kamulingue foram atraídos para a morte", *Folha* 8, 26 November 2013.
118. "Constitucional de Angola absolve condenado pela morte de Cassule e Kamulingue", Deutsche Welle, 28 October 2017.
119. "General Filó da Casa Militar Financia Esquadrões da Morte em Luanda", *Folha* 8, 30 March 2015.
120. Author interviews and correspondence with human rights activists from Huambo collecting evidence on the massacre, Johannesburg and Windhoek, June–December 2015.
121. Author interview with an activist investigating the massacre, Windhoek, November 2015.
122. "Genocide against 'New Light of the World' Adventists Church of Pastor / Prophet Jose Julino Kalupeteka", Huambo, 20 April 2015, report compiled by activists and church members.
123. Evidence was pointing to the possibility of these supporters who killed the police being infiltrated agents used to trigger the clampdown, author interview with Huambo activist, December 2015.
124. Author interview with an activist investigating the massacre, Windhoek, November 2015.
125. Evidence presented in the draft report of the massacre.
126. Author interviews and correspondence with human rights activists from Huambo collecting evidence on the massacre, June–December 2015.
127. Author interview with a human rights activist, Johannesburg, February 2016.
128. "Genocide against 'New Light of the World' Adventists Church of Pastor / Prophet Jose Julino Kalupeteka", op. cit.
129. Coroado, Herculano, "Angola demands apology from UN over Christian sect killings", Reuters, 16 May 2015.
130. They must collect 100,000 notarised signatures, supported by copies of identification cards, from at least a third of Angola's 18 provinces.

## 4. THE ANGOLAN ARMED FORCES: A STRAINED NATIONAL PILLAR

1. Estimates on the actual size of the FAA vary. This number was given by an FAA general but other sources such as the IISS Military Balance and defenceweb.co.za give different numbers.
2. Male citizens between the ages of 18 and 45 are called for mandatory service, and by the age of 30 to register for the reserve forces. Under the

General Law on Military Service, active service for the army is two years (which includes the instruction period) whilst for the navy and air force it is three years. Recruitment is the responsibility of each provincial government.

3. Internal FAA documents.
4. Ibid.
5. According to the 26 December 2014 Russian Federation Military Doctrine. Referenced in McDermott, Roger, "Putin Signs New Military Doctrine: Core Elements Unchanged", *Eurasia Daily Monitor*, Vol. 12, No. 2, via The Jamestown Foundation, January 2015.
6. Author interview with Western Defence Attaché, Pretoria, December 2014.
7. Cuba's military mission was commanded by Raul Menendez Tomassevich (1977–9) and then again (1981–3), by General Leopoldo Cintra Frias (1983–6) and again in 1989, and General Arnaldo Ochoa (1987–8).
8. Author interviews with FAA senior officers, Luanda, January 2015.
9. Author interview with a former advisor to CEMG, Lisbon, February 2019.
10. Author interviews with different military sources, Luanda, January 2015.
11. "Armed Forces of Angola (FAA)", globalsecurity.org. These figures are regarded as estimates. Details on the FAA arsenal were published by the South African online publication, https://www.defenceweb.co.za/; International Institute for Strategic Studies, 2014 Military Balance, but they are difficult to corroborate.
12. Information gathered through interviews with FAA generals and a small publication on the "Armed Forces of the Portuguese Speaking Countries Community (PALOP)" by Jose Mendonca da Luz and João Matias, "Forças Armadas Angolanas: natureza, contingents e estruturas", JANUS, 2013.
13. "General Nunda anuncia passos para a Reedificação das FAA", Angop, September 2014.
14. Author interviews with FAA officers, Luanda, February 2014.
15. Angolan Air and Air Defence Force, globalsecurity.org.
16. "Angola Country Study Guide: Strategic Information and Developments", Library of Congress, Washington, International Business Publications, 2015, p. 49.
17. Angolan Air and Air Defence Force, globalsecurity.org.
18. This included instruction on anti-aircraft defence and radar systems and pilot training for MIG-23, SU-22 and 25, MI-17, 25 and 35.
19. South Africa is the only other country in SADC to have this resource.
20. Author interview with an air force colonel, Luanda, January 2015.
21. Author interview with an FAA brigadier, Luanda, January 2015.

22. Caffrey, Craig and Fenella McGerty, IHS Jane's, "Analysis: Defence Budget Trends in Sub-Saharan Africa", December 2012.
23. "Russia will supply Angola with $1billion in weapons", *Rostec*, October 2013. https://rostec.ru/en/news/3266/. Accessed May 2021.
24. Military Balance, IISS, 2018.
25. Author interview with an FAA general, Luanda, January 2015.
26. Author interview with a military intelligence officer, Luanda, January 2015.
27. Author interview with a retired admiral, Luanda, January 2015.
28. Angolan Navy, globalsecurity.org.
29. Author interview with Western Defence Attaché, Luanda, January 2015.
30. "Piratas Atacam ao largo de Angola", *Voz da América*, 22 January 2014. https://www.voaportugues.com/a/piratas-atacam-ao-largo-de-angola/1835422.html. Accessed May 2021.
31. Mango Tchindele, Daniel, "Apresentado plano de Sistema Nacional de Vigilância Marítima", Angop, 25 November 2009.
32. "Government Creates National Maritime Surveillance System", Angop, 15 November 2019.
33. Angola Armed Forces, *Defence Web*, 5 February 2015.
34. Author interview with Western Defence Attaché, Pretoria, December 2014.
35. "Marinha de Guerra Angolana recebem 6 dos 17 navios comprados a Privinvest—Governo", *Observador*, 2 February 2019.
36. The "secret debt" referred to illicit loans worth over $2 billion, granted by Credit Suisse and VTB of Russia between 2013 and 2014 to three fraudulent security-related companies, Proindicus, Ematum (Mozambique Tuna Company) and MAM (Mozambique Asset Management). The loans were underpinned by state guarantees. Privinvest became the sole contractor for the three companies.
37. Author interviews with civil society and anti-corruption activists, August 2013.
38. "Future of the Angolan Defence Industry-Market Attractiveness, Competitive Landscape and Forecasts to 2019", US-based defence market report by Strategic Defence Intelligence, November 2014.
39. "Angola Military Spending", GlobalSecurity.
40. Author interview with FAA generals, Luanda, January 2015.
41. Author interview with an FAA general, Luanda, January 2015. The President was aware of these difficulties and how they threatened the FAA's ability to operate, yet chose not to address the matter given that the then Finance Minister Armando Manuel was a cousin.
42. Author interview with a military intelligence officer, Luanda, September 2019.

43. Author interview with a retired FAA general, Luanda, January 2015.
44. "Angola tem 320 multimillionarios", *Jornal de Negócios*, 26 April 2017.
45. Author interview with an FAA general, Luanda, September 2008.
46. Author interview with an SISM officer, Luanda January 2015.
47. Coppola, Frances, "Cobalt International Energy: Oil, Angola and Corruption", *Forbes*, 8 August 2014. "Daughters and Generals", *Africa Confidential*, Vol. 49, No. 14, 4 July 2008. Weiss, Michael, "The 750 Million Dollar Man", *Foreign Policy*, 13 February 2014.
48. Sanz, Miguel, "President Lorenço: business, arms deals and old ghosts", AfricaNews, 25 January 2019.
49. Detailed clearly in Burgis, Tom, 2015, *The Looting Machine: Warlords, Oligarchs, Corporations, Smugglers, and the Theft of Africa's Wealth*, New York: PublicAffairs.
50. Author interviews with soldiers, August 2012.
51. Ebertz, Utz and Müller-Koné, Marie, "Legacy of a resource-fuelled war: the role of generals in Angola's mining sector", Bonn International Centre for Conversion (BICC) report, June 2013.
52. "Angola", Government Defence Anti-corruption Index, International Defense and Security Programme, International Transparency, 2013.
53. Author interview with an investigative journalist, Johannesburg, January 2015.
54. Law (21/90).
55. "Nas Lundas generais têm exército privado. Promiscuidade e corrupção nas Forças Armadas Angolanas", *Folha* 8, 28 December 2011.
56. Blore, Shawn, Blore, Josée Létourneau, Josée and Smillie, Ian, "Diamond Industry Annual Review Republic of Angola", Partnership Africa Canada (PAC), 2007.
57. Sofia, Gloria, "Chefe dos Serviços Secretos de Angola Suspeito de Corrupção", Deutsche Welle, 12 March 2013.
58. Marques, Rafael, "Corruption Prerequisite for Government Contracts", Africa Files, September 2009; *Africa Confidential*, Vol. 15, No. 19, 25 September 2009 reports that Sadissa's Chief Executive (former Public Works Minister Jose Alberto Puna Zau) told local journalists that Sadissa "is a kind of NGO to help the comrade freedom fighters".
59. Author interview with a captain of military intelligence, Luanda, January 2015.
60. Author interview with a military intelligence officer, Luanda, January 2015.
61. Author interview with an SISM officer, 23 January 2015.
62. Marques de Morais, Rafael, "Angola: general awards himself more than 300 square kilometers of land", Maka Angola, 24 November 2014.

63. Author interview with a general within CEMG, Luanda, September 2012.

64. In a landscape of over 500 generals, the most senior Ovimbundu generals made up merely a handful. These included former CEMG Nunda, Lúcio Gonçalves Amaral (Army Chief), Geraldo Abreu Ukwatchitembo Kamorteiro (Deputy CEMG for Logistics and Infrastructure), General Samuel Kapinala Samy (President for the Superior Disciplinary Council of the FAA), Adriano Mackevela Mackenzie (Chief Director of Troop Training and Education), Peregrino Isidro Wambu Chindongo (CEMG Advisor on Legal Affairs), Lt. Gen. Wilson Sakai Muzengo (CEMG Advisor on Armament), Lt. Gen. Jaime Manuel Pombo Vilinga (Director of the Superior Military Institute IRTM), General David Wenda Catata (Deputy Army Chief), Lt. Gen. Job Sungeuet Longfellow (Chief of Penitentiary Services), General Kananay (Advisor to Army Chief), Brigadier Didimo Kapingana (Head of Operations in General Staff), General Jacinto Mbandua (Chief Director of Psychological Warfare) and General Artur Santos Pereira Vinama (Deputy Military Inspector).

65. Author interview with a military intelligence officer, Luanda, January 2015.

66. Author interview with a lawyer to MPLA elites, Luanda, September 2019.

67. Author interview with a retired FAA general, Luanda, January 2015.

68. Foreign Minister George Chikoty was retired as a brigadier according to an author interview with an FAA general, Luanda, January 2015.

69. Tabela de Valores, Caixa de Segurança Social FAA, Departamento de Contabilidade, Finanças e Contribuições, Ministério da Defesa Nacional, 14 June 2013.

70. "Ex-oficiais generais angolanos na reforma prometem aguardar por resolução no corte de pensões", *Diário de Notícias*, 14 February 2019.

71. "Oficiais reformados das FAA recebem pensões a partir de Dezembro", *Jornal O País*, 23 November 2019.

72. "Angola precisa de 108 milhões de euros para reintegrar mais de 117.000 ex-militares", *Observador*, 9 April 2019.

73. Author interview with a former deputy minister, Luanda, January 2015.

74. Author interview with a demobilised FAA brigadier, Luanda, January 2015.

75. "Angola gastou 293 milhões de euros com pensões para ex-militares em 2019", *Observador*, 28 January 2020.

76. "Mais de 9 mil oficiais das FAA recebem pensões", *Jornal de Angola*, 23 November 2019.

77. "Angola Ministry of Defense/Armed Forces of Angola (FAA)", GlobalSecurity.

78. See "Ninjas in Zimbabwe", March 25, 2007 Strategy Page, www. strategypage.com.

79. An assertion made by a captain in the Presidential Guard, interviewed Luanda, January 2015.

80. This was integral to the 2014 agreements. "Angola, CAR sign legal instruments for bilateral cooperation", Reliefweb (reliefweb.int), 5 May 2014.

81. "Affaire Mokoko: Tshisekedi et Lourenço ont-ils plaidé pour l'évacuation de l'opposant congolais?", *Jeune Afrique*, 9 July 2020.

82. Author interviews with military sources, 2008–2017; also see "Will the bad loser be squeezed out?", *The Economist*, 10 March 2011.

83. Angolan Foreign Minister George Chikoty's speech to Chatham House, 20 February 2012; it is unclear if this money was made available to Bissau as a repayable loan or if it was delivered as aid.

84. Author interviews with military sources, Luanda, 2015.

85. Sebastião Bernardo Cabouco, "Participação das Forças Armadas Angolanas em Operações de Apoio à Paz: Lições Aprendidas", thesis, Escola Superior de Guerra, Luanda, 2014, p. 18.

86. Author interview with an FAA general, Luanda, March 2015.

87. "Portuguese-speaking countries hold joint peacekeeping exercise", Agência Brasil, 25 September 2013. "Exercise Golfinho an example for other continental brigades", Boshoff, Henri, ISS Today, 13 October 2009. https://issafrica.org/amp/iss-today/exercise-golfinho-an-example-for-other-continental-brigades. Accessed May 2021.

88. "Angola: conditions for AU to certify FOMAC created", Angop, 5 June 2010.

89. "Angola, CAR sign legal instruments for bilateral cooperation", Angop, 5 March 2014. "Every time the President in CAR is in trouble of some sort she goes running to Luanda", author interview with a CAR UN official, Pretoria, May 2015.

90. Author correspondence with a military expert, 2015.

91. In the mid-1980s, Cuban troops, under the "tropical troops" unit of Major Alberto Garcia Mestre, bolstered the defences of Chevron's $1.3 billion investment in Cabinda against South African and UNITA sabotage activities. Brooke, James, "Cubans Guard US Oilmen in Angola", *New York Times*, 24 November 1986.

92. Author interviews with different political actors, Cabinda, November 2015.

93. Author correspondence with Cabindan activists, October 2013.

94. Author interviews with activists, Cabinda and Luanda, November 2015.

95. Author interviews with different FLEC supporters, November 2015.

96. "Estado de Sítio: Cafunfo sob fogo de Militares e Policiais", Maka Angola, 17 November 2018.

97. Author interviews and correspondence with Lunda activists and community representatives, November and December 2015.
98. See Rafael Marques de Morais' reports: "Lundas: as Pedras da Morte", 2005; "A Colheita da Fome nas Areas Diamantiferas", 2008, and his 2011 report that was transformed into the book *Blood Diamonds: Corruption and Torture in Angola*.
99. Allen, Michael, "The Blood Diamond Resurfaces", *Wall Street Journal*, 19 June 2009.
100. "Lunda Norte: protectorado revela lista de pessoas assassinadas pela polícia nacional", 17 August 2015, Club-K.
101. Author interview with a Lunda activist, December 2015.
102. Sharife, Khadija, and Grobler, John. Edited by Andelman, David A. and Fredrick, Yaffa, "Kimberley's Illicit Process", *World Policy Journal*, Winter 2013. http://worldpolicy.org/kimberleys-illicit-process/. Accessed May 2021.
103. Many Brazilian diamond interests were held under joint ventures with Odebretch, like the case of the Sociedade de Desenvolvimento Mineiro, whose equal partner was Endiama; Russian interests were mainly held with Alrosa, while Israeli interests diverged mostly with private investors Lev Leviev among others and Belgian interests are represented by Omega.
104. Endiama was the national diamond company, whose main private security company is Alfa-5.
105. Created in 1997, Gibraltar-registered company Trans Africa Investment Services (TAIS), was set up by Isabel dos Santos (75%) and her mother Tatiana Cergueevna Regan (25%) who in 2004 became the sole shareholder after her daughter transferred all her shares. It was renamed Iaxonh in 2001 (Marques 2011: 32–33).
106. SMC's shareholding was divided between Endiama (41%), ITM Mining (38%) and Lumanhe (21%); key Angolan generals had key interests in SMC and in the provision of security with their private company Teleservice (Marques 2011: 70–71).
107. Sociedade de comercialização de Diamantes de Angola (Sodiam) was a national company created by the Council of Ministers in 1999 to act as the main outfit to exert full control over the commercialisation of the stones; it was a subsidiary of Endiama. See Marques (2011: 31).
108. Angola Selling Corporation (Ascorp), created in 1999, was a venture between TAIS, the Goldberg Group and Leviev Wellox. Ascorp was created to become the only channel of sale and purchase of diamonds, which at a time of war required more organisation and control of the sector. Marques (2011: 32).

109. SML was a consortium created to explore diamonds in the Lunda Sul province. Its shareholding was as follows: Endiama (32.8 %), Russian multinational Alrosa (32.8%), Lev Leviev Holding (18%) and Odebretch (16.4), Marques (2011: 73).
110. Krawitz, Avi, "Angola, 100 years Later", Diamond.net, 28 June 2013.
111. "Produção de diamantes aumenta 5,6%", Rede Angola, 19 December 2015.
112. Author interview with Lunda civilian leader, December 2015.
113. "Operation Thunderclap: at least five dead in Separatist attack on Angolan prison", Maka Angola, 5 November 2019.
114. "Relatorio sobre o massacre do Cafunfu", Grupo Parlamentar da UNITA, 10 February 2021.
115. Call made by Benedito Daniel leader of the PRS opposition party. Quoted in "Igreja Católica angolana alerta para 'grave massacre' de manifestantes no Cafunfo", Observador, 1 February 2021.
116. Lai Men, Cristina and Maldonado Vasconcelos, Catarina, "Ocultação de crime em Angola? Familiares de mortos em Cafunfu denunciam furto de 20 corpis de morgue", TSF, 2 February 2021.
117. Local elections were always a key area for the opposition. They knew that of the 18 provinces the opposition could potentially win eight— with UNITA, PRS and CASA-CE winning Luanda, Huambo, Bengulea, Bie, Cabinda, Lunda Norte, Lunda Sul, and Moxico. In 2002 UNITA had two main political considerations for the government: the direct election of provincial governors as opposed to their nomination by the President and the direct control of finances of the governors. (Author interview with a member of the UNITA commission in 2002, Luanda, October 2019.) UNITA understood that as an opposition party it stood no chance of dismantling the centralised apparatus built around dos Santos. Instead, they focused on trying to seek influence at the provincial and local levels. At the time of going to press, no municipal elections have been held in Angola as a result.

## 5. CHANGING THE GUARD: JOÃO LOURENÇO'S PRESIDENCY

1. Costa, Gustavo, "Presidente Angolano anula contratos de $20 mil milhões de dólares à família de José Eduardo dos Santos", Expresso, 14 July 2018.
2. Author interview with leading dos Santos advisor, Luanda, September 2019.
3. IDREA 2018–2019, Instituto Nacional de Estatística, December 2019.
4. Author interview with opposition leader, Luanda, September 2019.
5. Roque, Paula Cristina, "Angola's elections trigger a crisis of legitimacy", ISS Today, 8 September 2017.

6. LUSA, "Vício nas eleições? UNITA põe algumas provas na mesa", *Correio Angolense*, 5 September 2017.

7. Author interview with a close advisor to dos Santos, Luanda, October 2019.

8. Author interviews with FAA generals and civilians, Luanda, October 2019.

9. Escom was a subsidiary of the Espirito Santo Group; see "A Honra do Espírito Santo e o Saque em Angola", Maka Angola, 17 August 2014.

10. Author interview with an intelligence officer, Luanda, September 2019.

11. "Quatro forças de segurança cuidaram do congresso do MPLA". Club-K, 17 June 2019.

12. Marques de Morais, Rafael, "General Disciplina Faz das FAA Exército do MPLA", Maka Angola, 15 June 2019.

13. Author interview with a retired FAA general, Luanda, October 2019.

14. "Nem os caixotes de lixo vão escapar à vigilância", *Folha 8*, 6 May 2020.

15. Ibid.

16. Author interview with a lawyer to Angolan elites, Luanda, September 2019.

17. See investigative report by Rafael Marques de Morais, "MPLA, Sociedade Anonima", Maka Angola.

18. Ibid.

19. Dan Keeler in the *Wall Street Journal*'s weekly Emerging & Growth Markets newsletter, 11 October 2020.

20. "Angolanos terão seis meses para repatriar fortunas sem serem alvo de investigação", *Observador*, 6 January 2018.

21. Study conducted by the Catholic University of Luanda.

22. Pearce, Justin, Didier Péclard and Ricardo Soares de Oliveira, "Angola's elections and the politics of presidential succession", *African Affairs*, Vol. 117: 466, January 2018, pp. 146–60.

23. "Unita elogia PR por ter divulgado montante desviado do Estado, mas Adalberto Costa Júnior e João Lourenço fazem contas diferentes", *Novo Jornal*, 12 October 2020.

24. Author interview with a former dos Santos advisor, Luanda, October 2019.

25. Author interviews with political elites, Luanda, September and October 2019.

26. Following the very public and widely condemned trials of political activists and youths, known as the "15+2" case, the celebration of 40 years of independence and the economic crises, President dos Santos and the MPLA passed an amnesty law that would cover crimes with up to 12 years' jail time.

27. Angola, BTI 2018 Country Report.

28. "Perto de 4 mil milhões de dólares voltam aos cofres do Estado", *Jornal de Angola*, 27 April 2019.
29. Ibid.
30. "Toda a verdade sobre o duelo entre Isabel dos Santos e Joaquim David", Maka Angola, 2 August 2017.
31. Patrick, Margot, Gabriele Steinhauser and Patricia Kowsmann, "The $500 Million Central Bank Heist—and How It Was Foiled", *Wall Street Journal*, 3 October 2018.
32. "Isabel dos Santos condemns abusive seizure of $442 million stake", International Consortium of Investigative Journalists, 7 April 2020. https://www.icij.org/investigations/luanda-leaks/isabel-dos-santos-condemns-abusive-seizure-of-442m-stake/#:~:text=Isabel%20dos%20Santos%20has%20denounced,abusive%E2%80%9D%20and%20%E2%80%9Cexcessive.%E2%80%9D. Accessed May 2021.
33. "PGR a 'Duas Velocidades' nos casos de corrupção", *Africa Monitor*, No. 1240, 19 March 2020.
34. "Os processos contra Isabel dos Santos em Angola", Maka Angola, 22 May 2020.
35. Hilary Osborne and Caelainn Barr, "The diamond deal that rocked Angola", *The Guardian*, 19 January 2020. https://www.theguardian.com/world/2020/jan/19/diamond-deal-that-rocked-angola-de-grisogono-luanda-leaks. Accessed May 2021.
36. Author interview, Luanda, October 2019.
37. These include former presidential spokesperson Aldemiro Vaz da Conceição, former foreign minister Assunção dos Anjos, and former petroleum minister Joae Maria Botelho de Vasconcelos, among others. "Obrigada e tchau, dos Santos", *Africa Confidential*, Vol. 59, No. 9, 4 May 2019. https://www.africa-confidential.com/article/id/12309/Obrigado-e-tchau%2C-Dos-Santos. Accessed May 2021.
38. "João Lourenço nomeia ex-arguido do caso "Burla Tailandesa" para casa de Segurança", *Observador*, 7 April 2020.
39. "Discontent takes wing", *Africa Confidential*, Vol. 59, No. 13, 29 June 2018. https://www.africa-confidential.com/article/id/12365/Discontent_takes_wing. Accessed May 2021.
40. Author interviews with generals and politicians, Luanda, September and October 2019.
41. "Angola Força generais a devolverem dinheiro", SÁBADO, 20 June 2019. https://www.sabado.pt/mundo/detalhe/angola-forca-generais-a-devolverem-dinheiro. Accessed May 2021.
42. "Corrupção: os tentaculos da Odebrecht em Angola e Moçambique", Deutsche Welle, 25 April 2017.

43. Author interview with an intellectual, Luanda, September 2019.
44. "Generais Dino e Kopelipa: Encenação de entrega de bens Maria Luísa Abrantes", Club-K, 15 October 2020.
45. "PGR a "Duas Velocidades" nos casos de corrupção", *Africa Monitor*, No. 1240, 19 March 2020.
46. "Switzerland froze $900 million from Angolan businessman—documents", Reuters, 2 September 2020.
47. Marques de Morais, Rafael, "Sonangol: o epicentro da pilhagem de São Vicente", Maka Angola, 14 September 2020.
48. "Caso Telstar: Que consequências para a governação angolana?", Deutsche Welle, 21 April 2019.
49. Marques de Morais, Rafael, "JLo emboscado no bairro dos Ministérios e das Mentiras", Maka Angola, 6 August 2019.
50. "Sodiam contrata empresa de Edeltrudes Costa", Club-K, 8 July 2020.
51. Author interview with a former oil executive, Luanda, September 2019.
52. Smith, Matt, "Discoveries Boost Angola Upstream Mood", Petroleum Economist, 27 August 2019.
53. Angola Country Report 2019, EIU.
54. Quaresma dos Santos, D., "Sonangol's Billion-Dollar Headache", Maka Angola, 21 July 2016.
55. Angola: First Review of the Extended Arrangement Under the Extended Fund Facility, International Monetary Fund, 29 May 2019.
56. "Some 32 state-owned enterprises earmarked for sale", Economist Intelligence Unit, 18 July 2019.
57. Angola Country Report, EIU, July 2020.
58. "FMI em Angola: Empréstimo a troco de quê?", Deutsche Welle, 19 June 2019.
59. Author interview with a military intelligence officer, Luanda, October 2019.
60. Author interviews, Luanda, September and October 2019.
61. Author interview with a military intelligence officer, Luanda, October 2019.
62. On the weekend of 27 September 2019, the daughter of the Speaker of Parliament, Fernando Dias dos Santos "Nando", held her wedding in Luanda in the lavish setting of a castle-like structure. The wedding reportedly cost over $2 million and was widely criticised across society for its obscene levels of luxury and because of the presence of the President. "Casamento de 2 milhões gera polémica", Club-K, 1 October 2019.
63. "12 milhões de Angolanos são tão pobres que não têm 500 kwanzas para comer", *Guardião*, 4 February 2020.

64. Cilliers, Jakkie; Oosthuizen, Marius; Kwasi, Stellah; Alexandre, Kelly; Pooe, TK; Yeboua, Kouassi; and Moyer, Jonathan, "Impact of Covid-19 in Africa: Ascenario analysis to 2030", Africa Report 24, Institute for Security Studies, July 2020.
65. Author interviews in Luanda, September 2019.
66. "Angola drought: millions at risk of starvation", Al Jazeera, 19 May 2019.
67. Author interviews conducted since 2008 in Angola.
68. There were two fundamental areas of contention and disagreement with the opposition regarding the holding of municipal elections. The MPLA floated the idea of "*gradualismo*" (gradualism), that would see the elections of different municipalities in a phased process. UNITA defended that any phased approach should entail the degrees of responsibilities that the central government could exercise while the municipal administrations were developing. The second area of disagreement was the level of responsibilities and supervision over local administrations. The ruling party defended the creation of a supervisory organ to monitor the local administrations. In contrast the opposition defended that the central government should ensure that the local administration abides by the laws established for the everyday running of its affairs. The polls were expected in 2020, but the ruling party was aiming to hold them only after the legislative polls in 2022 when it was able to control the results. Holding legislative and municipal polls at different times would break the MPLA's hegemonic stranglehold. It would also potentially improve the quality of polls and supervision of the process by opposition parties. Several laws have to be passed to prepare for the process, including legislating on its organisation, its functioning, powers of the municipalities, local finance, and the election of municipal assemblies.
69. 2019/20 Afrobarometer survey, https://afrobarometer.org/.
70. "Lourenço propõe revisão constitucional que pode permitir fiscalização do Governo pelo Parlamento", Voice of America, 3 March 2021.
71. Author correspondence with opposition member and MPLA dissident, March 2021.
72. "Angola: SINSE quer difamar Costa Júnior com associação a pedofilia", E-Global, 16 March 2021.
73. Ironically, the opposition's xenophobic slurs against dos Santos, claiming he was born in Cape Verde, were being slung against da Costa Júnior. They meant to disqualify him politically but also to create tensions within UNITA. The extraordinary irony was that UNITA had always used the MPLA "un-Africanness" against it while the ruling party had always depicted UNITA as a tribalist and backward party. "Lourenço, Bureau Politico e SINSE na Reacção a Cafunfo", *Africa Monitor*, No. 1286, 11 February 2021.

74. Author conversation with retired FAA general, 1 June 2021.
75. "Autoridades confiscam 40 milhões de dólares em nome do General Furtado", Club-K, 17 January 2011.
76. Author correspondence with officers in military intelligence, May 2021.

6. THE TIME OF MONSTERS: ANGOLA'S RESPONSE TO COVID-19

1. Antonio Gramsci, *Prison Notebooks*.
2. Author conversation with an Angolan intellectual, July 2020.
3. "Angola: witnesses describe horrific killings of teenagers by police", Amnesty International, 25 August 2020.
4. Angola Country Report, EIU, July 2020.
5. "Fragilidades das Cercas Sanitarias", PlataformaOSC-Angola, 16 August 2020. https://plataformaosc.org/fragilidade-das-cercas-sanitarias/.
6. National Defence and War Veterans; Transportation, Telecommunications and Information Technology; Industry and Commerce; Mineral Resources and Petroleum, Fisheries and Agriculture; Culture, Tourism and Environment.
7. Marques de Morais, Rafael, "O Estado da Saúde e o Berbequim de Pedreiro", Maka Angola, 29 July 2020.
8. "'Braço de ferro' entre médico e direção do hospital pediátrico pode chegar a tribunal", *Novo Jornal*, 15 August 2020.
9. "Dispara número de Mortes nos Hospitais do pais", *O País*, 15 March 2020.
10. "Em um mês, UNITA consta 4570 mortes em hospitais em Luanda", Deutsche Welle, 12 April 2016.
11. "Negócio à porta dos hospitais de Luanda: 'Um balão de sangue pode custar até 30 mil kz'", *Novo Jornal*, 7 May 2016.
12. "Covid-19: Africa CDC diz que é prematura qualquer avaliação da mortalidade elevada em Angola", *Novo Jornal*, 17 September 2020.
13. Author correspondence with a leading member of Angolan civil society, September 2020.
14. Author correspondence with an officer from military intelligence, September 2020.
15. "Covid-19: MINSA compra cinco laboratórios a China por seis milhões USD", *Novo Jornal*, 17 July 2020.
16. "Covid-19 em Angola: falta de testes agrava primeiros estragos da pandemia", *Expresso*, 1 May 2020.
17. "Angolan government relying Partner assistance to fight Covid-19", Centre for Strategic and International Studies, 24 June 2020. https://www.csis.org/analysis/angolan-government-relying-partner-assistance-fight-covid-19.

18. "Presidente da república aprova despesa de mais de 45,5 mil milhões de Kwanzas para contratação de médicos Cubanos", *Novo Jornal*, 6 June 2020.
19. "Sessenta e seis pacientes recebem alta no hospital de campanha de Viana", Angop, 22 October 2020.
20. "Governo disponibiliza mais de mil milhões de dólares para combater Covid-19", *Jornal de Angola*, 28 March 2020; "Financiamentos do PAC atingem 108 mil milhões", *Jornal de Angola*, 14 February 2020.
21. "Angola aprova programa de 420 milhões de dólares para famílias vulneraveis", Lusa, 14 May 2020.
22. "Covid-19: Governo fixa preços aos testes", *Novo Jornal*, 20 October 2020.
23. Angola Situation Report 5, August 2020, UNICEF.
24. "Fome mata 46 crianças por dia em Angola", *Novo Jornal*, 9 October 2020. https://novojornal.co.ao/sociedade/interior/fome-mata-46-cri-ancas-por-dia-em-angola-95044.html. Accessed 5 June 2021.
25. "Tempos sombrios em Angola: "E uma catastrophe", *Público*, 17 June 2020.
26. Numbers were more likely to be higher, given that these accounted for only the known numbers of four provinces. "Mais de 700 pessoas suicid-aram-se nos últimos seis meses, revela SIC", *Novo Jornal*, 29 September 2020.
27. "Economia Angolana afundou 5.1 % em 2020, a maior queda em quatro decadas", *Expansão*, 14 March 2021.
28. The country's national statistics institute (INE) surveyed the levels of poverty in 2018–19 and found that almost half of Angolans lived below the poverty line, with a higher incidence in rural areas.
29. "Tempos sombrios em Angola: "E uma catastrophe", *Público*, 17 June 2020.
30. "Covid-19. Angola arrisca ficar em recessão económica até 2023", *Expresso*, 31 May 2020. https://expresso.pt/economia/2020-05-31-Covid-19.-Angola-arrisca-ficar-em-recessao-economica-ate-2023. Accessed 5 June 2021.
31. "Angola's oil exploration evaporates as COVID-19 overshadows historic reforms", Reuters, 20 May 2020.
32. In the revised budget, spending continued to prioritise debt repayment (55%), government spending on salaries and other running costs (19%), followed by the social sector (17%), and defence (8%).
33. "Angola's Fiscal Deficit Target Achievable, but High Debt Persists", Fitch Ratings, 7 December 2020.
34. "Clinica dentária milionária e retirada da discussão do orçamento ango-lano", Deutsche Welle, 28 July 2020.

35. "USD 180 Milhões para unidade Orçamental do MDN", *Africa Monitor*, No. 1248, 14 May 2020.
36. "Novo Aeroporto de Luanda: Um elefante branco em Angola", Deutsche Welle, 9 September 2019.
37. "Discontent and protests in Luanda marks 3 years of Joao Lourenço's rule", *Ver Angola*, 28 September 2020.
38. Kamalata Numa, General Abilio, Facebook post, 25 October 2020. Accessed November 2020.
39. "Com petróleo a 60 USD, OGE 2021 tem uma 'almofada' de 3,61 mil milhões USD", https://mercado.co.ao/economia/com-petroleo-a-60-usd-oge-2021-tem-uma-almofada-de-361-mil-milhoes-usd-AG1008453. Accessed April 2021.

## CONCLUSION

1. The 1977 "coup" unleashed a massive purge and highlighted the importance of a strong Presidential Guard, a contained party and a shielded Presidency with centralising power. This initiated a move that would gradually create the Presidency's shadow government.

   The 1986 economic crisis took the country away from the disastrous distortions of state socialism which resulted in the economic redeployment of the elites in controlling resources. This began the process of economic stranglehold that would fuel the shadow government, the war and the patronage system.

   The 1992 elections and the mismanagement of the process securitised polls and revealed the utility of reactivating militias and the powerful paramilitary police (PIR). The Presidency became the parallel government, a reality that was very much consolidated when the 1997 government of national unity was inaugurated. The ruling class was, on one side, waging war with UNITA and, on the other, invalidating the parliamentary efforts and governing policies of the unity government, resulting in further shadowing.

   In 2002, the country faced chaos and a severe humanitarian crisis. Public order was achieved through the security forces, including civilian defence militias, and a rushed and mismanaged DDR process. Intelligence services and non-FAA units factored more prominently into the post-war strategy. Following the 2010 "hyper-presidentialist" constitution, the protests of 2011 instilled fear in the elites, unleashing a wave of brutality buttressed by intrusive surveillance and militarised political cells. The government's paranoia increased in 2014 with the fall in oil prices that set the country on a path of unrecoverable recession.

     While the 2017 presidential succession was politically managed to ensure continuity, internal rifts brought the need to further securitise to protect the new President.

2. Author virtual interview with an Angolan intellectual, July 2020.
3. "A Marcha do medo, da vergonha e das mentiras", *Folha* 8, 2011.
4. These leaflets read "Everyone still remembers how in 1992 UNITA rejected the results and plunged the country into war ... Do not contribute to the destruction of peace that was so tirelessly conquered".
5. Author interview with a Catholic priest in Huambo, January 2003.
6. Defamation campaigns and character assassination strategies were increasing against UNITA's new leader Adalberto da Costa Júnior, questioning his "Angolanness" and suggesting he aimed to violently destabilise the country. "Angola: UNITA culpa Governo por campanha de difamação contra o seu líder", Deutsche Welle, 24 March 2021. Opposition parties were allegedly created by UNITA members, with the MPLA's support, to split the vote.
7. Sears, Nathan Alexander, "The securitisation of Covid-19: three political dilemmas", Global Policy Journal blog, 25 March 2020.

# BIBLIOGRAPHY

Acemoglu, Daron; Robinson, James; Verdier, Thierry, "Kleptocracy and Divide-and-Rule: A Model of Personal Rule", *Journal of the European Economic Association*, Vol. 2, Nos. 2–3 (April–May 2004), pp. 162–92.

Aradau, Claudia, 2004, "Security and the Democratic Scene: Desecuritization and Emancipation", *Journal of International Relations and Development*, Vol. 7 (December), pp. 388–413.

Araújo, Raul Carlos Vasques, 2017, *O Presidente da República no Sistema Político de Angola 1975–2010*, Edições Almedina.

Balzacq, Thierry (ed.), 2011, *Securitisation Theory: How Security Problems Emerge and Dissolve*, New York: Routledge

Beale, Stephane, "On the Securitization of COVID-19", Pandemipolitics, 9 April 2020.

Blanes, Ruy Llera, 2016, "A febre do arquivo. O 'efeito Benjamin' e as revoluções angolanas", *Práticas da História*, Vol. 3, pp. 71–92.

Bigo, Didier, 2002, "Security and Immigration: Toward a Critique of the Governmentality of Unease", *Alternatives*, Vol. 27, No. 1 (February), pp. 63–92.

Bittencourt, Marcelo, 2011, "Fissuras na luta de Libertação Angolana", *METIS: História e Cultura*, Vol. 10, No. 9 (January/June), pp. 237–55.

Bonzela Franco, Marcelino, 2013, "A Evolução do Conceito Estratégico de Serviço de Inteligência e de Segurança dio Estado da República de Angola (1975–2010)", master's thesis, Instituto Superior de Ciências Sociais e Políticas.

Brownlee, Jason, 2007, *Authoritarianism in an Age of Democratization*, Cambridge: Cambridge University Press.

Burke, Anthony, 2002, "Aporias of Security", *Alternatives: Global, Local, Political*, Vol. 27, No. 1, pp. 1–27.

Buzan, Barry; Waever, Ole; de Wilde, Jaap, 1998, *Security: A New Framework for Analysis*, Boulder, CO: Lynne Rienner Publishers, pp. 50–1.

# BIBLIOGRAPHY

Cleary, Sean, 1999, "Angola—A Case Study of Private Military Involvement", in Cilliers, Jakkie, and Mason, Peggy (eds), *Peace, Profit or Plunder?*, Institute for Security Studies, pp. 141–74.

Castles, Stephen, 2005, "Nation and Empire: Hierarchies of Citizenship in the New Global Order", *International Politics*, Vol. 42, pp. 203–24.

Chabal, Patrick, and Vidal, Nuno (eds), 2007, *Angola: The Weight of History*, London: Hurst.

Cruz, Domingos, 2016, *Angola Amordaçada*, Lisbon: Editora Guerra e Paz.

Duffield, M., 2001, "Governing the Borderlands: Decoding the Power of Aid", *Disasters*, Vol. 25, No. 4, pp. 308–20.

Duncan, Jane, 2015, *The Rise of the Securocrats: The Case of South Africa*, Johannesburg: Jacana.

Elbe, Stefan, 2006, "Should HIV/AIDS Be Securitised? The Ethical Dilemmas of Linking HIV/AIDS and Security", *International Studies Quarterly*, Vol. 50, No. 1 (March), pp. 119–44.

Ezeokafor, Edwin, and Kaunert, Christian, 2018, "Securitisation Outside of the West", *Global Discourse*, Vol. 8, No. 1, pp. 83–99.

Faria, Paulo, 2013, *The Post-War Angola: Public Sphere, Political Regime and Democracy*, Newcastle upon Tyne: Cambridge Scholars Publishing.

Floyd, Rita, 2011, "Can Securitization Theory Be Used in Normative Analysis? Towards a Just Securitization Theory", *Security Dialogue*, Vol. 42: Nos. 4–5 (August), pp. 427–39.

Gastrow, Claudia, 2017, "Aesthetic Dissent: Urban Redevelopment and political Belonging in Luanda, Angola", *Antipode*, Vol. 49, No. 2 (March), pp. 377–96.

Gaudino, Ugo, "The Ideological Securitization of COVID-19: Perspectives from the Right and the Left", E-International Relations, 28 July 2020, https://www.e-ir.info/2020/07/28/the-ideological-securitization-of-covid-19-perspectives-from-the-right-and-the-left/

Glennon, Michael, 2015, *National Security and Double Government*, New York: Oxford University Press.

Gleijeses, Piero, 2013, *Visions of Freedom: Havana, Washington, Pretoria and the Struggle for Southern Africa, 1976–1991*, Chapel Hill: University of North Carolina Press.

Hallsworth, Simon, and Lea, John, 2011, "Reconstructing Leviathan: Emerging Contours of the Security State", *Theoretical Criminology*, Vol. 15, No. 2 (May), pp. 141–57.

Hansen, Thomas Blom, and Stepputat, Finn (eds), 2005, *Sovereign Bodies: Citizens, Migrants and States in the Postcolonial World*, Princeton, NJ: Princeton University Press.

Heywood, Linda, 2011, "Angola and the Violent Years 1975–2008: Civilian casualties", *Portuguese Studies Review*, Vol. 19, No. 1, pp. 311–32.

# BIBLIOGRAPHY

Hodges, Tony, 2004, *Angola: Anatomy of an Oil State*, Oxford: James Currey.

Holbraad, Martin, and Axel Pedersen, Morten, 2012, "Revolutionary Securitisation: An Anthropological Extension of Securitization Theory", *International Theory*, Vol. 4, No. 2, pp. 165–97.

Huntington, Samuel, 1985 [1957], *The Soldier and the State: The Theory and Politics of Civil-Military Relations*, Cambridge, MA: Harvard University Press.

Huysmans, Jeff; Dobson, Andrew; Prokhovnik, Raia (eds), 2006, *The Politics of Protection: Sites of Insecurity and Political Agency*, London: Routledge.

Jackson, Robert, and Rosberg, Carl, 1982, "Why Africa's Weak States Persist: The Empirical and the Juridical in Statehood", *World Politics*, Vol. 35, No. 1 (October), pp. 1–24.

Jensen, Soren Kirk, and Pestana, Nelson, 2010, "O papel das Igrejas na Redução da Pobreza em Angola", CMI Report, https://www.cmi.no/publications/3631-o-papel-das-igrejas-na-reduo-da-pobreza-em-angola.

Jones, Will; Soares de Oliveira, Ricardo; Verhoeven, Harry, 2013, "Africa's Illiberal State-builders", Refugee Studies Centre, Working Paper Series 89 (January).

Junior, Miguel, 2019a, *Popular Armed Forces for the Liberation of Angola: First National Army and the War (1975–1992)*, Author House.

————, 2019b, *The Formation and Development of the Angolan Armed Forces*, Author House.

Lasswell, Harold, 1941 [1997], *Essays on the Garrison State*, New York: Routledge.

Lima, Juliana, 2013, "From Arab Spring to a New Revolution in Angola: Postwar Political Movements and Protest in Luanda", *Afrique contemporaine*, Vol. 245, No. 1

Lipschutz, Ronnie D. (ed.), 1995, *On Security*, New York: Columbia University Press.

Mabeko Tali, Jean Michel, 2001, *Dissidências e Poder de Estado. O MPLA perante si próprio (1962–1977), Ensaio de História Política*, Luanda: Nzila.

Maier, Karl, 1997, "Angola: Peace at Last?", *Refugee Survey Quarterly*, Vol. 16, No. 2, pp. 1–23.

————, 2007, *Angola: Promises and Lies*, London: Serif.

Marques, Rafael, 2008, "Angola: Waiting for Democracy to fall from the Sky after the Elections", conference paper.

————, 2011, "Diamantes de sangue: corrupção e tortura em Angola", *Caderno CRH*, Vol. 26, No. 68 (May–August), pp. 407–8.

Martins, Vasco, 2017, "Politics of Power and Hierarchies of Citizenship in Angola", *Citizenship Studies*, Vol. 21, No. 1 pp. 100–1158.

Mateus, Dalila and Mateus Álvaro, 2007, *Purga em Angola*, Lisbon: Edições Asa.

McDonald, Matt, 2008, "Securitization and the Construction of Security",

*European Journal of International Relations*, Vol. 14, No. 4 (December), pp. 563–87.

McInnes, Colin, and Rushton, Simon, 2013, "HIV/AIDS and Securitisation Theory", *European Journal of International Relations*, Vol. 19, No. 1, pp. 115–38.

Meldrum, Andrew, 1992, "Angola: Hungry to Vote", Africa Report, Vol. 37, No. 6 (November), p. 26.

Messiant, Christine, 2007, "The Mutation of Hegemonic Domination", in Patrick Chabal and Nuno Vidal (eds), *Angola: The Weight of History*, London, Hurst.

————, 2000, "Prefacio", in Schubert, Benedict, *A Guerra e as Igrejas, Angola 1961–1991*, Basel: Schlettwein Publishing.

————, 2001, "The Eduardo dos Santos Foundation or How Angola's Regime is Taking over Civil Society", *African Affairs*, Vol. 100, No. 399 (April), pp. 287–309.

————, 2004, "Why Did Bicesse and Lusaka Fail?", *ACCORD* Issue 15, pp. 16–23.

Miranda, Jorge, 2010, "A Constituição de Angola de 2010", *Revista de Ciências Juridicas e Economicas*, Vol. 2, No. 1.

Moorman, Marissa, 2008, *Intonations: A Social History of Music and Nation in Luanda*, Athens: Ohio University Press.

Moura Roque, Fátima, 1994, *Angola em Nome da Esperança*, Lisbon: Bertrand Editora.

————, 1997, *Building the Future in Angola: A Vision for Sustainable Development*, Oeiras: Editora Celta.

————, 2000, *Building Peace in Angola*, Lisbon: Edições Universitárias Lusófonas.

Neto, António Pitra, 2008, *MPLA e as eleições legislativas de 2008: as nossas razões para a vitória; tópicos de estudo*, Luanda: Editorial Nzila.

Nelson-Pallmeyer, Jack, 1992, *Brave New World Order*, Maryknoll, NY: Orbis Books.

Olesker, Ronnie, 2018, "The Securitisation Dilemma: Legitimacy in Securitisation Studies", *Critical Studies on Security*, Vol. 6, No. 3, pp. 312–29.

Pacheco, Fernando, 2009, "Civil Society in Angola: Fiction or Agent of Change?", in Nuno Vidal and Patrick Chabal (eds), *Southern Africa: Civil Society, Politics and Donor Strategies*, Luanda: Media XXI; Lisbon: Firmamento.

Paredes, Margarida, 2010, "Deolinda Rodrigues, da Família Metodista à Família MPLA, o Papel da Cultura na Política", *Cadernos de Estudos Africanos*, Vol. 20, pp. 11–26.

Pawson, Lara, 2007, "O 27 de Maio Angolano Visto de Baixo", *Relações Internacionais*, IPRI.

# BIBLIOGRAPHY

Pearce, Justin, 2005, *An Outbreak of Peace: Angola's Situation of Confusion*, Johannesberg: David Phillip Publishers.

———, 2015, *Political Identity and Conflict in Central Angola 1975–2002*, Cambridge: Cambridge University Press.

———, 2016, "Youthful Dissent Challenges Angola's Old Elite", *Current History*, Vol. 115, No. 781, pp. 175–80.

Péclard, Didier, 1998, "Religion and Politics in Angola: The Church, the Colonial State and the Emergence of Angolan Nationalism 1940–1961", *Journal of Religion in Africa*, Vol. 28, No. 2 (May), pp. 160–86.

———, 2008, "Les chemins de la 'reconversion autoritaire' en Angola", *Politique Africaine*, Vol. 110, pp. 5–20.

Plaut, Martin, and Holden, Paul, 2012, *Who Rules South Africa?*, London: Biteback Publishing.

Porto, João Gomes, and Parsons, Imogen, 2003, "Sustaining the Peace in Angola: An Overview of Current Demobilisation, Disarmament and Reintegration", *ISS Monograph*, Vol. 83.

Purdeková, Andrea, 2011, "'Even If I Am Not Here, There Are So Many Eyes': Surveillance and State Reach in Rwanda", *Journal of Modern African Studies*, Vol. 49, No. 3, pp. 475–97.

Power, Marcus, and Alves, Ana Cristina (eds), 2012, *China and Angola: A Marriage of Convenience?*, Cape Town: Pambazuka Press.

Raskin, Marcus, 1976, "Democracy versus the National Security State", *Law and Contemporary Problems*, Vol. 40, No. 3, pp. 189–220.

Rodrigues, Cristina Udelsmann, 2010, "Youth in Angola: Keeping the Pace towards Modernity", *Cadernos de Estudos Africanos*, Vol. 18/19, pp. 165–179.

Roque, Paula Cristina, 2008, "Angolan Legislative Elections: Analysing the MPLA's Triumph", Situation Report, Institute for Security Studies.

———, 2009, "Angola's Façade Democracy", *Journal of Democracy*, Vol. 20, No. 4, pp. 137–50.

———, 2011, "Angola: Parallel Governments, Oil and Neopatrimonial System Reproduction", Situation Report, Institute for Security Studies.

———, 2013, "Angola's Second Postwar Elections: The Alchemy of Change", Situation Report, Institute for Security Studies.

———, 2017a, "Angola's Africa Policy", Policy Paper 98, Egmont Royal Institute for International Relations.

———, 2017b, "The Rebel Governance of the SPLM and UNITA. A Comparative Study on Parallel States in Angola and South Sudan", PhD thesis, University of Oxford.

———, 2020, "Angola's New President: Reforming to Survive", Report 38, Institute for Security Studies.

Schuilenberg, Marc, 2011–12, "The Securitization of Society: On the Rise of

Quasi-Criminal Law and Selective Exclusion", *Social Justice*, Vol. 38, Nos. 1–2, pp. 73–89.

Schubert, Jon, 2013, "Democratização e consolidação do poder político em Angola no pós-guerra", *Relações Internacionais*, Vol. 37.

———, 2017, *Working the System: A Political Ethnography of the New Angola*, Ithaca, NY: Cornell University Press.

Shubin, Vladimir, 2008, *The "Hot" Cold War: The USSR in Southern Africa*, London: Pluto Press.

Shearer, David, 1998, "Private Armies and Military Intervention", Adelphi Paper 316, International Institute for Strategic Studies.

Simpkins, Gregory, 1996, *Angola: A Chronology of Major Political Developments, February 1961–September 1996*, Alexandria, VA: Institute for Democratic Strategies.

Soares de Oliveira, Ricardo, 2011, "Illiberal Peace-building in Africa", *Journal of Modern African Studies*, Vol. 49, No. 2 (June), pp. 287–314.

———, 2013, "'O Governo Está Aqui': Post-war State-making in the Angolan Periphery", *Politique africaine*, Vol. 130, No. 2, pp. 165–87.

Tendi, Blessing-Miles, 2016, "State Intelligence and the Politics of Zimbabwe's Presidential Succession", *African Affairs*, Vol. 115, No. 459, pp. 203–24.

Thomashausen, Andre, 2014, "Super-Presidentialism in Angola and the Angolan Judiciary", Stellenbosch Constitutionalism Seminar paper.

Tomás, António Augusto, 2012, "Refracted Governmentality: Space, Politics and Social Structure in Contemporary Luanda", PhD thesis, Columbia University.

Turner, John W., 1998, *Continent Ablaze: The Insurgency Wars in Africa 1960 to the Present*, London: Arms and Armour Press.

Van Rythoven, Eric, 2020, "The Securitization Dilemma", *Journal of Global Security Studies*, Vol. 42, No. 3, pp. 815–54.

Vidal, Nuno, 2016, "O MPLA e a governacao: entre internacionalismo progressista marxista e pragmatism liberal-nacionalista", *Estudos Ibero-Americanos*, Vol 42:3, pp. 815–854.

———, 2019, "The Historical-sociological Matrix and Ethos at the Heart and Strength of MPLA's Modern Angola", *Tempo*, Vol. 25, No. 1, pp. 153–73.

Villegas, Harry, 2017, *Cuba and Angola: The War for Freedom*, London: Pathfinder Press.

Vines, Alex; Shaxson, Nicholas; Rimli, Lisa; Vidal, Nuno, "Angola: Drivers of Change", Chatham House/DfID, April 2005.

Vuori, Juha, 2008, "Illocutionary Logic and Strands of Securitisation: Applying the Theory of Securitisation to the Study of Non-democratic Political Orders", *European Journal of International Relations*, Vol. 14, No. 1, pp. 65–99.

# BIBLIOGRAPHY

————, 2011, *How to do Security with Words: A Grammar of Securitisation in the People's Republic of China*, dissertation, University of Turko.

Wæver, Ole, 1995, "Securitization and Desecuritization", in *On Security*, Ronnie D. Lipschutz (ed.), New York: Columbia University Press, pp. 46–87.

Weigert, Stephen, 2011, *Angola: A Modern Military History, 1961–2002*, New York: Palgrave Macmillan.

Williams, Michael, 2003, "Words Images, Enemies: Securitisation and International Politics", *International Studies Quarterly*, Vol. 47, No. 4, pp. 511–33.

Williams, Paul D., 2007, "Thinking about Security in Africa", *International Affairs*, Vol. 83, pp. 1021–38.

Wolfers, Michael, and Bergerol, Jane, 1983, *Angola in the Front Line*, London: Zed Books.

Wood, Elizabeth, 2000, *Forging Democracy from Below: Insurgent Transitions in South Africa and El Salvador*, Cambridge: Cambridge University Press.

Zakaria, Fareed, 1997, "The Rise of Illiberal Democracy", *Foreign Affairs*, Vol. 76, No. 6, pp. 22–43.

*Reports*

"Angola: Assault on the Right to Life", Amnesty International report, August 1993. https://www.amnesty.org/en/documents/AFR12/004/1993/en/. Accessed October 2020.

"Ending the Angolan Conflict: Our Times has Come to be Heard", National Society for Human Rights (NSHR), 29 March 2000.

"Angola: Arms Trade and the Violations of the Laws of War since the 1992 Elections", Human Rights Watch, November 1994.

"Between War and Peace—Arms Trade and Human Rights Abuses since the Lusaka Protocol", Human Rights Watch, February 1996.

"Angola Livro Branco sobre as Eleições de 2008", Instituto de Desenvolvimento Democratico, September 2009.

"Angola Unravels: The Rise and Fall of the Lusaka Peace Process", Human Rights Watch, September 1999.

"Struggling through Peace: Return and Resettlement in Angola", Human Rights Watch, August 2003. https://www.hrw.org/report/2003/08/15/struggling-through-peace/return-and-resettlement-angola. Accessed October 2020.

"Sustaining the Peace: An Overview of Current Disarmament, Demobilization and Reintegration", Institute of Security Studies, February 2003.

"UNAVEM II", 1996, *The Blue Helmets: A Review of United Nations Peace-keeping*, New York: UN, Department of Public Information.

Angola Peace Monitor 3:5, Action for Southern Africa, January 1997, 1–7.

# BIBLIOGRAPHY

https://reliefweb.int/report/angola/angola-peace-monitor-issue-no5-voliii-29-jan-1997. Accessed April 2021.

"Angola, behind the Façade of 'Normalization'. Manipulation, Violence and Abandoned Populations", Médecins Sans Frontières, November 2000.

"Angola: Sacrifice of a People", October 2002, Médecins Sans Frontières.

"Deception in High Places: The Corrupt Angola Russia Debt Deal", Corruption Watch UK and Associação Mãos Livres, 2013.

# INDEX

Note: Page numbers followed by "*n*" refer to notes

AAA (insurance company), 83, 189
AATA. *See* Associação Angolana de
  Autoridades Tradicionais
  (AATA)
Abrantes, Maria Luisa, 188
Acção Para o Desenvolvimento
  Rural e Ambiente (ADRA),
  237*n*26
Accounts Tribunal, 141
Action Plan for the Promotion of
  Employment (PAPE), 195, 211
Active Revolt (1974), 25
ADFL. *See* Alliance of Democratic
  Forces for the Liberation of
  Congo-Zaire (ADFL)
Africa
  FAA's interventions in, 21, 130,
    150–2
  securitisation strategy usage,
    17–18
African Centres for Disease Control
  and Prevention (CDC), 209
African Investment Bank (BAI), 83
African Union (AU), 81, 153
  African Capacity to Immediate
    Reaction to Crisis (ACIRC)
    programme, 156

*Agora* (newspaper), 44
agriculture, 195
Air Connection Express, 190
air force. *See* Força Aerea Angolana
  (FAN)
AJPD. *See* Associação Justicia, Paz
  e Democracia (AJPD)
Alicerses, Adolosi Mango Paulo,
  59, 180
Alliance of Democratic Forces for
  the Liberation of Congo-Zaire
  (ADFL), 67
Almeida, Alberto de, 210–11
Alpha 5 (firm), 65, 145
ANC (African National Congress)
  (South Africa), 19
Andulo, 69
Angola
  airlift capacity, 137, 155
  Brazil and Spain assistance for
    maritime security strategy, 139
  budget (2020), 213
  capital flight, 83
  China as important trading
    partner, 81–2
  and China securitisation con-
    trasts, 11–12

# INDEX

debt to GDP ratio, 213
diamond industry, 164
failed interventions in Côte
    d'Ivoire, 153, 155
40th anniversary of independence, 85
humanitarian aid to Bangui, 153
investment in Portugal, 83–4
a militarised society, 36
military interventions in
    Democratic Republic of
    Congo, 66–7, 151–3
national security state traits,
    14–15
nation-building exercise, 5–6, 8
political system, 7–8
post-conflict stabilisation
    strategy, 5–6, 8, 20–1
securitised state, emergence of,
    14–15
security apparatus role, 19–20
socio-economic system, 6–7,
    37, 156, 167, 194, 199, 201,
    205, 227, 228
SSR mission to Guinea Bissau,
    154
state and power control, 3–4
UN Human Development Index
    rank, 194
US as oil partner, 81
See also Covid-19 pandemic:
    Angola's response to
Angola rising, 79–86
Angola Selling Corporation
    (Ascorp), 253–4n108
"Angolagate" deal, 62
Angolan Armed Forces. See FAA
    (Angolan Armed Forces)
Angolan Civil War (1975–2002),
    4–5, 26, 49
Angolan Civil War (1992–4), 50,
    61–5, 144

Angolan Civil War (1998–2002),
    50, 68–72
Angolan diamonds, 67
Angolan identity, 4–5
Angolan navy. See Marinha de
    Guerra (MG)
Angolan Social Communications
    Regulatory Body, 110
"Angolan Spring", 118–19, 218
Angolanidade (Angolanness), 24–5,
    227
Angolense (newspaper), 44
Angosat (satellite), 104
Anstee, Margaret, 56
anti-corruption, 86, 181–90, 223
Anti-Crime Unit, 118
Arab Spring (2011), 3, 46, 102,
    118, 120
arbitrariness, 96–7
Areal Defence Region (RADS),
    137
Associação Angolana de
    Autoridades Tradicionais
    (AATA), 42
Associação Justicia, Paz e
    Democracia (AJPD), 237n26
Attorney General's office (PGR),
    182, 183–4, 187
AU. See African Union (AU)
authoritarianism, 7, 10, 173, 216

Bailundo, 69
Bakongo (ethnic group), 38–9, 40,
    60, 178
    Bloody Friday massacre (22 Jan
    1993), 60
Banco Angolano Investimento
    (BAI). See African Investment
    Bank
Banco Comercial Português (BCP),
    83
Banco Económico, 187

Banco Espirito Santo (BES), 188
Banco Internacional de Credito
 (BIC), 83, 186
Banco Português de Negócios
 (BPN), 83–4
Baptista, Alves Bernardo ("Nito
 Alves"), 25–6
Bastos de Morais, Jean-Claude,
 184–5
Batalhão da Guarda Presidencial
 (Presidential Guard Battalion).
 *See* Presidential Guard
BATOPE (Batalhão Técnico
 Operativo), 110
Beirão, Luaty hunger strike, 123,
 124
Bemba, Jean-Pierre, 152
Bembe, António Bento, 158
Benguela province, 125
Benguela Railway project, 80
Bento, Bento, 122
Berlin Conference, 157
Bermuda Triangle (bank), 69
Beye, Alioun Blondin, 64
BFA bank, 186
BGI (firm), 209
Bicesse Agreement (1991), 28, 31,
 38, 51–61, 62, 64, 100, 221
 breakdown of, 20, 52
Bloco Democrático, 214
Boe region, 154
Boma, Estanislau, 158
BPV. *See* People's Vigilante
 Brigades (BPV)
Branch Energy (firm), 65
Brazil, 81, 84, 120, 139
 diamond interests, 253n103
Brazzaville, 67, 152–3
budget (2021), 215
"Burla Thailandesa" scandal, 187
"business as usual" approach, 204,
 214

"business generals", category of,
 144–7
Cabinda, 21, 109
 Cabindan Liberation Front
  (FLEC), 1
 Comando Militar para a
  Independência de Cabinda
  (CMLC), 158
 DDR processes (2006), 150
 FAA deployment in, 129, 153,
  156, 157–62
 oil revenues, 160
 peace agreement (2006), 159,
  160
 Portuguese rule, 157
 struggle for independence/
  autonomy, 157–62
 US oil interests in, 157
*caenches*, 120
Cafunfo, 215
Caixa de Segurança Social das
 Forças Armadas Angolanas (the
 FAA Social Security Bureau),
 149
*Capital, A* (newspaper), 44
CAPs. *See* Committees of political
 action (CAPs)
Cardoso, Frederico, 190
Carneiro, Higíno, 184
Carvalho, André Mendes de
 "Miau", 39
Casa Civil (Civil Cabinet of the
 Presidency), 9, 32, 88
Casa de Segurança. *See* SCP (Casa
 de Segurança/Security Cabinet
 of the Presidency)
Casa Militar, 32, 92
CASA-CE. *See* Convergence for
 National Salvation—Electoral
 Coalition (CASA-CE)
Casimiro, Carbono, 121

Cassule, Isaías, assassination of, 21, 104, 121–3, 225
Castro, Fidel, 133
Catholic Church, 45–6, 160
Catóca mine, 164
Causa Solidária, 43
CCFA. See Joint Commission for the Formation of the Armed Forces (CCFA)
CCPM. See Political and Military Joint Commission (CCPM)
CCVCF. See Joint Ceasefire Verification Monitoring Commission (CCVCF)
CEMG. See Chief of General Staff (CEMG)
Central African Republic (CAR), 153, 156
Central Bank, 34, 182, 184, 185, 199
Centre for Electronic and Public Security (CESP), 181
Centro de formação Especial de Inteligência do Serviço de Informações (CFECIS), 106, 107
Centros de Instrução Revolucionária (CIR) (Centres for Revolutionary Instruction), 133
cesta básica, prices of, 212
Chacal special forces, 94, 96, 98
Chad, 17
"Cherokee", Arsénio Sebastião, 120
"Cheu", Mauricio, 122–3
Chief of General Staff (CEMG), 131–2, 134
Chiluba (Frederick) corruption trial (2009), 176
Chimbili, Eliseu Sapitango, 59
China International Fund (CIF), 82, 97, 187, 188–9

China Petroleum and Chemical Corporation (Sinopec), 82
China Sonangol, 82
China
    loans to Angola, 80, 81
    securitisation, 11–12
    as trading partner of Angola, 81–2
Chitunda, Jeremias Kalandula, 59
Chivukuvuku, Abel Epalanga, 39, 200
Chokwe (ethnic group), 39, 40, 162, 167
Christian Coalition of Angola, 46
churches, 35, 42, 166
    highlighting the risk of malnutrition, 196
    influence on the political consciousness, 45
    MPLA control over, 45–6
CIF. See China International Fund (CIF)
CIM. See Service of Military Counter-Intelligence (Contra Intelligência Militar, or CIM)
CIPE. See Inter-ministerial Commission for Electoral Process (CIPE)
CIR. See Centros de Instrução Revolucionária (CIR) (Centres for Revolutionary Instruction)
citizenship, 229
    hierarchy of, 172–3
civil society, 20, 23, 35–6, 166
    on biosecurity measures, 209
    as counterpower, 41–2
    on Covid-19 public health response, 208
    highlighting the risk of malnutrition, 196
    and Kalupeteca massacre, 127
    political space for, 32

strengthening efforts, 41
class distinctions, 40
clientelism and patronage, 6, 226, 230
CNE. *See* National Electoral Commission (CNE)
Cobalt International Energy, 144
Cold War, 28, 49, 132
COMINT (Combined Communications Intelligence Systems), 103–4
Commission to Memorialise the Victims of the Conflict, 198–9
Committees of political action (CAPs), 29, 120
Community of Portuguese Speaking Countries (CPLP), 155
"Felino exercises", 155
Congo, Democratic Republic of (DRC), 66, 96, 151–3
Covid-19 cases, 209
FAA military intervention in, 151–2, 160–2
Congo, Jorge, 161–2
Congolese army, 161
Constitution (2010), 33, 34, 87, 90
constitutional revision laws (1991–2), 32
Convergence for National Salvation—Electoral Coalition (CASA-CE), 39, 174, 175
streets protest, 119–20
Copenhagen school, 11
corruption, 22, 81, 84, 99, 173
amount of money lost (2002 and 2014), 182
avenues for, 92
Lourenço fighting against, 181–90, 223
Costa Junior, Adalberto da, 38, 199–200, 262n6
Côte d'Ivoire, 151, 153, 155

Council of National Security, 90
Council of the Revolution (Conselho da Revolução), 30
coup (1977). *See* massive purge (27 May 1977)
Covid-19 pandemic, 19, 115, 162, 171, 202, 218, 224, 231, 233
Covid-19 pandemic: Angola's response to, 22, 203–16
arrests for breaching restrictions, 206
cost for testing, 211
death rate, 209
emergency procedures, 203
FAA deployment in Luanda, 206
government officials infected by, 210
healthcare system, decentralisation of, 207–8
impacts on economy, 211
insufficient testing, 209
ministers and secretaries of state replacement, 207
and oil collapse (Apr 2020), 171, 205, 212–16
pandemic response strategy with foreign assistance, 210
PPE, lack of, 208
public health emergency, militarisation of, 206–7
quarantine, imposition of, 206
securitisation and, 204, 205–6
social distancing, 211
state of emergency declaration, 206
and suicide levels, 212
"super-ministries", creation of, 207
unemployment, 211, 212
CPPA. *See* People's Police Corps of Angola (CPPA)

# INDEX

Credit Support Programme (PAC), 211
Criança Futuro, 43
Crocker, Chester, 56
Cuango river, 163, 166
Cuba, 132
  military mission, 132, 133, 134, 247n7
  modus operandi, 89
  troops withdrawal, 94

da Costa, Edeltrudes, 114–15, 190
da Silva, Mário Leite, 186
David, Joaquim Duarte, 184
DDR process (1992), 57, 65, 70, 75, 77, 261–2n1
De Beers (firm), 164
de Sousa, Caetano, 112
Death Squadrons, 122
Defence and Security Council (DSC), 31, 90
defence budget, 140, 141–2
Defence Cooperation Agreement (2010), 139
DeGrisogono (firm), 186
democracy, 15, 18, 33, 173, 197, 219
  multi-party democracy, 60, 220
Democratic Party for Progress—Angolan National Alliance (PDP-ANA), 38–9, 55
democratisation, 232
demolition campaigns (2002), 85
desecuritisation, 204, 231–3
Destacamento de Protecção da Casa de Segurança. See Reconstruction Protection Unit (DPCS)
diamond industry/mining fields, 162–7
  exports, 164

FAA generals access to Lundas provinces, 144–5, 163–4
human rights abuses in mining, 163
  See also Lundas provinces and curse of diamonds
"Dino", General Leopoldino Fragoso de Nascimento, 144, 187
Direcção de Informação e Segurança de Angola (DISA), 99–100
Directorate for Criminal Investigation (DNIC), 117, 118
Directorate for Investigation of Economic Activities (DNIIAE), 117
Directorate for Military Counter-Intelligence (DPCIM), 108
Directorate for Operational Military Intelligence (DIMO), 108
Directorate for the Investigation of Illicit Actions (DIIP), 117
Directorate of Information and Security, 26
"Disciplina", General Egídio de Sousa Santos, 110, 132, 179–80
divide-and-rule strategy, 159
Dokolo, Sindika, 186
"Dolphin" military exercises, 155
donor conference, 81
dos Santos era, end of, 21, 169–70, 171, 223
dos Santos, Isabel, 85, 170, 185–6
dos Santos, José Eduardo, 2, 9, 14, 22, 23, 35, 51, 55, 78, 89
  administration and oil crisis (2014), 85
  assessment commission into SIMPORTEX activities, 141
  background, 30

"blank cheque" to, 33
counter-power building, 223
electoral campaign (1992), 55
on "15+2" book club coup (Jun 2015), 123
foreign deployments, 150–1
as head of state, 29
help to remove Lissouba, 152
his Presidency, 29–35
infrastructure projects, 80–2
on Kalupeteca massacre (2015), 127
last decrees (Jul 2017), 169, 176–7
Lusaka Accord, breakdown of, 68
as Minister of Planning, 30
Moscow trip, 68
moved to Barcelona, 95, 175–6
parallel army, creation of, 93–8
parallel organs of power, 79
patronage system, 29–32
personalisation of power, 29–32
replacement, 171, 172
retirement, 169, 172
RMCs appointment, 31
strengthening praetorian guard, 93–8
took over Presidency, 27
vision for Angola, 79–86
war against UNITA, 29
youth demonstrations against, 46–7, 119
dos Santos, José Filomeno "Zenu", 85, 176, 184–5
DPCIM. See Directorate for Military Counter-Intelligence (DPCIM)
DPCS. See Reconstruction Protection Unit (DPCS)
DSC. See Defence and Security Council (DSC)

Eastern Revolt of Daniel Chipenda (1969–1974), 25
Economic Community of Central African States (ECCAS), 155
economic crisis (1986), 261–2n1
economic crisis (2015), 3
economic growth (2002–8), 79–80
economic recession, 169, 190–3, 194
economy, diversification of, 192
ECOWAS (Economic Community of West African States), 153
election (1992), 28, 32, 33, 39, 50, 51, 54, 55–7, 201, 261–2n1
election (2008), 3, 39, 40, 43, 111, 118
election (2012), 114, 171
election (2017), 39, 115
election (2022), 202, 230–1
elections, 7–8
and citizenship, 229
electoral debacle (1992), 111
electoral fraud, 1–2
electoral misconduct (2017), 174–5
irregularities in, 112, 113
objectives of, 111
parallel tabulation process, 115
Endiama (diamond company), 192, 253n104
Eritrea, 17
Ethiopia, 17, 18
European Union, 210
Executive Outcomes (EO), 62
Export-Import Bank (Exim Bank) (China), 81, 107
External Intelligence Service (SIE), 91, 99, 101, 105–7
budget, 93
centre for communications attached to Presidency, 105
under General Miala, 106, 107

UNITA neutralise efforts, 106
extrajudicial killings, 60, 163
of youths (Viana and Cacuaco),
117–18

FAA (Angolan Armed Forces), 21,
41, 54, 61–2, 75–6, 89, 93,
129–67, 218, 223
"business generals", category of,
144–7
capabilities of, 130–1
CEMG of, 131–2, 134
command of, 130–4
commissars, role of, 178
composition of, 130–4
creation of, 53
deployment in Cabinda, 129,
153, 156, 157–62
discontent, 149–50
domestic role in Lunda Norte
operation, 156, 162–7
domestic role in Lunda Sul
operation, 130, 156, 162–7
during Covid-19, 206
extravagances of commanding
officers, 146
foreign deployments, 150–6
interventions in Africa, 21, 130,
150–2
José Maria's insistence on
counter-surveilling, 109–10
leadership, 130
Lourenço changing of guard,
177
military ethos of, 132
Military Inspector's Office, 145
military interventions in
Congos, 151–2, 160–2
military loyalty ensuring
strategy, 143
military officials' involvement in
business deals, 145

military regions (RM), 134–5
military spending and corruption, 140–4
as national institution, 134
Operation Restoration, 69
Operation Hexagono, 69
Operation Quissonde (Brave
Ant), 70
Operation Triangulo, 69
organisational structure of,
134–40
partisan deployment of, 179–80
pathologies and threats for, 130,
140–50
peacekeeping missions (2014–
15), 167
political instruments for national
defence, 156–67
post-war re-edification programme, 133, 135–40
"purifying", 224
recapture of lost territory, 62
recruitment, 147–8
reform attempts, failure of, 140
reliance on Russian equipment,
133
response to Kalupeteka clampdown, 126, 127, 128
retirement of generals, 147,
148–50
Soviets and Cubans influence
over, 132–4
Soviets influence on military
assistance, 132–4
as state founding pillar, 21, 129
structure of, 130–4
under General Matos, 131–2
UNITA personnel removal, 148
Faceira, General António Emílio,
145
Faceira, General Luís Pareira, 145
factionalism, 171, 177

FALA. *See* Forças Armadas de
Libertação de Angola (FALA)
Falcone, Pierre, 62, 70
FAN. *See* Força Aerea Angolana
(FAN)
FAPLA. *See* Forças Armadas
Populares de Libertação de
Angola (FAPLA)
FEACC. *See* Forças Especiais de
Apoio ao Comandante em Chefe
(FEACC)
Feijó, Carlos, 34
Ferreira, Julia, 175
FESA. *See* Fundação Eduardo dos
Santos (FESA)
"15+2" book club coup (Jun
2015), 21, 121, 123–4, 225
dos Santos on, 123
Figueredo, Elisio, 70
Finance Ministry, 142, 190, 211
FLEC (Frente de Libertação do
Enclave de Cabinda), 1, 135,
153, 157–61
FLEC-Renovada, 158
FNLA. *See* National Front for the
Liberation of Angola (FNLA)
*Folha 8* (newspaper), 44, 45
FOMAC, 155–6
Força Aerea Angolana (FAN),
136–8
air force accidents, 138
procurement deal with Israel,
138
Forças Armadas Angolanas. *See*
FAA (Angolan Armed Forces)
Forças Armadas de Libertação de
Angola (FALA), 53, 69, 133,
134
Forças Armadas Populares de
Libertação de Angola (FAPLA),
53, 59, 60, 99, 132, 133, 134,
151

Forças Especiais de Apoio ao
Comandante em Chefe
(FEACC), 98
foreign aid, 17–18
Foreign Direct Investment, 83
formal economy, 37
Forum Cabindês para o Dialogo
(FCD), 159
Franque, Luis Ranque, 158
Freitas, Ermelinda, 121
FRELIMO. *See* Mozambique
Liberation Front (FRELIMO)
Frente de Libertação do Enclave de
Cabinda. *See* FLEC (Frente de
Libertação do Enclave de
Cabinda)
*From Dictatorship to Democracy: A
Conceptual Framework for Liberation*
(Sharp), 123
Fundação Eduardo dos Santos
(FESA), 43
Furtado, Francisco Pereira, 200–1
Futungo de Belas (Luanda), 31, 60,
64, 66

Gabinete de Obras Publicas
(Cabinet of Public Works), 92
GAE. *See* Group of Special FAA
Forces (GAE)
GALP (energy company), 185
"Ganga", Manuel de Carvalho,
119–20
GAPI (Presidency's intelligence
service), 200
Garcia, Norberto, 184, 187
*garimpeiros* (informal miners), 163,
164, 165
Gaydamak, Arkady, 62
Gbagbo, Laurent, 153–4
GCP. *See* Groups of Political
Combat (GCP)

GDP (Gross Domestic Product), 190, 213
GEFI (Sociedade de Gestão e Participações Financeiras), 182
General Law on Military Service, 247–8n2
Global Witness report, 69–70
GOI. *See* Grupo Operativo de Inteligência (Operational Intelligence Group, GOI)
Government of National Unity (GURN), 33, 218, 222
dissolution of, 33–4
inauguration of, 65–6
"*gradualismo*" (gradualism), 258n68
*Grande Familia do MPLA* (MPLA's Great Family), 25
GRN Office of National Reconstruction, 97
Grós, General, 183–4
Group of Special FAA Forces (GAE), 155
Groups of Political Combat (GCP), 120
Grupo Operativo de Inteligência (Operational Intelligence Group, GOI), 108, 109
Guardia Civil (Spain's Rural Anti-terrorist Group), 54
Guinea Bissau, 151, 153, 154
security sector reform (SSR) programme, 154
Guinean armed forces, 154
Gulf of Guinea, 139
GURN. *See* Government of National Unity (GURN)
Guterres, Antonio, 81, 162

Halloween massacre (1992), 13, 28, 57–60, 199
Harare, 151
historical revisionism, 198, 226–7

Hospital Pedro Maria Tonha "Pedale", 98
hospitals, inadequacies and limitations of, 207, 208
Houphouët-Boigny, Felix, 153
Huambo massacre (2015), 94
Huambo province, 74
Huambo siege, 61, 63
Huambo, 98
Human Rights Watch, 96
human surveillance, 45
humanitarian crisis (2002–4), 50–1, 72–9
emergency assistance, end of, 72–3, 75
HUMNIT (Human Collection and Analysis Intelligence), 104

ICIJ. *See* International Consortium of Investigative Journalists (ICIJ)
IDPs. *See* internally displaced populations (IDPs)
"Iko" Carreira, General Henrique Teles, 26, 106
IL-76 aircraft, 137, 155
IMF. *See* International Monetary Fund (IMF)
"Implacável", Diógenes Malaquías, 109
INDRA (Spanish company), 113, 114
inequality, 85, 171, 172–3
infant mortality rate, 61
inflation, 83, 149
informal economy, 37
Information and Security Directorate of Angola. *See* Direcçao de Informacão e Seguranca de Angola (DISA).
Institute for Social and Professional Reintegration of Ex-soldiers (IRSEM), 75, 149

Integrated Municipal Programme for Rural Development and to Combat Poverty (PMIDRCP), 196–7

Integrated Plan for the Acceleration of Agriculture and Fishing (PIAAPE), 195

Integrated Programme for Municipal Intervention (PIIM), 196, 197, 211

"Intelligence Community", 106

intelligence services
domestic intelligence (SINSE), 102–5
external intelligence (SIE), 105–7
harassment of, 1–3
military intelligence (SISM), 107–10
motto of, 98
power and mandates, 99
surveillance role, 223

Interactive Empreendimentos Multimedia, 44

Inter-ministerial Commission for Electoral Process (CIPE), 114

internally displaced populations (IDPs), 72, 73, 74, 75, 76, 78

International Consortium of Investigative Journalists (ICIJ), 185

International Monetary Fund (IMF), 191, 192, 196

IOM (International Organization for Migration), 75, 76

IRSEM. See Institute for Social and Professional Reintegration of Ex-soldiers (IRSEM)

Jamba, 2, 69

João Carneiro, Manuel, 189

Joint Ceasefire Verification Monitoring Commission (CCVCF), 53

Joint Commission for the Formation of the Armed Forces (CCFA), 53

Joint Commission in the Peace Process, 75

Joint Military Commission (JMC), 75

Jornal de Angola (newspaper), 44, 56, 238n9

José Maria, General Antonio, 32, 70, 99, 102, 106–7, 127, 177, 179
architect of fabricated book club coup, 124
national defence strategy, 109
revenge trial, 179
UNITA personnel removal from FAA, 148

Jovem Justiceiros, 58

judicial system
ill-preparation of, 184
militarisation of, 178

Kabango, Ngola, 38

Kabila, Joseph, 152

Kabila, Laurent, 151, 152

Kalupeteca massacre (2015), 21, 121, 125–7, 128
closing of religious organisations, 127
dos Santos on, 127
PIR teams deployment, 125–6

Kalupeteka, José Julino, 125, 127

"Kamorteiro", Abreu Muengo Ukwachitembo, 70

Kamulingue, Alves, assassination of, 21, 104, 121–3, 225

Kangamba, Bento, 120

Keched devices, 102

Kenyan Supreme Court, 174–5

Kenyatta, Uhuru, 174
Kilamba Kiaxe city, 80
Kimberley Process (KP)
    Certification Scheme, 164
Kimberley Process (KP), 163–4
Kinshasa, 67, 152, 163
Kissassunda, Ludy, 99
kleptocracy, 85–6
"Kopelipa", Manuel Hélder Vieira
    Dias, 68, 70, 90–1, 95, 97, 99,
    107, 114, 117, 144, 145, 187
    as dos Santos' "Machiavellian
        point-man", 91
    helping President, 91–2
    replacement of, 177
Kuando Kubango, 98, 137
Kuangana, Eduardo, 39
Kuito siege, 61, 63, 64
Kwanhama, 94
kwanza (Kz), 237n27
Kwanza Norte, 113
"Kwenda" programme, 211

Laborinho, Eugénio, 181
landmines, 72, 73
Law for the Coercive Repatriation
    of Assets, 184
Law of Voluntary Repatriation,
    184
Lemos, Ambrósio de, 117
Lesotho, 156
Liquefied Natural Gas (LNG), 83
Lisbon Stock Exchange, 83
Lisbon, 84
Lissouba, Pascal, 67, 152
LNG-Angola project, 178
"Lohango" exercise (2014), 155
Lopes, Filomeno Vieira, 121
Lourenço, João, 21–2, 68, 96,
    117, 223, 234
    Academia de Ciências Sociais e
        Tecnologias, creation of, 107
    adjustment in SCP, 98
    Angosat-3 project contract,
        104–5
    constitutional review process
        announcement (Mar 2021),
        199
    dismantling dos Santos family's
        grip on economy, 22
    elected as President, 169, 172
    FAA divide during his
        Presidency, 148
    grip on SCP, 177
    meeting with top oil companies,
        190–1
    and Privinvest deal, 140
    securitisation strategy, 22
Lourenço's Presidency, 22,
    169–202
    aeroplanes purchase for TAAG,
        213–14
    airport construction announce-
        ment, 213
    allowed for burial and memorial
        construction, 199
    Bakongo commanders in key
        positions, 172
    "business as usual" approach,
        204, 214
    dialogue with civil society and
        youth, 197–8
    economic recession and poverty,
        169, 190–3
    economic reforms, 191–3
    economic strategy, 174
    employment-generating sectors
        development, 173
    fighting against corruption,
        181–90, 223
    instrumentalisation of demo-
        cratic procedure and prin-
        ciples, 173
    job creation, 195–6

MPLA campaigns, 174
multisector commission,
    creation of, 182–3
national awards by, 198
non-oil revenues generating,
    192–3
political reform and reconcilia-
    tion, 170–1, 197–202
presidential transition (2017),
    171–6
rapid economic growth, 172–3
reforms of, 170–1
securitisation of non-military
    sectors, 170
security and military chiefs,
    changing of, 176–81
security apparatus leadership
    changes, 169–70, 176–81
social tensions and austerity,
    193–7
youth streets protests (26 Sep
    2020), 214–15
See also Covid-19 pandemic:
    Angola's response to
Luanda
counter-march, 102
Covid-19 cases, 209, 210
defended by FAPLA and
    Presidential Guard, 60
FAA deployment during
    Covid-19, 206
oil economy, 85
own satellite system, 104–5
slums of, 36
social unrest (Feb 2015), 97–8
UNITA returned to, 51
war veterans march (June
    2012), 119
youths meeting (Independence
    Square), 119
Luanda Leaks (Jan 2020), 185

Luanda massacre. See Halloween
    massacre (1992)
Lubango, 119
Luemba, Francisco, 161, 162
Luena Accord (Apr 2002), also
    known as Luena Memorandum
    of Understanding (MoU), 30,
    70, 75, 201
Lulo mine, 165
Lumanhe company, 145
Lunda Norte, 21, 113, 209
    FAA deployment in, 156, 162–7
    massacre in (30 Jan 2021), 166
Lunda Sul, 21, 113
    FAA deployment in, 130, 156,
    162–7
Lunda-Chokwe kingdom, 165
Lundas provinces and curse of
    diamonds, 144, 162–7
    diamond exports, 164
    diamond mining and human
        rights abuses in, 163
    garimpeiros (informal miners)
        mass deportation, 163
    massacre in (30 Jan 2021), 166
"Lungo", João Antonio Santana,
    110, 180
Lusaka Protocol (1994), 33, 65–8,
    70, 130
    breakdown of, 65–8
Luso-Angolans, 24
"Luta", João Francisco Kinguengo,
    123
Lutucuta, Silvia, 207
Luzia jail attacks (Saurimo, Nov
    2019), 165–6
Lwini Social Solidarity Fund, 43

MacKenzie, General Adriano
    Makevela, 145, 148
MSTelcom telecommunications,
    83

# INDEX

Maka Angola, 189
"Malakito", Jota Filipe, 165
malaria, 209
malnutrition, 71–2, 196
    Severe Acute Malnutrition
    (SAM), 211–12
Mangueira, Archer, 193
man-made famine (2002), 71–2
Manuel Junior, Domingos, 178
Manuel, Jesus, 97
Manuvakola, General Eugénio, 67
Marikana massacre (2012), 18
"marimbondos", 194
Marinha de Guerra (MG), 138–40
Maritime Surveillance System
    (SINAVIM), 139
Marques de Morais, Rafael, 44–5,
    198
Martins, Sebastião, 103, 104, 200
Marxism, 32
Marxism-Leninism, 27
Massano, João Pereira, 201
massive purge (27 May 1977), 13,
    25, 26, 261–2n1
Matos, General João de, 54, 68,
    69, 90, 131–2
Maua, José João, 94
Mauritius Leaks, 144
Mbilingue, Dom Gabriel, 46
Mbkassi, Antonio "Mosquito", 70
Mbundu/Creole constituency, 24
Media Novo group, 44
media, 35
    MPLA control over, 44–5
    MPLA own media outlets,
    creation of, 43–4
    on MPLA's "philanthropic"
    organisations relations, 43
Melo, Ricardo De, 44
Memorando de Entendimento para
    a Paz e Reconciliaça ao da

Provincia de Cabinda (1 Jul
    2006), 159, 160
Menongue, 119
Miala, General Fernando, 70, 103,
    105, 178
    arrest of, 106
    SIE under, 106, 107
    SINSE under, 178–9
MIC. See Movimento
    Independentista de Cabinda
    (MIC)
military corruption, 130, 140–50
Military Intelligence (SIM), 101
Military Professional Resources
    Incorporated, 62
"Ministries Neighbourhood"
    project, 189
Ministry for Assistance and Social
    Reintegration (MINARS), 75, 77
Ministry for Economy and
    Planning, 211
Ministry of Defence (MOD), 93,
    105, 116
    anti-fraud service, 145
    on retirement processes
    mismanagement, 148–9
Ministry of Health, 93, 208
Ministry of Interior, 93, 101, 105
    police organs under, 116, 117
Ministry of Security (MINSE), 100
MINUSCA. See UN
    Multidimensional Integrated
    Stabilisation Mission in the
    Central African Republic
    (MINUSCA)
Missão de Cooperação Técnico-
    Militar a Guiné-Bissau
    (MISSANG), 154
MONUA, 66, 67, 68
Moracén, Rafael, 26
Moscow, 132, 133
Mount Sumi massacre, 125–7, 225

MOVICEL (telecom services), 104
Movimento do Protectorado Lunda
 Tchokwe (MPLT), 165, 166
Movimento Independentista de
 Cabinda (MIC), 162
Movimento Popular de Libertação
 de Angola. *See* MPLA
 (Movimento Popular de
 Libertação de Angola)
Moxico, 70
Mozambique Liberation Front
 (FRELIMO), 151
Mozambique, 140, 151
Mpalabanda, 159
MPLA (Movimento Popular de
 Libertação de Angola), 4, 15,
 16, 19, 23, 24–9, 87, 219
 "Angolagate" deal, 62
 attention towards the Sobas,
 42–3
 Bicesse Agreement (1991), 28,
 31, 38, 51–61, 62, 64, 100,
 221
 bureaucracy and administration,
 collapse of, 27–8
 *caenches*, use of, 120–1
 central actors of, 24
 centralised control, 25, 27
 Committees of political action
 (CAPs), 29, 120
 Congress IV, 68
 control over churches, 45–6
 control over NGOs, 43–4
 corporatism and assimilation, 8,
 227
 defamation campaign, 200
 Defence and Security Council
 (DSC), 31, 90
 economic collapse, 27–8
 election (2008), 39, 40
 election (2017), 174–5
 electoral campaign (1992), 55
 electoral campaign cost, 112
 electoral slogan, 24
 FNLA military defeat
 (Quifangondo, 1976), 38
 fragmentation within, 171, 177,
 178–81, 202
 fraudulent practices, 173
 "*gradualismo*" (gradualism),
 258n68
 as guarantors of peace, 13
 Halloween massacre (1992), 13,
 28, 57–60, 199
 human surveillance, 45
 leadership, 25–6, 172
 legislative elections campaign
 (2008), 112–13
 "as the legitimate heir of
 resistance", 35
 membership, 27, 32
 militaries restructuring, 50
 military ethos, 51
 military heroism, 40
 military victory, 222
 "a monolithic political system"
 establishment, 25
 multiple threats to, 88
 own media outlets, creation of,
 43–4
 party-state system, 7–8, 24, 31
 People forced to join, 74
 *poder popular* (popular power),
 26, 58
 political monism, 220
 political power de-linkage,
 16–17
 polls favour of, 111–12
 post-nationalism, emergence of,
 227
 post-war congress (2003), 79
 power restructuring within,
 173–4
 racial divides within, 106

reason for securitisation policy,
50
rebellion against the Portuguese,
24
Regional Military Councils
(RMCs), 31
restructuring attempts, 32
securing political sovereignty,
28–9
slogan for 2012 polls, 114
slogan for 2017 election, 115
Soviets help to, 132–3
state-building exercises, 6
synonymous with corruption, 24
20-year Friendship and
Cooperation treaty with
Soviet Union, 27
ungoverned territory, state
administration in, 77–8
UNITA military threat to, 31
UNITA war against, 37–8
VII Extraordinary Congress,
179, 180–1
vision for a new Angola, 227
MPLT. See Movimento do
Protectorado Lunda Tchokwe
(MPLT)
MPU. See United Patriotic
Movement (MPU)
Mugabe, Robert, 19
music, as form of protest, 46–7
musseques (slums), 85, 206

Namibia diaspora youth protest (7
Mar 2011), 102
Nascimento, Dom Alexandre do,
46
Nascimento, Lopo do, 68
National Agency for Petroleum,
Gas and Biofuels (ANPG), 191
National Directorate of the Popular
Police, 116

National Doctors Syndicate
(SINMEA), 209
National Electoral Commission
(CNE), 56, 112, 113, 114, 175
national tally centre, 115
National Front for the Liberation
of Angola (FNLA), 38, 55, 174,
175
internal factionalism, 38
military defeat (Quifangondo,
1976), 38
National Institute of Military
Aviation, 137
National Patriotic Alliance (APN),
175
National Reconstruction Cabinet
(GRN), 91–2
National Security Council, 131
National Statistics Institute (INE),
194
Naval Academy, 139
Naval War Institute, 139
Nazaki Oil and Gas, 144
neo-patrimonialism, 4, 5–6, 16–17
nepotism, 96
Neto, Agostinho, 25, 99, 221
coup against Neto, 26
death of, 27
dos Santos learned from, 30
Neto, General Armando da Cruz,
69, 132, 145
"Ngongo", Leal Monteiro, 78
NGOs (Non-Governmental
Organisations), 35, 42–3, 222
as "chains of transmission", 43
closedown of operations, 71
humanitarian assistance, 73
MPLA control over, 43–4
"Ninjas". See Rapid Reaction
Intervention Police (PIR)
("Ninjas")
Nito Alves "coup" (1977), 133

Nito Alves. *See* Baptista, Alves
  Bernardo ("Nito Alves")
Northern Aerial Defence Region
  (RADAN), 137
NOS (telecommunications
  company), 185
Numa, General Abilio Kamalata,
  54, 59
Nunda, General Geraldo
  Sachipengo, 70, 132, 147, 179
Nzita, Emmanuel, 161

O Nosso Soba (Our Soba), 42–3
*O Pais* (newspaper), 44
OCHA, 73, 76
Octavio, Eduardo, 104
ODC. *See* Organisation for Civil
  Defence (ODC)
Odebrecht (firm), 188
OECD. *See* Organisation for
  Economic Cooperation and
  Development (OECD)
Office for National Reconstruction
  (Gabinete de Reconstrucção
  National, GRN), 82
Office for Special Infrastructure
  Works, 98
oil boom, 83, 84
oil collapse (Apr 2020), 171, 205,
  212–16
oil crisis (2014), 85, 93, 97, 115,
  169, 190–1, 218
oil dependency, 215–16
oil industry, 190–1
  reforms, 191–2
oil prices, fall of (1986), 27
oil production, 190
oil rents, 15
oil windfall (2004–13), 173
oil-backed loans, 81
Oligarchs, 15
One Belt One Road initiative, 82

OPEC (Organization of the
  Petroleum Exporting
  Countries), 212
Operation Restoration, 69
Operation Broom, 158–9
Operation Crab, 200
Operation Hexagono, 69
Operation Quissonde (Brave Ant),
  70
Operation Triangulo, 69
opposition, 2, 4, 7–8, 9, 18, 20,
  21–4, 35–47, 56, 79, 103, 104,
  113–15, 119–25, 130, 174,
  175, 178, 197, 199–202, 208,
  213, 228, 231–3
Organisation for Economic
  Cooperation and Development
  (OECD), 84
Organisation of Civil Defence
  (ODC), 60–1, 78
Ouattara, Alassane, 153, 154
Ovimbundu (ethnic group), 38,
  58, 60, 74
  soldiers and officers in FAA, 147–8

Pa, Sam, 187–8
PAC. *See* Credit Support
  Programme (PAC)
Pacavira, Rosa, 196
Paihama, General Kundy, 100, 135
Panama Papers, 144
"Panda", Alfredo Mingas, 117
PAPE. *See* Action Plan for the
  Promotion of Employment
  (PAPE)
Paradise Papers, 144
parastatals, privatisation of, 192
Partido de Renovação Social (PRS),
  39–40, 165, 174, 214
Partido do Renascimento
  Angolano—Juntos por Angola
  (PRA-JA), 39

party-state system, 7–8, 24, 31
patrimonial system, 5–6, 16–17
patronage system, 6, 10, 30, 32, 42, 79, 83, 87, 188, 195, 205, 219, 226, 230, 233, 261–2n1
PDP-ANA. *See* Democratic Party for Progress—Angolan National Alliance (PDP-ANA)
Pena, Elias Salupeto, 59
People's Assembly (Assembleia do Povo), 30
People's Defence Organisation, 132
People's Police Corps of Angola (CPPA), 116
People's Vigilante Brigades (BPV), 58, 60–1
Pereira, General Apolinàrio José, 201
personal protective equipment (PPE), 208, 210
"Petroff", Santana Andre Pitra, 116
PGR. *See* Attorney General's office (PGR)
phone tapping, 104
PIAAPE. *See* Integrated Plan for the Acceleration of Agriculture and Fishing (PIAAPE)
PIIM. *See* Integrated Programme for Municipal Intervention (PIIM)
PIR. *See* Rapid Reaction Intervention Police (PIR) ("Ninjas")
PMIDRCP. *See* Integrated Municipal Programme for Rural Development and to Combat Poverty (PMIDRCP)
police
    command structure, 116–17
    extrajudicial killings of youths (Viana and Cacuaco), 117–18

as instrument of repression, 115–16
and phantom threats, 115–28
restructuring programme plan (2003), 116
and threat of protests, 118–19
Police Reserve Force, 118
Political and Military Joint Commission (CCPM), 53, 56, 57
Political Bureau (MPLA), 31
political pluralism, 33, 35
political transition (1990s), 32, 49, 134
population, 35
    structure their lives, 36–7
    war for independence, 37
Port Buba project, 154
Portugal, 37, 53, 81, 187–8, 210
    Angola investment in, 83–4
    protectorate treaty (127th anniversary), 166
Portuguese imperialism, 157
Portuguese Securities and Market Commission, 185
poverty rate, 212
poverty, 190–3, 229
PRA-JA. *See* Partido do Renascimento Angolano—Juntos por Angola (PRA-JA)
Presidency
    arbitrary control, 3–4, 8–9
    authoritarian control, problem of, 233
    centralisation of power, 16, 50
    centralised control, 27
    control over Angolan economy, 84
    degree of autonomy, 12
    elites and security forces link, 220
    as guarantors of peace, 13

and intelligence services,
102–10
military victory over UNITA, 20
parallel armies usage, 86, 87, 88
as a parallel state, 86
political relations stabilising
capacity, 7–8
post-war order, 34–5
President as ultimate arbitrator
of state power, 34
retain control of forces, 60
securitised policy, emergence
of, 20
shadowing strategy, dangers of,
130
social awakening, afraid of,
228–9
supra-structures of, 88–93
Presidential Decrees, 90
Presidential Guard, 9, 26, 41,
93–8, 150, 232
first unit, creation of, 94
in Kinshasa, 152
mission of, 26
pay and conditions of, 96–7
security apparatus changes, 177
Presidential Security Cabinet. *See*
SCP (Casa de Segurança/
Security Cabinet of the
Presidency)
presidential transition (2017),
21–2, 171–6, 261–2n1
Privinvest (Middle Eastern
company), 140
Protecção Civil, 78
Protectorado da Lunda Tchokwe,
165
protests (2013), 95, 96
Provedor da Justiça (Ombudsman),
116
PRS. *See* Partido de Renovação
Social (PRS)

Public Procurement Laws (2010),
141

Qatar, 210
Queensway group, 82
Queiroz, Francisco, 198

Rabelais, Manuel, 44, 184
Radio Ecclesia, 44
Radio Global, 44
Radio Mais, 44
Radio Nacional de Angola, 44
Rapid Reaction Intervention Police
(PIR) ("Ninjas"), 54, 58, 59, 63,
65, 98, 117, 119, 124, 125,
127, 155, 161, 261–2n1
deployment in Kalupeteca
massacre, 125–6
first operation in civilian areas,
60
Reconnaissance Service RETO,
108
Reconstruction Protection Unit
(DPCS), 94, 97, 98
reconstruction, 92
refugees, 72, 73, 74, 75, 76, 78
Regional Military Councils
(RMCs), 31
'resource curse', 85
Revolutionary Council, 100
Revolutionary Front for the
Integration and Sociological
Independence of Lunda-
Chokwe, 165–6
"Revus", 46, 119
RKK Energia, 104
RMCs. *See* Regional Military
Councils (RMCs)
Roberto, Holden, 38
Rome, 46
Roque Santeiro market (Luanda),
37

Rosoboronexport (Russian defence company), 104
ruling elites
  interests in diamonds, 164
  revenue and capital, 15
  securitisation, 17–18
  securitising governance, 3–4
  threat to, 222
Russia, 53
  as Angola chief military ally, 81
Rwanda, 17, 18, 152

SADC Standby Force Brigade (SADCBRIG), 155
SADC. *See* Southern Africa Development Community (SADC)
Sadissa (firm), 145–6
Sakaita, Eloy, 106
Salazar, Antonio de Oliveira, 34
Samakuva, Isaias, 38, 79
Samba Hospital (Luanda), 208
Samba Panza, Catherine, 153
Saneamento Económico e Financeiro (Economic and Financial Rehabilitation programme), 28
Sango, General André Oliveira, 107
Santos, Fernando da Piedade Dias dos "Nando", 100, 103, 257n62
São Vicente, Carlos, 189
Saracen International employing Executive Outcomes personnel (firm), 65
Saraiva, Rogerio, 112, 114
Sassou-Nguesso, Denis, 67, 151, 152
Saudi Arabia, 81
Saurimo, 164
Savimbi, Jonas Malheiro, 28, 32, 68, 69

acceptance of electoral results (1992), 56
death of, 30, 70
electoral campaign (1992), 55
funeral of, 199
UNITA, founding of, 37
SCP (Casa de Segurança/ Presidential Security Cabinet), 8–9, 12, 21, 82, 88, 101–2, 169, 223–4, 231
  Cabinda file under, 92
  cabinet, 220
  control of elections, 89, 111–15
  control over FAA, 131
  creation of, 90
  fears of, 147
  GRN run by, 92
  influence over national budget, 93
  intelligence service's role, 89, 98–102
  Lourenço grip on, 177
  on national security threats, 14
  parallel army, 21, 93
  priorities for state security, 101
  as secretariat for the Presidency, 90
  structures of, 89–93
  wide-angled approach, 95
Sebastião, General Pedro, 177–8, 190, 206
"secret debt", 249n36
Secretaria da Defesa (Defence Secretariat), 32
securitisation, 4–5, 9, 50
  Africa securitisation strategy usage, 17–18
  as architecture of power, 10
  in China, 11–12
  clientelism and patronage, 226, 230

and Covid-19 pandemic, 204, 205–6
defining moments of crisis and political threats, 217–18
'democratic bias', 11–12
desecuritisation, 204, 231–3
impact on nation's identity, 226–8
infrastructure building to support form of governing, 13–14
legacies of, 22, 204, 226–34
limitation of, 11–13
massification of war machines, 221
need to manage fear, 228
in non-security areas, 11
objectives of, 10–11
part of a transitory process, 11
as part of everyday politics, 219–20
political calculations, 222
in political landscape, 18
political power de-linkage, 16–17
and political threats, 221
as a process and infrastructure, 225–6
securitised state traits, 12–16
shadow government securitisation strategy usage, 5–6, 220
social and ethnic stratification, 15
socio-economic inclusion, 229–30
as strategy to protect the President, 223
structure of, 13–15
surveillance strategies, 18
survival of shadow power, 13
threat of economic hardship, 230

threat-centred management approach, 218–19
under the guise of humanitarianism, 17–18
war mentality underpinned, 218
weakening of militarised ethos, 223
wealth from the extractive industries, 15
securitised state
features of, 12–16
strength of, 223–4
securocrats, 9, 217
rise of a generation of, 14–15
rise of power, 18
Semanário Angolense (newspaper), 163
Serqueira, General José Lourenço, 96, 98, 177
Service for Criminal Investigation (SIC), 117, 166
Service of Military Counter-Intelligence (Contra Intelligência Militar, or CIM), 105–6
Services for Internal Security (SINFO, later SINSE), 101, 113, 114
Serviço de Inteligência e Segurança Military (Military Intelligence Service) or SISM, 91, 99, 107–10, 123, 152
during the civil war, 108
took over surveillance system, 110
under José Maria, 107–9
unofficial objective of, 109
Sese Seko, Mobutu, 66, 152
Seventh Day Adventist Light of the World Church, 125
Severe Acute Malnutrition (SAM), 211–12

shadow government and edifice of power, 21, 49–86, 87–128
control of elections, 111–15
domestic intelligence (SINSE), 102–5
external intelligence (SIE), 105–7
intelligence services, 98–110
military intelligence (SISM), 107–10
parallel structures of, 88
police and phantom threats, 115–28
Praetorian Guard, 93–8
SCP supra-structure, 89–93
securitisation strategy, 5–6, 220
Sharp, Gene, 123
SIC. *See* Service for Criminal Investigation (SIC)
SIE. *See* External Intelligence Service (SIE)
SIMPORTEX, 91, 141, 145
Simulambuco, Treaty of (1885), 157
SINFO. *See* Services for Internal Security (SINFO, later SINSE)
Sinopec International, 82
SINSE. *See* State Security and Internal Intelligence Service (SINSE)
SISM. *See* Serviço de Inteligência e Segurança Military (Military Intelligence Service) or SISM
social distancing, 211
Sociedade Mineira do Cuango (SMC), 145
Société Ivoirienne de Raffinage (SIR), 154
Sodiam (Sociedade de comercialização de Diamantes de Angola), 186, 190, 253n107

Sonangol (oil company), 69, 82–3, 85, 92, 144, 154, 170, 185
piracy attack on oil tanker (Feb 2014), 139
restructuring of, 191
Sonangol Group, 82–3
Sonatrach (oil company), 83
South Africa, 2
Covid-19 first wave, 209
securitisation in political landscape, 18–19
South Korean Eximbank, 181
South Sudan, 17, 18
South Sudan's National Security Service (NISS), 18
Southern Africa Development Community (SADC), 155, 156
sovereign wealth fund (SWF), 85, 169, 185, 211
Soviet Union, 132–4
help to MPLA, 132–3
MPLA 20-year Friendship and Cooperation treaty with, 27
Spain, 139
Spatial Strategy for Angola (2016–25), 105
'state of exception', 33
State Security and Internal Intelligence Service (SINSE), 91, 99, 102–5, 122, 124, 200
functions of, 103
surveillance ability extension, 104
surveillance systems upgrade, 103–4
under Miala, 178–9
state-owned enterprises (SOEs), 192
Stockholm International Peace Research Institute, 141
Superior Military Council, 90

TAAG (national airline), 175, 192, 213

TAIS. *See* Trans Africa Investment Services (TAIS)

Tati, Alexandre, 158, 161

Tati, Raul, 161

Technical Group (TG), 75

technocrats, 9, 30, 31, 89, 169, 234

Teixeira, General Eusébio de Brito, 146

Teleservice (firm), 145

Televisão Public de Angola (TPA), 44

Telstar (firm), 189

Tiago, Nzita, 158, 161

Tonet, William, 45

Trans Africa Investment Services (TAIS), 253n105

Tshisekedi, Felix, 152

"Tucayano", Benilson Pereira, 122

Turismo hotel, 57

TV Palanca, 44

TV Zimbo, 44

Tyaunda, Alfredo, 94

Uganda, 17, 18, 152

UGP Instruction Centre (Benfica), 96

UGP. *See* Unidade de Guarda Presidencial (UGP)

UN (United Nations), 56, 68, 76
  humanitarian crisis and assistance, 72
  mission in Angola, 52–3

UN Angola Verification Mission I (UNAVEM I), 52

UN Angola Verification Mission II (UNAVEM II), 52–3, 54, 56

UN Angola Verification Mission III (UNAVEM III), 65, 66

UN Human Development Index (HDI), 194

UN Human Rights Commission, 126

UN Multidimensional Integrated Stabilisation Mission in the Central African Republic (MINUSCA), 156

UN Security Council (UNSC), 52, 62
  oil embargo, 64
  "Resolution 1127", 67
  "Resolution 696", 53
  "Resolution 793" (1992), 56
  "Resolution 864" (September 1993), 52

unexploded ordnance (UXOs), 73

UNHCR (United Nations High Commissioner for Refugees), 75, 127

União dos Povos Angolanos (UPA), 38

UNICEF (United Nations Children's Emergency Fund), 196, 210

Unidade de Guarda Presidencial (UGP), 94, 95–6, 97, 122, 179

Unidade de Segurança Presidencial (USP), 94, 95–6, 120, 179

Unidade Operativa Especial (Special Operational Unit), 94

UNITA (União Nacional para a Independência Total de Angola), 5, 20, 21, 27, 40, 41, 104, 197, 221
  acceptance of electoral results (1992), 56
  and election (2017), 174–5
  Bicesse Agreement (1991), 28, 31, 38, 51–61, 62, 64, 100, 221

combatants and their families in quartering areas, 76
combatants left FAA, 65
constitutional revision laws acceptance (1991–2), 32
criminal charges against Kopelipa, 114
defeat in 2002, 38, 50
demobilisation of, 76–7, 149, 218
diamond revenues, 144
electoral campaign (1992), 55
entry into GURN, 33
FAN operation against, 137
forces removal from diamond areas, 68
founding of, 37
generals withdrawal from FAA, 56
Halloween massacre (1992), 13, 28, 57–60, 199
integration of generals into FAA, 65, 66
intelligence and surveillance capacities, 100
internal power struggles, 79
Kuito siege, 61, 63, 64
leadership, 38, 70, 78–9
membership, 38
militaries restructuring, 50
military defeat, 78
military hospital medical assistance, 109
oil town of Soyo, capture of, 60
on ghost ballot stations, 113–14
parallel tabulation process, 115
participation in the unity government, 65–6
personnel removal from FAA, 148
polls (2008), 38
post-war congress (2003), 79
public burial of Savimbi, 199
returned to Luanda, 51
SIE neutralise efforts, 106
SISM track on communications and movements, 110
soldiers integration into FAA, 70
streets protest, 119–20
territorial control, 61
top command, 132
top leadership, killing of, 59
troops levels of training, 133–4
UN arms embargo on, 62
war against the MPLA, 37–8
wartime state in Jamba, 31, 38
youth streets protests (26 Sep 2020), 214–15
UNITA-Renovada (Renovated-UNITA), 67
United Patriotic Movement (MPU), 121
United States (US), 53, 156
Angola as oil partner, 81
humanitarian assistance, 210
oil interests in Cabinda, 157
UNITEL (telecom services), 104
Universal Church of the Kingdom of God, 45
UNSC. See UN Security Council (UNSC)
"us or them" approach, 4
USP. See Unidade de Segurança Presidencial (USP)

Vaal da Silva, Carlos Hendrick, 145
Valleysoft (company), 113
Van Dunem, José Vieira Dias, 26
VAT tax, 193
Vicente, Manuel, 95, 144, 145, 171, 187
Victor, M'fulumpinga N'landu, 39

# INDEX

Vieira Dias, Filomeno de Nascimento, 46
"Vietnam", General Mateus Miguel Angelo, 146–7

*Wall Street Journal*, 163, 182
Wambu, General Peregrino Chindondo, 148
war for independence, 37
World Bank, 195, 210, 211
World Food Programme (WFP), 63, 74

Xa-Mutemba (municipality), 163

yellow fever outbreak (2015–16), 208
youths
demonstrations against dos Santos, 46–7, 119
extrajudicial killings of (Viana and Cacuaco), 117–18
music as form of protest, 46–7

Namibia diaspora youth protest (7 Mar 2011), 102
"Revus" (revolutionary youths group), 46, 119
streets protests (26 Sep 2020), 214–15
unemployment, 36, 195

Zaire, 62, 66–7
Angola 24th regiment deployment in, 67
"Zé Grande", José Luís Caetano Higino de Sousa, 107, 109, 181
Zecamutchima, José Mateus, 165, 166
"Zenu", José Filomeno dos Santos, 85, 176, 184–5
Zimbabwe African National Union—Patriotic Front (ZANU-PF), 19, 151
Zimbabwe, 19, 96, 151
Zuma, Jacob, 18
Zumba, Zenobio, 123